CW00836236

About the Auth

Sheldon Nemoy is a master designer—a teacher as well as a lifelong student of design and its relationship with technology. He is president of The Thornhill Group, one of the Los Angeles area's premier computer-based design agencies. As president of Thornhill, Sheldon has been instrumental in introducing desktop design technologies to Los Angeles's professional book, periodical and corporate publishing communities. As a design and electronic publishing consultant, he has worked extensively for major domestic and international clients. Throughout his career, Shel has enjoyed sharing his expertise with those around him. He currently teaches desktop publishing and design in the Computer Graphics Department at UCLA Extension and is a featured international seminar speaker.

Jan Weingarten was brought in to revise the third edition of this book. She's a software trainer, consultant and writer in Seattle, Washington. Her most recent book is *Teach Yourself WordPerfect 6.0 for Windows*. In addition, she has authored or co-authored books on Windows 3.1, WordPerfect for DOS, Lotus 1-2-3 for Windows, Paradox for Windows, Microsoft Word 6.0 for Windows and Excel 5.0 for Windows.

C.J. Aiken is a writer, editor, desktop publisher and student of the book arts. She has written on topics ranging from the decorative arts to wildlife, from desktop publishing to circadian rhythms. Her articles have appeared in travel, design and general-interest magazines as well as books. She is former managing editor of Access Press Ltd. and *Reason* magazine.

Acknowledgments

Many people contributed their knowledge, advice and encouragement on this project, and with these people we happily share credit for this book.

First, we would like to thank the CorelDRAW artists whose outstanding work appears in our "Gallery" chapters. Many talented Corel users submitted work for *Looking Good With CorelDRAW!*, and we're sorry we couldn't include it all.

We are indebted to Steve Oblas for his helpful troubleshooting suggestions for Chapter 9. Steve specializes in marketing , communication, design and corporate and network publishing on PC systems.

Shane Hunt of Slimy Dog Graphix in San Dimas, CA, and Nicole Ledoux of The Solutions Factory in Yorktown Heights, NY, supplied how-to information, general Corel know-how and some late-night laughs. Thanks to both of them.

At Ventana Press, the concept of this book originated with Elizabeth Woodman; Diane Lennox provided timely promotional support, and the ready editorial, technical and production support team—including Pam Richardson, Marion Laird, Diana Merelman, John Cotterman, Karen Wysocki and Marcia Webb—guided our progress.

At Corel Corp., our point men were Jeff Johnson and Michael Bellefeuille. In addition, they were able to direct us to others within Corel, and we are grateful to all those we made contact with for their prompt and enthusiastic assistance.

Finally, we express our profound appreciation to Jan Weingarten, who updated this third edition with great care and insight.

Shel Nemoy and C.J. Aiken

Colophon

The black-and-white pages of this book were produced with PageMaker on a 486-50MHz PC with 16mb of RAM. The color gallery pages were produced using CorelDRAW 4.0. The Video system used is a Cornerstone Dual-Page 120 grayscale monitor driven by an ImageExcel controller.

The body type is Palatino 11/13. Headline type is ITC Stone Sans from Digital Typeface Corporation. All pages were output directly to film using a Linotronic 530 imagesetter.

Looking Good With CorelDRAW was researched and produced on equipment supplied by the following vendors:

SuperMatch • Wacom • Colorado Tape Systems • Dell Computer

Contents

SECTION I: Graphic Building Blocks

CHAPTER 1

CHAPTER 2

CHAPTER 3

CHAPTER 4

CHAPTER 5

SECTION II: CorelDRAW in Action

CHAPTER

6

CHAPTER

7

CHAPTER

SECTION III: Troubleshooting

CHAPTER

SECTION IV: Appendices

APPENDIX

APPENDIX B

Introduction

A new tool—constituting a potential revolution in the future of art—has arrived: the electronic computer.

— Carl Sagan
Introduction, *Art and the Computer*

Something unprecedented is happening in art and design, and PC artists powered by high-performance graphics software packages such as CorelDRAW are at the forefront of the revolution that's underway. For evidence, simply skim the pages of *Looking Good With CorelDRAW!* and you'll see some of the stepping stones of this new discipline—sophisticated works created entirely on the computer.

DRAWING 2001

This quantum leap in the production process is a subject worth pondering. For thousands of years, people created two-dimensional drawings and paintings in basically the same way—by hand. Since the first cave dweller left a muddy hand print on the wall at Lascaux, art has been made by dipping a stick (finger, pen, sable brush) into color (mud, blood, Winsor & Newton watercolors), and applying that color to a surface (animal skin, plaster, woven fiber).

Today we can create and produce drawings and paintings within a single medium—electricity. Illusion keeps us rooted in tradition—we still use brush (mouse, tablet and pen), paint (digital color) and surface (computer-screen display). But computer art has colors and curves that look and "feel," emotionally, very different from anything that has come before. Just as the new technology of oil paint, replacing egg tempera, allowed

15th century artists to achieve realistic lighting effects, textures and depth of field, computer art will allow 21st century artists and designers—you—to achieve results so far only imagined.

With Version 3.0, Corel introduced three new programs to its dynamic creative package. CorelCHART is a full-featured charting program that converts data into visual images for use as illustrations. CorelPHOTO-PAINT lets artists create bitmap art from scratch, or import and manipulate photographs. Corel-SHOW lets users combine images into presentations that can be displayed on the computer screen or other projection media.

Now, Version 5.0 continues the tradition of beefing up the program with each new release. Drag-and-drop editing, the ability to use an object as a lens, up to three light sources for 3D extrusions and user-controlled screen redraws are just a few of the many new tools and special effects. Version 5.0 also adds CorelQUERY, which allows you to extract data from several different database formats and use that data to create charts in CorelCHART or Corel Ventura. And with Version 5.0, Corel Ventura, Corel's full-featured page layout program, and ARES Font Minder, an excellent font management utility, are also included in your CorelDRAW package.

If we as designers of computer-generated art are pioneering art's future, the PC is our spaceship and Corel is our fuel. We have some exciting new worlds to explore.

COMPUTER ART AS A WORLDWIDE PHENOMENON

PC artists have discovered a powerful ally in CorelDRAW software. This feature-packed program makes computer art-work and design accessible to everyone—from the budding artist, to the experienced traditional artist who is a computer neophyte, to the experienced artist who is also an experienced computer user. Winner of numerous prestigious awards world-wide, CorelDRAW is the top-selling graphics software package available today.

The phenomenal growth of the Association of Corel Artists & Designers (ACAD) offers good evidence of CorelDRAW's universal appeal. Started in 1991, ACAD serves as an educational and networking association. Today the association has over 4,500 ACAD members in 90 chapters around the world, including the USA (in 27 states and Puerto Rico), Argentina, Australia, Austria, Belgium, Brazil, Canada, Cyprus, England, Germany, Indonesia, Italy, Korea, the Netherlands, New Zealand, Portugal, Singapore and Switzerland. More chapters are being added weekly. You'll find ACAD's address in Appendix B.

WHO NEEDS THIS BOOK?

We created *Looking Good With CorelDRAW!* to serve as a "design companion," a source book of ideas and techniques for the working artist, designer and desktop publisher. Our goal is to offer a useful combination of information and inspiration. Although this book will provide the most benefit for readers who have a working knowledge of CorelDRAW basics, even Corel newcomers will find it useful as a source book.

For your convenience, *Looking Good With CorelDRAW!* includes a quick how-to guide to Corel tools and techniques (Chapters 2, 3, 4 and 5). But the heart of the book is its illustrations and galleries—and the possibilities they suggest for expanding and refining your own creative techniques. As a source of inspiration and information, this book offers as much when you flip from page to page, searching for an idea, as when you read step-by-step how to master a new CorelDRAW technique. It will serve you equally well whether you're designing a straightforward logo or creating a complex illustration.

WHAT'S INSIDE?

Chapter 1 introduces the CorelDRAW package: how to set up your program; the various ways you can use CorelDRAW; and the many sources available for creating and manipulating artwork. You can produce entirely within CorelDRAW; you can also import clip art and scanned images from outside sources.

Chapters 2, 3 and 4 review CorelDRAW's basic tools and techniques. In Chapter 2, roll-up windows are reviewed and several new roll-ups are introduced. Graphics effects covered in Chapter 2 include envelopes, contours, welds, extrusions, blends and, new in Version 5.0, intersection, trim and presets.

Chapter 3 explores working with lines, from basic Freehand and Bézier drawing techniques to the creation of special effects such as custom arrowheads, calligraphic lines and PowerLines. Color is a big part of Chapter 3, with DRAW's available fill styles discussed—uniform, fountain, bitmap and PostScript. In addition, working on Layers is introduced.

In Chapter 4, CorelDRAW's expanded and improved text-handling features are discussed, along with ways to style both Artistic and Paragraph text. Styles allow you to apply preset style parameters to objects or pages, and DRAW's desktop publishing functions, which include multipage documents, master pages and page templates.

In Chapter 5, the techniques covered in Chapters 2, 3 and 4 are combined in step-by-step guides to creating sophisticated effects such as chrome and neon, drop shadows, highlights and customized type. Object Data, a feature that allows information to be linked to graphic objects, is also discussed.

Chapter 6 features a stunning gallery of CorelDRAW black-and-white art selected from the portfolios of some of the most talented and imaginative artists working on the PC. Chapter 7 showcases CorelDRAW artwork in color.

Chapter 8, "How They Did It," offers a step-by-step explanation of how some of the "master artists" who use CorelDRAW created the artwork featured in Chapters 6 and 7, the gallery sections.

Although CorelDRAW is noted for its ease of use, Chapter 9 anticipates the inevitable occurrence of problems. The main focus here is on troubleshooting strategies and workarounds that can save time, money and headaches.

Appendix A looks at Corel's expanded package: PHOTO CD, PHOTO-PAINT, CHART, SHOW, MOVE, MOSAIC and TRACE. New to Version 5.0 are QUERY, Ventura and ARES Font Minder.

CONVENTIONS USED

To make our how-to sections as easy to follow as possible, we have incorporated a few visual aids and text conventions you'll need to be familiar with:

Icons—Wherever possible, Corel icons ( ) have been included in the text to provide a quick visual reference.

Keyboard shortcuts—A key combination within parentheses often follows an instruction. Here's an example of one of these keyboard shortcuts: In the instruction "Access the Preferences menu [Ctrl]+[J]," pressing [Ctrl] and [J] simultaneously will automatically access that menu.

Key symbols—To indicate which key to strike, we've included key symbols [Ctrl]+[L] in the text.

Apply and OK—These are shorthand for "Click the Apply button," or "Click the OK button."

Handles—We refer to handles this way:

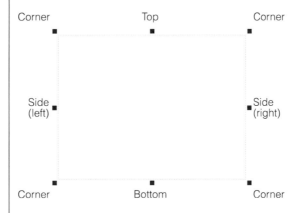

SYSTEM & SOFTWARE REQUIREMENTS

Corel is a program for power users and should be operated in the **Windows 3.1** environment. You need a **pointing device**—mouse, trackball or pen.

The faster your system, the more you'll be able to take advantage of Corel's advanced capabilities. And the faster your system, the more work you'll get done. A 486 or Pentium system with 16 megabytes of RAM should keep you happy. Short file-loading times and fast screen-redrawing are just two benefits of a powerful system.

Your **monitor** is also a key systems component. A large screen with a super VGA or 24-bit card, while not essential, will allow you to use Corel's fine-line drawing and incredible color capabilities to the fullest extent at an efficient pace.

A 300 DPI **laser or inkjet printer** will let you proof your work; a color printer is ideal but not necessary.

A **CD-ROM drive** is quickly becoming an essential part of a "hot" graphics system, both for resourcing and for storage. A CD disk's high storage capacity allows inexpensive delivery of applications as well as storage of massive resources. Developments in image access—notably the introduction of Kodak's PHOTO CD imaging service and the photographic resources this process will make available to CorelDRAW users—make CD drives even more essential for PC designers.

SYSTEM PROFILE

At the Thornhill Group, we eagerly pursue advances in PC technology. Over the years we have explored much of this technology, using our knowledge to build a central PC system that as a working tool is both time- and cost-efficient.

Today we use a Dell Dimensions P60V/XPS (Pentium) multimedia personal computer. This PC was designed for multimedia applications like those in the Corel 5.0 package. It is outfitted with 32 megabytes of RAM and a 450-megabyte Seagate hard drive. Several factory-installed components make it ideal for graphics-intensive and multimedia work, including Creative Labs's Multi-spin CD-ROM drive, a Sound Blaster 16 sound card and a #9GXE HawkEye video adapter. This high-powered system is so fast that it makes creating complex graphics a true pleasure, and while we work we can also listen to our favorite CDs!

Our printer is a Newgen TurboPS/480 with PostScript compatibility. Our scanner is a MicroTek ScanMaker 600Z. For graphics, we use Wacom's UD-1212 graphics tablet with cordless pen. Finally we have a Colorado Jumbo 250 tape backup system.

THE COMPANION DISKS

We've prepared a *Looking Good With CorelDRAW Companion Disk Set* (3 1/2- or 5 1/4-inch format) that you can purchase separately (see ordering information in the back of this book).

These disks feature an onscreen gallery of selected artwork from this book in .CDR file format. As you see these pieces draw on your screen, you'll discover how the artist constructed the elements and how the final image came together.

We've included an eclectic gallery of useful clip art from some of the industry's top sources. Each image is ready for immediate use in CorelDRAW. Art includes patterns, symbols, backgrounds and borders; logos; and theme illustrations.

The disk set includes a special collection of TrueType fonts supplied by Linotype-Hell.

To get you started designing with CorelDRAW, we've included a gallery of basic customizable templates, including forms for disk labels and report covers.

For more information on the disk, see "Companion Disks Sneak Preview" in the back of the book.

MOVING ON

Looking Good With CorelDRAW! is written and organized to serve a broad spectrum of computer artists. In fact, it's not even necessary to consider yourself an "artist" to enjoy and profit from the information and visual treats you'll find in the pages of this book. Almost everyone likes to look at interesting pictures—and almost everyone would like to be able to express themselves visually. But it's not easy to get started when you sit down and face a big white sheet of paper or a blank screen. With CorelDRAW, plus the guidance you'll find in this book and some practice and patience on your part, you can have a lot of fun becoming "graphic."

Newcomers to CorelDRAW and/or Windows software will probably want to follow the traditional path—start reading at Chapter 1 and continue sequentially through to the end of the book. Once the fundamentals are familiar, the creative process can begin.

Experienced CorelDRAW users may prefer to skim some of the chapters and sections, focusing primarily on new and upgrade features.

Computer artists at all levels can refer to the gallery chapters over and over for creative inspiration. Every successful artist "goes to school on" other artists. As long as you don't copy someone else's work and call it your own, you're free to gather your ideas and express them in your own way.

So, let's get started.

—Sheldon Nemoy & C.J. Aiken
Los Angeles, CA

SECTION I: GRAPHIC BUILDING BLOCKS

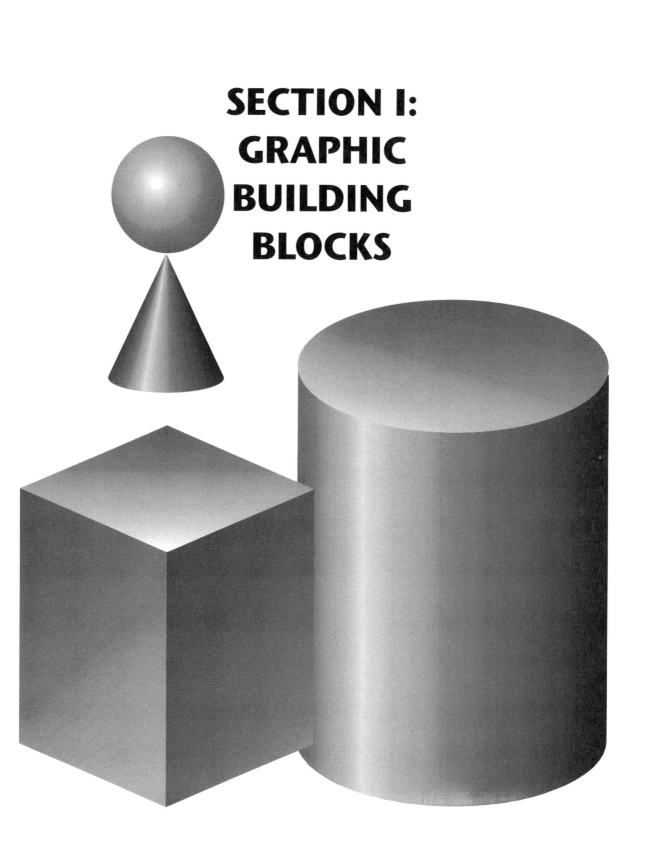

The Best Gets Better

Art is a lie that makes us realize truth.

—*Pablo Picasso*

In a single glance, the broad cross-section of artists whose works are featured in the gallery chapters of *Looking Good With CorelDRAW!* says a lot about CorelDRAW itself:

Radim Mojzis, a designer in the Czech Republic, creates logos and brochures with CorelDRAW. Marshall (Sam) Blight, an Australian artist and musician, designs the posters and packaging for his musical group. U.S. designer Gerry Wilson has created an intricately detailed drawing using blend and duplicate features. Italian designer Amadeo Gigli produces posters and technical documents in CorelDRAW at his Rome office. Puerto Rican artist William R. Clegg achieves an "exact feeling of expression" in his traditional-style florals produced in CorelDRAW and Corel PHOTO-PAINT.

The works of these and other artists showcased in this book range from the abstract to the technically precise, from the practical to the experimental. Several artists have had extensive art and design training, while others came to computer art from other backgrounds, such as editing or marketing.

Of course, the common denominator among this international talent pool is that each artist has found that CorelDRAW provides the graphics tools they need.

Corel's popularity has grown steadily since its initial release in 1989. Today it is the world's bestselling graphics software. The program's awards and citations are numerous. The winning entries in Corel-sponsored art contests are stunning.

Three things in particular ensure that CorelDRAW will stay at the forefront of art on the desktop. First, Corel's programs are easy to use. Interaction between your pointing device and onscreen dialog boxes and roll-up windows makes it easy to manipulate line, shape and color. Second, CorelDRAW offers superior text-handling. In 4.0, CorelDRAW's text capabilities were expanded considerably, with features such as text wrap, bullet text and text flow. Third, several tools—for instance, layering and tiling—make it possible to create complex full-color drawings on the PC.

THE CORELDRAW PACKAGE

Corel's graphics package includes six complete programs. Together, this collection provides artists, designers, desktop publishers and animators with fingertip access to some of the most exciting technology available.

CorelDRAW: Corel's drawing program gives every PC user the ability to create superior computer-generated artwork; and with 5.0, these drawing features have been greatly enhanced. Among the highlights of this upgrade are such desktop publishing features as drag and drop, the ability to use an object as a lens, preset effects and up to three light sources for 3D extrusions, square fountain fills, user-controlled screen redraws and additional text attributes, including underline and strikeout. The user interface now includes tabbed dialog boxes, a ribbon bar, and the ability to access INI switches such as automatic backup without leaving CorelDRAW. In addition, Version 5.0 allows you precise control over color displays through its new color management system, which allows you to calibrate your monitor, printer and scanner for more accurate onscreen images. Part of CorelDRAW's strength lies in the fact that it is a vector-based, object-oriented program, which means razor-sharp images and faster printing.

CorelDRAW 5.0 contains seven powerful utilities, four of which are new in Version 5.0:

ARES FontMinder: A font management utility that gives you complete control over all your fonts. You can create custom font groups, and even install fonts and activate them without having to restart Windows.

Adobe Acrobat Reader: Lets you view, print and share electronic documents in PDF format (Adobe's Portable Document Format). This utility is especially useful if you plan to use Corel Ventura (included in your CorelDRAW package), which supports Adobe Acrobat.

Corel QUERY: You can extract data from several different database formats and use it to create charts in CorelCHART. The data can also be imported into Corel Ventura.

TagWrite: A document tag conversion utility for use with Corel Ventura. It includes support for SGML (Standard Generalized Markup Language) and RTF (Rich Text Format), as well as many other document formats.

In addition, current CorelDRAW users are probably familiar with CorelTRACE, which lets you import bitmapped images and trace them automatically for use in CorelDRAW. Silhouette and woodcut tracing methods are now available. The scanning module in CorelTRACE and CorelPHOTO-PAINT lets you extract text from a bitmap. And last but not least, CorelMOSAIC helps you manage your graphics files. In Version 5.0, you can access MOSAIC from a roll-up within most of CorelDRAW's applications. (We'll talk more about MOSAIC later in this chapter.)

In Corel's 3.0 upgrade, three groundbreaking programs were added to the Corel package. With 4.0 each of these programs was improved and expanded. And Version 5.0 piles on additional enhancements:

CorelCHART: Lets you convert data into high-impact graphics for presentations and publications. The program includes a sophisticated Data Manager and dozens of chart display options. Version 5.0 gives you 10 new chart types and three-dimensional text effects. The spreadsheet capabilities have been greatly expanded—your spreadsheets can now have up to 16,384 rows and 240 columns, and there are more than 300 new functions.

CorelMOVE: Gives you an animation program that lets you create "actors" as multiple cels (cels are the basic visual component of animation files), then combine these cels into animated movies. MOVE includes the ability to record sounds to use with your animations. The biggest enhancement in Version 5.0 is "morphing," which lets you create way cool sci-fi effects that make it look like one object is melting into another (just like *Terminator 2*). As if that weren't enough, you can now create your actors in CorelDRAW through its new frame mode and then bring the actors into MOVE. And MOVE now supports QuickTime for Windows animations.

CorelPHOTO-PAINT: Lets you create bitmapped images as well as enhance and manipulate artwork and photographs. The 5.0 upgrade adds improved masking control, new brush styles and the ability to create custom brushes, onscreen text entry and drag-and-drop editing.

CorelSHOW: Offers all kinds of images that you can select and compile into a "slide show" on your computer screen or other projection medium. Version 5.0 adds speaker notes, a one-disk runtime player and direct text entry.

And as icing on the cake, all packages of CorelDRAW 5.0 include **Corel Ventura**, Corel's robust page layout program.

Kodak PHOTO CD: Corel is committed to keeping DRAW users up-to-date with developments in the booming computer imaging industry. One ongoing development is Kodak's PHOTO CD system, which transfers a photographic image to digital information for the PC. These digitized photos are stored on CDs and readable via a CD-ROM drive. (See Appendix A for more information.)

You can open PHOTO CD images through Corel-MOSAIC for use in DRAW, PHOTO-PAINT, CHART and MOVE (if you have a CD-ROM drive). You can then manipulate the photo images in a variety of ways and export them—for instance, to a page layout program.

Autographix Slide Service: Corel also features software to support Autographix Slide Service bureaus around the world. This service lets you convert Corel-created documents to high-quality 35mm slides, prints, posters or transparencies. Your Corel files can be transferred to the service bureau via modem or disk.

Corel's comprehensive graphics package, the PHOTO CD technology and Autographix image processing are three exciting elements of the revolution in art being inspired by computers. We'll discuss each in Appendix A ("Corel's Creative Collection"), but let's get started with the heart of Corel's creative power: CorelDRAW.

SETTING UP: DEFAULTS & PREFERENCES

CorelDRAW lets you customize many of the functions that affect program operation and screen display. Before you begin working, read through this section to find out how to specify custom defaults. Whenever you begin an extensive project, you may want to return to this section to refresh your memory as to which customization options are available.

The options are arranged by CorelDRAW 5.0 menus to make it easier for you to locate them. If you're using Version 4.0, you'll find instructions in a separate paragraph, preceded by a special icon, just below the 5.0 instructions.

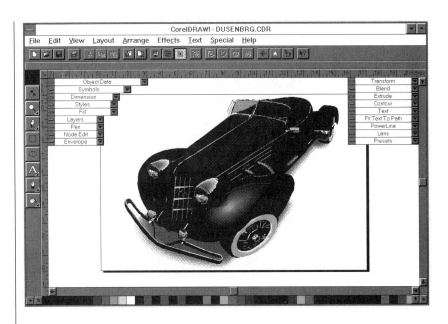

Figure 1-1: Your Corel-DRAW Opening Screen.

View Menu

Rulers: Turn on or off by choosing View, Rulers.

4.0 Choose Display, Rulers.

Toolbox: To release the toolbox from its default position at the left side of the screen, choose View, Toolbox, Floating. You can then drag the toolbox's title bar to reposition the toolbox any-where in your working area. To hide the Toolbox, deselect Visible from the cascading Toolbox menu.

4.0 Choose Display, Floating Toolbox.

Color Palette: Choose View, Color Palette to select which palette you want to use or to turn off the palette display. The choices are None, Uniform Colors, Custom Colors, Standard Colors, FOCOLTONE Colors, PANTONE Spot Colors, PAN-TONE Process Colors and TRUMATCH Colors.

4.0 Choose Display, Color Palette. The choices are No Palette, Custom Palette, Pantone Spot Colors, Pantone Process Colors and TruMatch Process Colors.

Roll-ups: Open the Roll-ups dialog box by choosing View, Roll-ups. From the Start Up Setting drop-down list, choose No Roll-ups to leave all roll-ups closed when you start CorelDRAW. All Roll-ups Arranged stacks closed roll-ups at the upper corners of your editing window. Save on Exit makes the roll-ups reappear as you left them when you last exited DRAW. Choose Custom and then Save Custom to save a custom roll-up arrangement with any name you choose.

4.0 Choose Special, Preferences, Roll-ups. The No Roll-ups and All Roll-ups Arranged options are the same. Appearance of Roll-ups on Exit is the same as Save on Exit. And Current Appearance of Roll-ups displays roll-ups as they are when you make this choice. Version 4.0 does not contain a Custom option.

Wireframe: To toggle between an image and its wireframe mode, choose View, Wireframe (or press Shift+F9).

4.0 Choose Display, Edit Wireframe (or press Shift+F9).

Bitmaps: For faster screen redraws in Wireframe view, turn bitmap display off by deselecting Visible from the cascading View, Bitmaps menu. When this option is turned off, bitmaps display as empty triangles. You can also toggle High Resolution display on or off.

4.0 Toggle Show Bitmaps on or off from the Display menu.

Color Correction: To control the amount of color correction used when you print your drawings, choose View, Color Correction. From the cascading menu, select None, Fast, Accurate or Simulate Printer.

4.0 This option is not available in Version 4.0.

Full-Screen Preview: Choose View, Full-Screen Preview to toggle between your work page and a clean-screen, full-color display.

4.0 Choose Display, Show Preview.

Text Menu

Text roll-up: To specify a default font for your current project, first make sure you don't have any objects selected, then choose Text, Text roll-up (or press Ctrl+F2). Corel remembers your last setting after each session. If you're in Artistic Text mode (selected from the toolbox), you can select alignment, typeface, type style and type size. Click the Paragraph button to choose spacing and alignment. If you are in Paragraph Text mode (at the toolbox), you can also choose hyphenation, tabs, indents and bullet text. These defaults will last for the current CorelDRAW session.

PowerType: To control text capitalization and have DRAW automatically replace abbreviations with words you specify, choose Text, Type Assist. Any settings you make in this dialog box are in effect for the current session and all future sessions (until you change them). While you're inputting artistic or paragraph text, you can tell DRAW to capitalize the first letter of all sentences, correct initial capitalization errors (when you don't let up on the Shift key quickly enough and end up with the first two letters of a word capitalized) or capitalize the names of days of the week.

Another handy shortcut in this dialog box is Change Straight Quotes to Typographic Quotes—you can just use the quote keys on the keyboard and they'll automatically be converted to typographic quote marks. The Replacement Text option can save you a lot of extra typing. For example, if you have to type "CorelDRAW Version 5.0" over and over, you could enter "cd" in the Replace text box and "CorelDRAW Version 5.0" in the With text box. Then, whenever you type "cd," Corel will automatically replace those characters with the full phrase. Another handy use for Replacement Text is automatic correction of typos. Suppose you habitually type "hte" instead of "the." You can tell Corel to automatically make the correction for you as you type.

4.0 The Type Assist options are not available in Version 4.0.

Special Menu (Preferences Dialog Box)

Open the Preferences dialog box by choosing Special, Preferences or by pressing Ctrl+J. Then select the tab that contains
the option you want to change.

> **4.0** Same instructions to get to the Preferences dialog box,
> but the dialog box doesn't contain tabs—you choose
> command buttons instead. And several of the options
> found in Preferences in 5.0 are located elsewhere in 4.0.

General Tab

Place Duplicates and Clones: You can specify horizontal/
vertical placement of an object's duplicate or clone. H=0, V=0
places the duplicate directly over the original. Specify an offset
placement to create effects such as shadowing. Use plus (+)
numbers to move the duplicate to the right and up, minus (-)
values to move it to the left and down.

> **4.0** The Place Duplicates and Clones option is in the main
> Preferences dialog box.

Nudge: Arrow keys (up, down, left and right) let you move
(nudge) a selected object. The Nudge option in Preferences lets
you set the increment of movement from 0.001 to 2 inches.

> **4.0** Nudge is in the main Preferences dialog box.

Constrain Angle: This lets you specify the amount of constraint
when you use the Ctrl key to rotate, skew, draw straight lines in
Freehand mode or adjust control points in Bézier mode.

> **4.0** Constrain Angle is in the main Preferences dialog box.

Miter Limit: Set minus values for beveled joints, plus values for
right-angled joints.

> **4.0** Miter Limit is in the main Preferences dialog box.

Undo Levels: You can choose the number of levels you want
available for this function. Set up to 99 levels of Undo. Choose a
lower setting to save memory. (The default setting is 4.)

`4.0` Undo Levels is in the main Preferences dialog box.

Right Mouse Button: Your secondary mouse button is always used to leave a copy of an object as you drag it. You can also assign a second function to this button: Object menu, 2x Zoom, Character (Character dialog box), Edit Text, Full Screen Preview (toggles between the working page and full-screen preview), or Node Edit (selects the Shape tool).

`4.0` Choose Mouse from the Preferences dialog box.

View Tab

Auto-Panning: (On or Off) Auto-panning lets the window scroll as you drag beyond its limits.

`4.0` Auto-Panning is in the main Preferences dialog box.

Interruptible Refresh: (On or Off) Allows you to interrupt a screen redraw by pressing any key or clicking the mouse button. The redraw continues as soon as you perform any other action, or when you manually refresh the screen by clicking on a scroll bar thumb, choosing View, Refresh Window or pressing Ctrl+W.

`4.0` Interruptible Display is in the main Preferences dialog box. This does the same thing as Interruptible Refresh.

Manual Refresh: (On or Off) Allows you to redraw the screen at any time by clicking a scroll bar thumb, choosing View, Refresh Window or pressing Ctrl+W.

`4.0` There is no manual refresh option in Version 4.0.

Cross Hair Cursor: (On or Off) When this box is checked, the mouse pointer turns into a set of crosshairs.

`4.0` Cross Hair Cursor is in the main Preferences dialog box.

Bitmap Thumbnail on Rotate: (On or Off) When this box is checked, rotated bitmaps are displayed as thumbnails to increase the speed of screen redraws.

`4.0` This option is not available in Version 4.0.

Preview Fountain Steps: Choose a lower number for faster redraw and printing times; choose a higher number for more subtle gradations.

4.0 Choose Display from the Preferences dialog box. You can override this preferences setting by changing the Steps setting in the Fountain Fill dialog box.

Show Objects When Moving: If you check this box to display objects onscreen as you move them, you can then specify a delay value (in milliseconds) in the Delay to Draw When Moving text box.

4.0 This option is not available in Version 4.0.

Show Status Line: (On or Off) When this option is selected, you can choose to position the status line at the top of the window (instead of in its default position at the bottom). You can also reduce the size of the status line by selecting Small Size and select Show Menu & Tool Help to display information about menu and toolbar items on the status line.

4.0 Choose Display, Show Status Line to toggle the status line display on or off. Version 4.0 doesn't give you the option of changing the position of the status line—it's placed just below the menu bar. And the Show Menu & Tool Help option is not available in Version 4.0.

Show Ribbon Bar: (On or Off) The ribbon bar contains buttons for several commonly used commands (such as Print, Save, Open, Align, Wireframe and Full Screen Preview). There are also buttons that open the Symbol and Mosaic roll-ups.

4.0 There is no ribbon bar in Version 4.0.

Show Pop-up Help: When this option is selected, help information for menus and toolbar items displays on the status line.

4.0 This option is not available in Version 4.0.

Curves Tab

4.0 All options in the 5.0 Curves tab (except Minimum Extrude Facet Size, which is not available in 4.0) are located in the Preferences – Curves dialog box in 4.0. Just choose Curves from the Preferences dialog box.

Freehand Tracking: Determines how accurately freehand Bézier curves will be drawn. A higher number creates a less accurate, smoother curve; a lower number, a more detailed thus rougher curve.

Autotrace Tracking: Determines how accurately Bézier curves will be drawn in Autotrace.

Corner Threshold: Determines whether a curve drawn in either Freehand or Autotrace mode is a smooth corner or a cusp.

Straight Line Threshold: Determines when a line will be considered a straight line or a curve. (Lower numbers are more likely to produce curves.)

AutoJoin: Lets you set the distance at which nodes will be automatically joined.

AutoReduce: Lets you set the sensitivity of the auto-reduce function (see Chapter 2, "Tools & Effects"), with a larger number meaning more nodes will be removed. The value must be between 0.001 and 1.000 inches.

Min. Extrude Facet Size: Determines the facet size CorelDRAW uses to render and print drawings that include extrusions.

Text Tab

Edit Text On Screen: (On or Off) When this option is checked, you can edit text directly on the screen. Otherwise you can edit text in the Text dialog box. Onscreen text editing has been speeded up and enhanced in Version 5.0.

4.0 In Version 4.0, you cannot turn off onscreen text editing.

Show Font Sample in Text roll-up: (On or Off) When this option is checked, the Text roll-up displays a sample of the currently selected font.

4.0 This option is not available in Version 4.0.

Minimum Line Width: Specify the number of characters you want as a minimum line width.

4.0 This option is not available in Version 4.0.

Greek Text Below: Save screen redraw time by making all paragraph text below a certain point size an approximation (where you can't actually read the text). Set a higher number for faster redraw. This setting does not affect printed type.

4.0 Choose Display from the Preferences dialog box.

Clipboard: You can save time when exporting files that contain a lot of calligraphic outlines by deselecting the Calligraphic Text option. Choose Text in Metafile if you want text attributes to be copied to the Clipboard along with the text.

4.0 These choices are not available in Version 4.0.

PANOSE Font Matching: When you open a CorelDRAW file or import text files (or graphics files that support text) that use fonts you don't have on your system, PANOSE Font Matching automatically substitutes the font that most closely resembles the unavailable font.

4.0 PANOSE Font Matching does not occur in Version 4.0.

Advanced Tab

Backup: You can direct Corel to make a backup copy whenever you save a file, and you can specify the number of minutes between automatic backups, as well as the directory in which backup files are saved.

4.0 Version 4.0 does create automatic backup files, but you have to go to the CORELDRW.INI file to change the backup settings. CORELDRW.INI can be accessed through Notepad or any text editor.

Preview Colors: Control your screen color display by choosing 256-Color Dithering or Windows Dithering. Choose Optimized

Palette for Full-Screen Preview to load your adapter's palette.

4.0 Choose Display from the Preferences dialog box.

Layout Menu
4.0 The following options are also found on the Layout menu in Version 4.0.

Page Setup
4.0 All of the options in this section are available in the Page Setup dialog box. Choose Layout, Page Setup.

Size Tab: Choose from 18 standard paper and envelope sizes. There's even a Slide option that gives you a work area with the dimensions of a 35mm slide. Or choose Custom and specify a paper size up to 30" by 30". Choose Set From Printer to automatically select the paper size currently set in the Printer Setup dialog box (File menu). The Size tab is also where you specify orientation (Portrait or Landscape).

Layout Tab: The default configuration is Full Page (see more about this option in "CorelDRAW's Desktop Features" later in this chapter and in Chapter 4's "Desktop Publishing" section). You can choose from five additional configurations, all of which divide a sheet of paper into either two or four pages.

Display Tab: Choose Facing Pages to view facing pages of a multipage document (indicate Left First or Right First). Select a color from the Paper Color drop-down to specify a background screen color for your drawings (the background color will not print—this setting affects only your screen display). Select Show Page Border to display the page outline. You should activate this setting before printing to make sure all of your drawing falls within the printable portion of the page. Choose Add Page Frame to get a printable colored frame or background the same size as your page.

Double-click anywhere in the printable page border to open the Page Setup dialog box.

Double-click on the ruler to open the Grid Setup dialog box.

Grid & Guidelines

Grid Setup: Choose Layout, Grid & Scale Setup (or press Ctrl+F3 to open the Layers roll-up, double-click on Grid and then choose Setup). In the Grid Setup dialog box, you can specify Drawing Scale, Grid Frequency, Grid origin, Show grid and Snap To Grid.

4.0 Choose Layout, Grid Setup.

Double-click on any guideline to open the Guidelines Setup dialog box.

Guidelines Setup: Before you change the guidelines settings, make sure no object is selected. Then choose Layout, Guidelines Setup (or press Ctrl+F3 to open the Layers roll-up, double-click on Guides and then choose Setup). In the Guidelines Setup dialog box, you can specify horizontal or vertical guidelines, add, move or delete guidelines (in the Guideline position field), toggle the display of guidelines on or off (Show Guidelines) and toggle Snap To Guidelines on or off.

4.0 Choose Layout, Guidelines Setup.

COREL'S CREATIVE TOOLS

By manipulating image, color and type, you can create artwork as spectacular as the examples you'll see in *Looking Good With CorelDRAW*'s gallery sections.

Working With Images

Part of Corel's power is the creative flexibility it gives artists and designers at every level of ability. Even if you boot up CorelDRAW knowing what you want, you can approach your project in several ways:

- You can import art as a scanned bitmapped image.
- You can use ready-made clip art.
- You can create art from scratch using Corel's expanded family of utilities.

Each kind of art has advantages and disadvantages, and each has its place in your library of visual resources. Whichever source you choose, the tools you'll find in DRAW, TRACE and PHOTO-PAINT will let you manipulate your artwork in many ways to achieve your creative goals.

Vector Images Versus Bitmapped Images

Because image format is a fundamental concept and an important issue for computer artists, here is a brief outline.

Computer imaging programs create art in two ways. **Bitmapped images** (also called raster or paint images) are created as though your screen were divided into a superfine grid. An image is created by making each tiny square on that grid either black or white. (This can create a stair-step pattern, which is usually not visible unless the image is greatly enlarged.)

Vector images (also called object-oriented or draw images) are defined by two points joined mathematically. This allows smooth, sharp lines.

Figure 1-2: Vector images.

Figure 1-3: Bitmapped images.

Generally, of the two formats, bitmapped images offer greater subtleties of shading and texture; but they also demand more memory and take longer to print. Vector images, on the other hand, give you sharper lines and quicker reproduction time.

Clip Art

The fastest way to "create" art is to bring ready-made images into your work from Corel's clip art and symbol libraries. (The clip art libraries must be copied to your system's hard drive when you install CorelDRAW.) These files give you thousands of pieces—from simple icons to sophisticated illustrations. If you have a CD-ROM disk drive, even more clip art is supplied on the CD that comes with the program.

CorelDRAW clip art is actually a compilation of work from more than a dozen clip art "houses," which accounts for the quality and variety of artwork. Other clip art sources include those that offer monthly "subscriptions" (so that you can continue to add to your library); those that specialize (e.g., road safety or medical graphics); and those that offer color as well as black-and-white artwork.

Clip art is available in both image formats. Vector (EPS) files can be imported into and edited in DRAW. Use PHOTO-PAINT and TRACE to import and edit bitmapped (TIFF, PCX, BMP, GIF) files.

The main advantage of clip art is that it's ready now. You don't need artistic skill or extra time to use clip art as an illustration. Just pop it into place. And don't forget: many handy symbols—from universal and professional icons to borders, map guides, ad balloons, logos and backgrounds—are available as clip art.

On the other hand, many people feel that clip art looks "canned." With CorelDRAW, no problem—just call up your image and, using the clip art as a base piece, manipulate it till you've eliminated the "canned" look.

Figure 1-4: Clip art used as illustration.

Mike Pfeiffer, Keenan-Nagle Advertising, Allentown, PA, USA

Figure 1-5: "Improved" clip art.

Nicole Ledoux, The Solutions Factory, Yorktown Heights, NY, USA

Images From Outside Sources

You can bring images into CorelDRAW from several sources including works created in paint programs (PHOTO-PAINT and others) and scanned artwork.

- Bitmapped art can be imported directly into DRAW as a graphic element. These images can be resized (with some distortion) but not modified.

- With CorelTRACE, you can trace bitmapped images for conversion to vector images for use in DRAW. This allows you to modify and resize an image yet retain its sharpness.

- You can use DRAW's Autotrace utility to create a rough tracing of an image. Just select the object, then access the Pencil tool ℓ . The Autotrace utility becomes active. Click on the area you want traced to begin the process.

- Bitmapped objects can be imported directly into PHOTO-PAINT for modification at the bit level. To bring a vector image (i.e., one created in DRAW) into PHOTO-PAINT, you must export it as a bitmapped file. (See Appendix A for more about CorelPHOTO-PAINT.)

CCAPTURE: Corel's Screen Capture Utility

Corel provides a screen capture device, which lets you print what you see on your screen (live area). You have three options:

- Press Ctrl + F3 to capture the entire desktop.

- Press Alt+Print Screen to capture the window that is currently displayed.

- Hold Alt +Pause to print a selected section of the window (a bounding box appears).

The captured screen resides on the Windows Clipboard from which you can paste the image into PHOTO-PAINT and save as a bitmapped file. To disable CCAPTURE, simply double-click the program icon again.

Creating Artwork From Scratch

Of course, Corel loves original artwork. Indeed, most of the pieces in our gallery pages were created entirely in Corel-DRAW, line by line, fill by fill. These are testaments to the versatility of the program as well as to the individual artists' talent, patience, ingenuity and computer skills!

Figure 1-6: Compare works created in DRAW (left) and PHOTO-PAINT (right).

Photo Retouching

With CorelPHOTO-PAINT's full-feature editing, photographs become an important source of manipulatable art for the desktop. Scan in a photograph and edit it with toolbox features such as Smudge, Tint and Airbrush. Apply patterns and special effects, clone sections, control brightness and contrast, etc.

Figure 1-7: Photo
retouched with
PHOTO-PAINT.

Robert Fletcher, Monterey, CA, USA

WORKING WITH TYPE

CorelDRAW gives you a wealth of sophisticated text-handling
options, from styling available typefaces to creating your own
characters. With DRAW's Text and Fit Text To Path roll-ups, it's
easy to apply special effects. You can turn your type upside
down, apply shadows, fill characters with colors and patterns—
even shape characters node by node. You can also use large
blocks of informational text (called Paragraph text) in
CorelDRAW, fine-tuning typographic features such as character
kerning and letter and line spacing. DRAW also lets you style
text with bullets, indents and tabs. You can even wrap text
around graphic objects. And there's both a Spell Checker/
Dictionary and a Thesaurus to help you polish your prose.

Version 5.0 gives you the ability to use true underlining and
strikeout, selectively apply attributes to multiple paragraphs
and justify artistic text. And one of the more powerful productivity enhancements for text is Type Assist, which is discussed
in "Setting Up: Defaults and Preferences" earlier in this chapter.

Available Fonts

Corel's collection of programs supports TrueType fonts (TTF), the Windows font format. These fonts appear onscreen just as they'll look on your printouts; so you don't have to install separate software for screen fonts and printer fonts. (Read more about TrueType fonts in your Windows manual.) Windows also supports PostScript fonts through Adobe Type Manager (ATM). With these type systems (TTF and ATM), all fonts are available to all Windows applications including the Corel collection.

Precise screen display and the ability to scale without distortion are two advantages of TrueType. In addition, many printers that don't support PostScript will print TrueType fonts. ATM allows printing of PostScript fonts on non-PostScript printers.

In addition to its extensive selection of TrueType fonts, Corel also provides musical, Greek, math and geographic symbols. In fact, the CD-ROM disk offers more than 825 different typefaces and thousands of symbols.

Arabia

Casablanca

COPPERPOT

Cupertino

Fujima XB

Kastler

Memorandum

Mystical

Switzerland

UMBRELLA

Figure 1-8: Sampling of Corel fonts.

Creating & Customizing Type

CorelDRAW makes it easy to create new typefaces and customize existing ones. Use the Layers function to provide a template to guide you as you build each special character in your alphabet. After you have created a character set, simply export it as an Adobe Type 1 font or a TrueType font. Also, sophisticated options such as precise character spacing and word spacing are built-in features. (Refer to your *CorelDRAW User's Guide* for specific instructions.)

If you created a typeface with Corel prior to the 3.0 release, you need to take special precautions to save your work, due to Corel's adoption of the TrueType system. FontMonger, an ARES product, lets you convert your WFN fonts (created in pre-3.0 CorelDRAW) to TrueType and PostScript fonts. And ARES Font Minder, which is included in your CorelDRAW package, will help you keep track of all those custom typefaces.

Color Control

Corel gives you a multitude of colors, as well as lots of ways to apply color to your artwork and type. Choose from several models, including

- CMYK Color Model
- RGB Color Model
- HSB Color Model
- Grayscale
- Uniform Colors
- FOCOLTONE Colors
- PANTONE Spot Colors
- PANTONE Process Colors
- TRUMATCH Colors

In addition, you can create your own colors by controlling percentages of CMYK—cyan, magenta, yellow and black; RGB—red, green, blue; or HSB—hue, saturation and brightness; and, finally, percentage of tint.

For convenience, you can collect colors in custom palettes. You can even designate a palette to load automatically when you open CorelDRAW.

CORELDRAW'S DESKTOP FEATURES

For the desktop designer and publisher, creating the artwork is only half the job. You still need to apply it to a publication—a brochure, newsletter, book or article. CorelDRAW provides the features of a page layout program so that you can complete your entire publishing project using the Corel package. And if the tools supplied by DRAW aren't enough, Version 5.0 is packaged with Corel Ventura, a full-featured page layout application.

Multipage Documents

CorelDRAW lets you create documents up to 999 pages long. At the Layout menu, choose Insert Page to create a multipage document, or Delete Page.

A page counter at the bottom of your Editing Window indicates which page you're currently working on and keeps track of the total number of pages in your project.

The Layers roll-up in CorelDRAW lets you set up a Master Page with standardized settings, such as margins, and repeating information, such as graphics, headers and footers.

Several preset page layout formats are provided or the Layout tab in the Page Setup dialog box. These include

- Full page: this is the default style.
- Book: prints two pages per sheet.
- Booklet: prints two pages per sheet.
- Tent card: prints two pages per sheet, with a top fold indicated.
- Side-fold card: prints four pages per sheet with left-side fold indicated.
- Top-fold card: prints four sides per sheet with top-fold indicated.

Facing Page View

To view facing pages, choose Layout, Page Setup, Display, Facing Pages.

4.0 Choose Layout, Page Setup, Facing Pages.

Automatic Imposition

Upon printing, CorelDRAW will automatically reorder pages for correct imposition.

Text-Styling Features

CorelDRAW contains a superior arsenal of text-handling tools (see more about text in Chapter 4, "Text & Publishing"). The following are just a few of Corel's text features:

- Text flow: When you indicate a beginning frame, text will automatically flow into subsequent frames. As frames are sized, text reflows to fill each frame.
- Column settings: Choose column and gutter widths. You can have up to eight columns on a page.
- Text wrap: You can shape type around an object by applying an envelope to the text then modifying the envelope with the shape tool.
- Bullet text: Simply click a button to turn Paragraph text into Bullet text. Then click the Bullet icon. You can choose a customized bullet from a symbols display menu at the dialog box.
- Tabs and indents: Use preset tabs and indents, or customize your settings at the Tabs or Indents dialog box (Paragraph dialog box under Text menu).

In addition, CorelDRAW lets you extract text from a drawing, edit it in your word processing program, then return it to the drawing.

Color Prepress

CorelDRAW provides an automated prepress process that gives you sophisticated previewing options. You can create spot color and four-color process separations. For color analysis, a densitometer (a printed indication of one color's density when printed) can print separately on each CMYK page, or print as progressive proofs combining two or more CMYK colors. Available prepress controls include dot gain, trapping and overprinting. (See Chapter 9, "More Helpful Information," for more about CorelDRAW's color prepress features.)

MANAGING YOUR COREL IMAGES

Your Corel programs pack so much visual information into so tiny a space that information management deserves your special attention. Corel provides several features to help you manage and manipulate images and data. (In addition to MOSAIC and the Graphics Database, both part of CorelDRAW, Corel's other programs feature information management devices, including CHART's Data Manager and MOVE's Library function, both discussed in Appendix A.)

CorelMOSAIC

If you have, or plan to have, an extensive collection of graphics files, you'll find MOSAIC an invaluable utility. Essentially, MOSAIC is a handy graphics librarian, designed to make handling these often-bulky files easier. In Version 5.0, MOSAIC can be accessed as a roll-up directly from most of the Corel applications.

With MOSAIC, you can

- Organize your files into a "library" for easy management.
- Display miniature representations, or "thumbnails," of several files at once.
- Group, name and print multiple thumbnails.

- Perform batch operations, such as printing, importing/exporting and copying.
- Compress files to save disk space.

Figure 1-9: CorelMOSAIC Thumbnail Gallery showing part of Corel's CD-ROM clip-art collection.

The Object Data Graphics Database

One of DRAW's most useful new features is Object Data, a database keyed to graphics objects.

Think of our gallery artist who creates floorplans as presentations to his interior design clientele. An Object Data worksheet could store information on each piece of furniture: manufacturer, style, color, dimensions, price, etc.

To create your database, CorelDRAW provides the Object Data roll-up window. Use the secondary mouse button and click on the object you want to attach the database to, then select Object Data roll-up on the Object menu. Database information is displayed as editable columns on a worksheet. All or part can be printed.

MOVING ON

Now that you know more about the contents of your Corel-DRAW 5.0 package, we're sure your mouse finger is getting itchy. With your setup Preferences complete, you're almost ready to discover for yourself just how graphically powerful the new Corel programs can be.

But before you start your next computer masterpiece, the following three chapters will review CorelDRAW's basic tools, and provide shortcuts and tips for increasing your productivity.

Tools & Effects

*Technique is merely a means,
not an end in itself.*

— M.C. Escher

All aspiring artists and designers, including those who create on the computer, begin their training by learning to use the basic tools of their craft. The next three chapters are a review of your basic CorelDRAW artist's tools. Like pencils, brushes and paints, these tools allow you to create and manipulate lines and shapes, add dimension and texture, and instantly apply special effects.

CorelDRAW's menus give you access to several manipulation modes, for example, Stretch, Mirror, Move and Rotate. By accessing functions through these menus, submenus and dialog boxes, you can control your artwork "by the numbers"—that is, by specifying precise values for such elements as line weights, angles, percentages, etc.

But CorelDRAW also gives you fast-and-easy ways to create, such as roll-up windows, which we'll explore in this chapter. You'll probably want to keep this information nearby when you start working at your computer. We've provided not only step-by-step instructions but plenty of examples to show how these tools can be used.

This quick reference guide is project-based. It is not meant to be comprehensive or in-depth (your *CorelDRAW User's Guide* covers all the details of your software program). But when you leaf through *Looking Good With CorelDRAW!* and say, *"That's what I want to do . . . "* you'll find a quick step-by-step to guide you.

ABOUT ROLL-UP WINDOWS

First introduced in Version 3.0, roll-up windows have proven themselves so useful that CorelDRAW has continued to add additional roll-ups to its arsenal in each new version. There are now 19 roll-ups: Blend, Contour, Envelope, Extrude, Fill, Fit Text to Path, Layers, Node Edit, Object Data, Pen, PowerLine, Style, Symbols, Text; and, new in 5.0, Dimension, Lens, Presets, Transform and Mosaic.

Roll-up windows provide shortcuts to many special effects. The windows can remain open on your page, or they can be neatly tucked into a corner, ready for immediate access. In Chapter 1, "The Best Gets Better," we covered how to set up your preferences for roll-up windows.

While each roll-up window controls different functions, they all work the same way:

- To roll up or down: Click the arrow in the top right corner.
- To move: Drag the window at the title bar.
- To arrange: Click the button in the top left corner. Choose Arrange to close your window and move it to the top corner of your work area; or choose Arrange All to close all active windows and arrange them in the top corners of your work area.
- To apply: After you've chosen functions within a window, click Apply to carry out those functions.
- To close: Double-click the top left corner (the Close button) to close the window.

    If you need help with any roll-up, all you need to do is either
- Press and hold `Shift`+`F1` and click on the roll-up.
- At the Close button, click once to access the Control menu and choose Help. (Click twice to close the roll-up.)

All roll-up windows on this page are new to version 5.0.

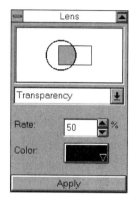

Figure 2-1: The Dimension, Lens and Presets roll-up windows.

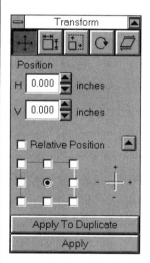

Figure 2-2: The Transform and Mosaic roll-up windows.

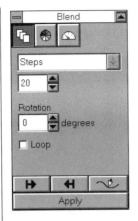

Figure 2-3: The Blend, Countour and Envelope roll-up windows.

Figure 2-4: The Extrude and Fill roll-up windows.

Figure 2-5: The Fit Text To Path, Layers and Node Edit roll-up windows.

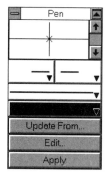
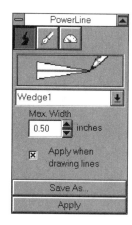

Figure 2-6: The Object Data, Pen and PowerLine roll-up windows.

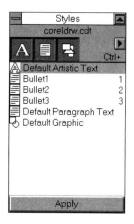
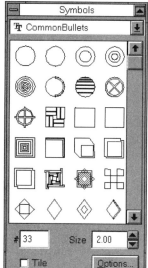
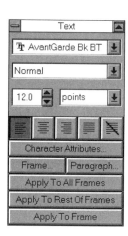

Figure 2-7: The Styles, Symbols and Text roll-up windows.

USING YOUR CORELDRAW TOOLS

CorelDRAW's basic tools make graphics manipulations really simple, whether you're customizing type or building graphic elements by sizing, duplicating and adding color. These same manipulations, if performed in a traditional design studio, would be time-consuming and costly. But on your computer screen, you can see the effects immediately, and you can continue to refine your artwork until it's just right.

CorelDRAW's intuitive interface and power shortcuts make using this program a natural for traditional artists. First, Corel gives you many familiar tools; for example, drawing with the Freehand Pencil tool mimics traditional drawing, and the Rectangle and Ellipse tools are like drawing with a template.

In addition, Corel's powerful performance makes keyboard and mouse manipulations easy. For example, simply click once to select an object, then resize or reshape it with one mouse motion. A double-click gives you instant access to skewing and rotating. Shortcuts include toggling between tools, and quick keyboard access to menus and dialog boxes.

Shaping

Use the Shape tool ✦ to change an object's outline. By selecting an object in Shape Tool mode, you activate nodes on the object's outline. Move these nodes to reshape the object, or double-click on a node to activate control points for shaping.

To round corners on squares and rectangles:

1. Draw a square or rectangle using the Rectangle tool ☐ .

2. Access the Shape tool ✦ (F10).

3. Select the object, and nodes appear. (If you're working in wireframe mode, select the outline.)

4. Drag a corner node; it will split into two nodes, with the corner curving between them.

5. Release the mouse button when you have the desired shape.

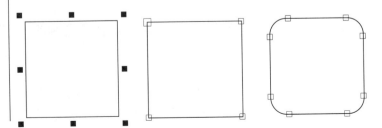

Figure 2-8: Rounding corners on squares and rectangles.

To create arcs and wedges:

1. Draw a circle or ellipse with the Ellipse tool ◯ (F7).
2. Access the Shape tool ⟋ (F10).
3. Select your object and a node appears. (If you're working in wireframe view, click on the outline.)
4. To create an arc, drag the node *outside* the outline. To create a wedge, drag the node *inside* the outline.
5. Release the mouse button when you have the desired shape.

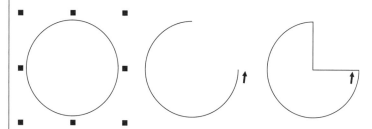

Figure 2-9: Creating arcs and wedges.

To reshape rectangles and ellipses:

1. In Pick Tool mode ↖ , select your object.
2. Convert to curves Ctrl+V.
3. Access the Shape tool ⟋ (F10).
4. Drag nodes to shape the object.

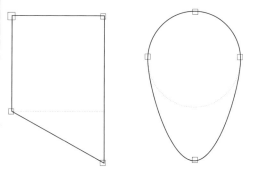

Figure 2-10: Reshaping rectangles and ellipses.

To shape curve objects:

Note: All objects created with the Pencil tool ℓ are curve objects.

1. Select the object.

2. Access the Shape tool ⬈ (F10).

3. Drag a node to reshape the desired portion of the outline. To drag several nodes, select the desired nodes with a marquee, or hold down the Shift key and click on the nodes. When you drag any single selected node, all selected nodes will move. Click on a node to access control points. You can drag a control point to shape your object as well.

Hold Ctrl when dragging nodes or control points to constrain your drag to a vertical or horizontal movement.

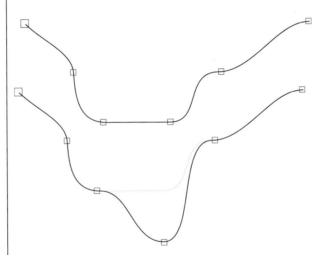

Figure 2-11: Shaping curve objects.

To add nodes:

In Shape Tool mode ⬈ , access the Node Edit roll-up by double-clicking on the object. Click on the place you want to add a single node and choose the Add button ⊞ (or click the ⊞ on your numeric keypad). Your object will be redrawn with the new node.

Figure 2-12: The Node Edit roll-up.

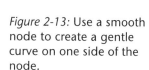 **You can only add nodes to curve objects. If you want to add nodes to a rectangle or ellipse, first convert it to a curve.**

To add new nodes halfway between existing nodes:

1. In Shape Tool mode 𝄖, select the object.

2. Double-click on a node to access the Node Edit roll-up.

3. Marquee select an area with two nodes.

4. Click the Add button ⊞.

5. To add multiple nodes, hit the ⊞ again. This will double the number of nodes added.

Note: The node will be added between the two pre-existing nodes and all line segments will be equal lengths.

To specify node type:

Click on the node you want to specify, or marquee-select several nodes. From the Node Edit roll-up, choose the node type: Cusp, Smooth, Symmetrical.

Figure 2-13: Use a smooth node to create a gentle curve on one side of the node.

Figure 2-14: Use a cusped node to create a sharp curve on one side of the node.

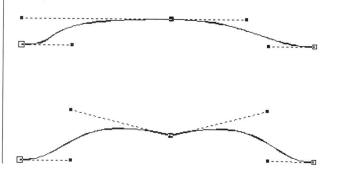

Figure 2-15: Use a symmetrical node to create symmetrical curves on either side of the node.

Figure 2-15: Use a symmetrical node to create symmetrical curves on either side of the node.

To delete nodes:

You can delete nodes simply by selecting your node and hitting the minus button ⊟ on the Node Edit roll-up, or by using the Delete key. To delete several nodes, marquee-select and hit the minus button ⊟.

Node Options

Along with the new buttons for adding ⊞, deleting ⊟, breaking [Page Up] and joining [Home] nodes, you can also select:

- Auto-Reduce: This automatically deletes nodes so that the curve isn't effected.
- Stretch: Select at least two nodes and click this button. Handles appear that let you stretch and scale the selected section of your curve.
- Rotate: Select at least two nodes and click this button. Handles appear that let you rotate and skew the selected section of your curve. Drag corner handles to rotate, middle handles to skew.
- Pressure Edit: This option is for editing PowerLines, which we'll discuss in Chapter 3, "Lines & Fills."
- Elastic Mode: Select multiple nodes and drag one node. As you move the mouse, the movement of the selected area is like elastic expanding and contracting.

Node Editing Shortcuts

[Tab]: Selects one node forward.

[Shift]+[Tab]: Selects one node back.

[Home]: Selects first node in selected object.

[End]: Selects last node in selected object.

Use the Shape tool to reshape objects. You can reshape by grabbing a line as well as a node or handle.

Shaping Text

1. Create text using the Text Tool mode 𝔸 (F8).
2. Select in Pick tool mode ↖ and convert to curves Ctrl + V .
3. Use the Shape tool ⟨ (F10) to reshape text by manipulating nodes.

Figure 2-16: Created text.

To shape objects and text:

1. Create or import an object.
2. Convert the object to curves if necessary.
3. Select multiple nodes with a marquee.
4. Drag the selected area.
5. Refine the shape by manipulating nodes.
6. Insert the text.
7. Convert the text to curves.
8. Use nodes to manipulate the text.

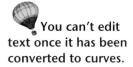 **Paragraph text cannot be converted to curves. You can only shape Artistic Text.**

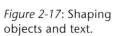 **You can't edit text once it has been converted to curves.**

Figure 2-17: Shaping objects and text.

Effects

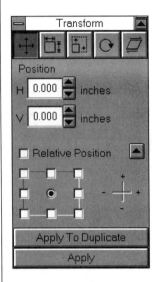

Figure 2-18: All of the effects in this section can be accessed through the Transform roll-up window. Choose Effects, Transform Roll-up or press Alt+F7.

4.0 The Transform roll-up is not available in Version 4.0.

Stretching and scaling are among the manipulations you can use to transform the shape of objects. *Stretch* changes an object's height or width ↔ . *Scale* changes both height and width proportionally ✛ .

1. In Pick Tool mode ▶ , select your object(s).

Figure 2-19:
Cupid selected.

2. Hold the mouse button down and drag a handle to stretch your object—left or right side handles to make it wider/ narrower, top or bottom handles to make it taller/shorter.

Figure 2-20: Cupid
stretched and squeezed.

Hold the mouse button down and drag a corner handle to scale
your object.

Figure 2-21: Cupid scaled.

3. When your object is the desired shape or size, release the
   mouse button.

Hold ⌈Ctrl⌉ to stretch or scale in 100% increments.

Hold ⌈Shift⌉ when dragging a top, bottom or side handle and your
object will stretch in opposite directions. Hold ⌈Shift⌉ when
dragging a corner and your object will scale in all four directions (relative to the center point).

Figure 2-22: Cupid
constrained.

Press Ctrl + Shift and your object will scale in 100% increments from the object's center point.

Figure 2-23: Cupid scaled from center.

Flip & Mirror

Flip creates a reversed mirror image; mirror leaves the original and creates a reverse image.

To flip an object:

1. Drag the handle *across* the object.
2. To flip to the *right* or the *left*, drag the opposite side handle across the object. To flip an object *in place* (i.e., create a reversed image with the same center point as your original), hold Shift down.

Hold Ctrl to constrain the object to its original size.

Figure 2-24: Cupid flipped.

To mirror:

1. Drag a handle *across* the object. *As you drag*, click the right mouse button to leave the original (or press + on the numeric keypad).

Hold [Ctrl] to constrain the object to its original size.

Figure 2-25: Cupid
mirrored.

To scale, repeat and mirror:

1. Select the object.

2. Scale, leaving the original. (Choose Apply & Duplicate
   instead of Apply.)

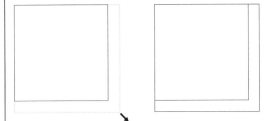

Figure 2-26: Square scaled.

To ensure that
your outline scales
automatically with your
object, choose Scale
With Image in the
Outline Pen dialog box
(F12).

3. Press [Ctrl]+[R] to repeat the scaled image several times.

Figure 2-27: Squares
resized and repeated.

4. Select all objects. Press [Ctrl]+[L] to combine. (Or choose
   Arrange, Combine.)

5. Choose fill, no outline.

Figure 2-28: Square combined and filled.

6. Mirror, leaving the original.

Figure 2-29: Square mirrored.

Note: "White" areas are actually transparent. Background elements will show through.

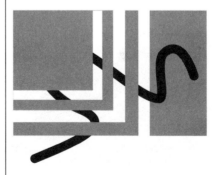

Figure 2-30: Background object visible through transparent (white) areas.

Rotate

The Rotate/Skew option on the Effects menu lets you turn your object around a center point.

Watch the Status Line for the angle of rotation.

1. In Pick Tool mode ↖ , access the Rotate/Skew option by double-clicking on the object. (If working in wireframe view, select the outline.)

Figure 2-31: Jet airplane rotated around its center point.

2. Move the cursor to a corner handle so that the ✛ icon becomes activated.

3. Drag the handle in the desired direction.

4. When your object is in the desired position, release the mouse button.

To customize the degree of rotation, choose Special, Preferences, General (or press Alt + J). (In Version 4.0, Constrain Angle is in the main Preferences dialog box.)

Hold Ctrl to rotate in the constrain angle you specified on the Preferences menu.

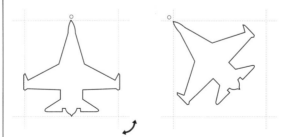

Figure 2-32: The jet's center of rotation has been changed.

To change the center of rotation:

1. To move the center of rotation ⊙, select the object's center point with your cursor and drag it to the desired location.

Radial Symmetry

Use the repeat call to create a symmetrical design that rotates around a center point. Many natural objects, such as flowers, are radially symmetric.

When moving the center point, hold Ctrl down to constrain the center point to one of the eight handle points or the center; this can be handy when you need to relocate the exact center.

1. Using the Pick tool, access Rotate/Skew mode by double-clicking on your object. If desired, select and move the center point.

2. Rotate 15 percent. Retain the original by clicking the right mouse button as you rotate (or press + on the numeric keypad).

3. Press Ctrl + R to repeat.

4. Choose fill, no outline ✕.

5. Press Ctrl + C to combine (or choose Combine on the Arrange menu).

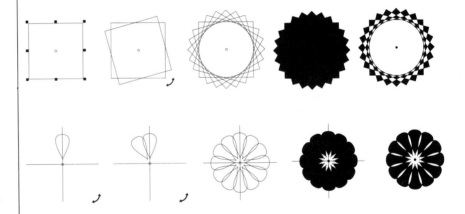

Figure 2-33: Examples of radial symmetry.

Figure 2-34: A different kind of radial symmetry.

Skew

Skewed objects that are bitmaps display as gray on your screen. The white corner triangle shows the bitmapped object's orientation.

1. In Pick Tool mode ↖, access the Rotate/Skew option by double-clicking on the object. (If working in wireframe view, select the outline.)

2. Move the cursor to a top, bottom or side handle ↔. The ┼ cursor becomes activated.

3. For horizontal skewing, choose a top or bottom handle. Drag the handle left or right. For vertical skewing, choose a side handle. Drag the handle up or down.

4. When the object is slanted at the desired angle (see the Status Line), release the mouse button.

Hold Ctrl down to constrain the skew to the constrain angle you specified on the Preferences menu.

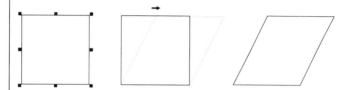

Figure 2-35: Skewing to create a slant.

Creating Op Art

1. Skew, leaving the original.
2. Press Ctrl + R to repeat.
3. Select all.
4. Press Ctrl + L to combine. (Or choose Arrange, Combine.)
5. Fill your object.

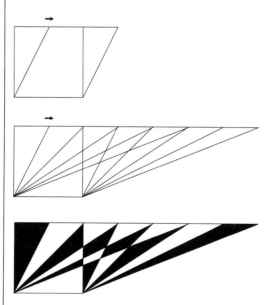

Figure 2-36: Op art created by combining several objects.

Creating Shadows

A simple way to add the illusion of depth is to give your object a shadow. Use the skew transition to position the shadow.

1. Select an object. Fill it, but remove any outline.
2. Skew, leaving the original.
3. Fill the skew with 20% gray.
4. Send the skew to the background [Shift]+[Page Down].
5. Select the skew and size appropriately.

To leave the original object, click the right mouse button or press [+] on the numeric keypad.

Figure 2-37: Q with a skewed shadow.

Scale, Copy & Combine

Figure 2-38: Image created using Scale, Copy and Combine.

Figure 2-39: Image created using Scale, Copy, Combine and Mirror.

To revert to your original object, choose Effects, Clear Transformations.

Special Effects

Corel makes it very easy to add visually interesting special effects to any object, including type. "Enveloping" makes an object conform to an unusual shape. The extrusion and perspective functions immediately pull an object into 3D view. Blending lets you transform one object or color into another.

Envelope

The Envelope effect has its own roll-up (accessible via the Effects menu or by pressing $\boxed{\text{Ctrl}}$ + $\boxed{\text{F7}}$).

Figure 2-40: The Envelope roll-up window.

To Add New:

1. In Pick Tool mode ↖ , select the object.

2. Choose Effects, Envelope Roll-Up or press `Ctrl`+`F7`.

3. Select the envelope style (see illustrations).

Figure 2-41: A Straight Line envelope ◁

Figure 2-42: A Single Arc envelope ◁

Figure 2-43: A Two Curves envelope ◁

Figure 2-44: An Unconstrained envelope ⋏

4. Select Add New. A bounding box in the chosen shape will appear around your object.

5. Grab a handle with your cursor and drag in the desired direction.
   - Top and bottom handles move only up/down.
   - Left and right side handles move only left/right.
   - Corner handles move up/down *and* left/right.
   - Handles on unconstrained envelopes move in all directions.

6. Click on Apply.

7. To clear an envelope, choose Edit, Undo or Effects, Clear Envelope or press Ctrl + Z.

Hold Ctrl down when you drag and the selected handle *plus* its opposite will move in the direction of the drag.

Figure 2-45: Dragging the envelope with the Ctrl key down.

Hold Shift down when you drag and the selected handle and its opposite will move away from each other.

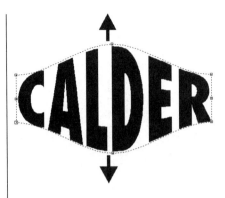

Figure 2-46: Dragging the envelope with the Shift key down.

Press Ctrl + Shift . When you drag, all four corners or sides will move away from each other.

Figure 2-47: Dragging the envelope with the Ctrl and Shift keys down.

To apply a second envelope while retaining the shape of the first:

Select the object, choose the second envelope shape and choose Add New.

Figure 2-48: Adding a second envelope. (The object on the right has two envelopes.)

Add Preset: Click this bar to access a menu of preset envelope forms. Choose one and click Apply.

Create From: This option lets you use the shape of any object as an envelope shape.

1. Create the new envelope shape you want to apply to your object.

2. Select the object.

3. Select Create From.

4. With the pointer that appears, indicate the new envelope shape.

5. Click Apply.

Figure 2-49: Object and new envelope shape.

Mapping Options: This affects the way DRAW makes an object conform to its envelope.

- Original: Compares handles on selected object to handles of envelope.

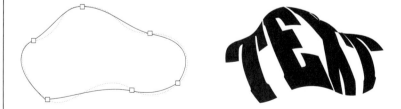

Figure 2-50: Original mapping option.

- Putty: Fits an object to its envelope by compressing from corners only.

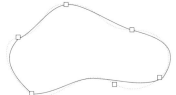 

Figure 2-51: Putty mapping option.

- Horizontal: Fits an object to its envelope by compressing primarily from the sides.

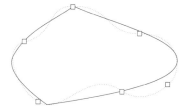 

Figure 2-52: Horizontal mapping option.

- Vertical: Fits an object to its envelope by compressing primarily from the top and bottom.

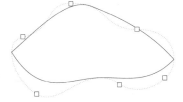 

Figure 2-53: Vertical mapping option.

• Text: Automatically activated when you apply an envelope to Paragraph Text.

🎈 **Use an envelope to wrap Paragraph Text inside an object.**

Ye, mine   leove
süstren, ne schulen   habben no best bute
kat one. Ancre, thet haveth eihte thuncheth bet
husewif, ase Marthe was, than ancre; ne none-weis ne
mei heo beon Marie mid grithfulnesse of heorte. Vor
theonne mot heo thenchen of the kues foddre and of
heordemmonne huire, oluhnen thene heiward,
warien hwon me pünt hire, and yelden, thauh,
the hermes. Wat Crist, this is lodlich
thing hwon me maketh mone in
tune of ancre eihte.

Figure 2-54: Text mapping option.

Keep Lines: When activated, this retains the linearity of the enveloped object—lines stay straight instead of curving to conform to the envelope.

Figure 2-55: Vertical mapping option with Keep Lines applied.

🎈 **To access the nodes on your original object, remove the envelope or reconvert your object to curves** `Ctrl`+`Q`.

Fitting Text to a Shape

1. Create a shape (closed object).
2. Place your text within the shape.
3. With text highlighted, open the Envelope roll-up (Effects, Envelope Roll-Up or `Ctrl`+`F7`).
4. Click on the Unconstrained Envelope button (the last one on the right).
5. Choose Add New.
6. Use handles and control points to shape the text against the outline.

7. Choose Apply.

For precision, convert the text to curves and use the Node Edit tool to fit the text to the outline. If desired, delete the original shape.

Figure 2-56: Fitting CALDER to a shape.

Perspective

In 1-point perspective, an object appears to recede toward a single vanishing point:

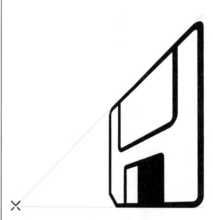

Figure 2-57: 1-point perspective showing vanishing point.

In 2-point perspective, the object appears to recede toward two vanishing points:

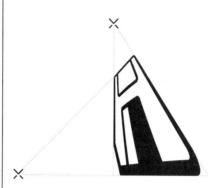

Figure 2-58: 2-point perspective showing vanishing points.

1. In Pick Tool mode ▶ , select your object.
2. Choose Effects, Add Perspective. A bounding box with corner handles appears around your object, and the cursor changes to a Shape tool ▶ cursor. When the cursor is over a handle, it changes to a cross ┼ .

Figure 2-59: Train: original object with no perspective.

3. To create 1-point perspective, drag a handle.

Figure 2-60: With 1-point perspective.

Use Ctrl to constrain your handle to the vertical or horizontal.

Figure 2-61: With constrained 1-point perspective.

Use `Ctrl` + `Shift` to move opposite handles away from each other.

4. To create 2-point perspective, drag on the diagonal.

Figure 2-62: With 2-point perspective.

Watch your **Status Line for the coordinates of your vanishing points; "very far" indicates your vanishing point is off your screen.**

5. Click and drag on a vanishing point ✕ to change perspective. (If you move the vanishing point ✕ too close, the object will revert to its original perspective.)

6. Release the mouse button to draw the new perspective.

To create multiple perspectives:

Choose Add Perspective again to create multiple perspectives.

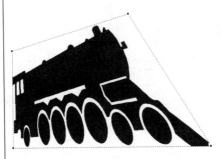

Figure 2-63: With multiple perspectives.

To clear perspective:

Choose Effects, Clear Perspective. Repeat for each layer of perspective applied.

To copy perspective:

Select the object you want a perspective copied *to*, then choose Effects, Copy, Perspective From. The mouse pointer turns into a thick arrow. At this point, click on the outline of the object whose perspective you want to copy.

You can't copy an object's perspective if you've added other effects to the object since you added the perspective.

Contour

This effect applies concentric shapes radiating within or around a selected object. These appear much like the lines of a contour map.

To give your contour lines a smooth, blend-like look, turn off the line attributes ✕ on the Pen tool flyout menu.

Figure 2-64: The Contour roll-up window.

The Contour roll-up (access by choosing Effects, Contour Roll-Up or by pressing Ctrl + F9) lets you specify several parameters:

To Center: Creates contour lines from the outline inward to the center of the object. Number of steps is determined automatically as a function of the Offset value.

Figure 2-65: Contour, center offset.

Inside: Creates contour lines from the object's outline inward.

Figure 2-66: Contour, inside offset (left) and Contour, outside offset (right).

Outside: Creates contour lines from the object's outline outward. Note that this selection will make your object larger.

Figure 2-67: Blended contours.

 **Groups of objects, bitmaps and OLE-linked objects cannot be contoured.**

Offset: Specify the distance you want between contour lines (7.2 to 720 points).

Steps: Specify the number of steps (number of contour lines) you want applied to the object.

Outline & Fill: Click to display a color palette. Choose the color you want your contour steps to blend to.

Using Contour to Create an Outline, Drop Shadow & Graduated Fill:

1. Set type at 100 points.

2. Select No Fill and apply a black outline.

3. From the Contour roll-up, choose
   • Outside
   • Offset .05 points
   • Steps "1"

4. Apply.

5. From the Arrange menu, choose Separate.

6. Select the contour (outline), apply a linear fill and remove the outline.

7. Select the contour and fill with white.

8. Select the contour, duplicate, fill with black, send to back and offset.

Figure 2-68: Contour with Fountain Fill, Outline and Drop Shadow.

Weld

When you weld two or more overlapping objects (you can weld as many as you like), three things happen:

- The objects' outlines are joined at the points they intersect.
- Any interior lines are eliminated.
- When you select the objects in sequence, the new weld object takes on the attributes (fill, outline, etc.) of the last object you select. When you use marquee-selection, the new object uses the attributes of the first object you select.

To weld:

1. Select two or more objects.

2. To weld objects across layers, activate the Multilayer selection on the Layers roll-up.

3. Choose Arrange, Weld.

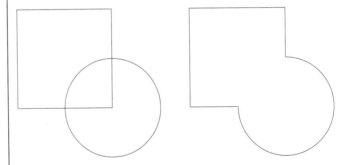

Figure 2-69: Two objects (left) with the Weld feature applied (right).

Intersect

When you intersect two or more overlapping objects (you can intersect as many as you like), the following happens:

- The objects' paths are joined at the points they intersect.
- A new object is created that uses only the intersected area.
- When you select objects in sequence, the new object takes on the attributes (fill, outline, etc.) of the last object you select. When you use marquee-selection, the new object uses the attributes of the first object you select.

To intersect objects:

1. Select two or more objects.

2. To intersect objects across layers, activate the Multilayer selection on the Layers roll-up.

3. Choose Arrange, Intersect.

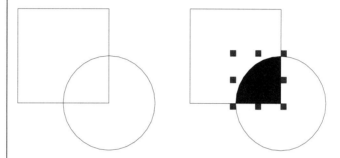

Figure 2-70: Two objects (left) with the Intersect feature applied (right). This feature is new to Version 5.0.

Trim

When you trim two or more overlapping objects (you can trim as many as you like), the following happens:

- The objects' paths are separated at the points where they intersect.
- The trimmed object is reshaped by the other selected objects.
- If you select objects in sequence, the object you select last is the one that gets trimmed. When you use marquee-selection, the first object you create is trimmed by the other objects.

To trim an object:

1. Select two or more objects.

2. To trim objects across layers, activate the Multilayer selection on the Layers roll-up.

3. Choose Arrange, Trim.

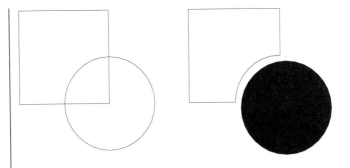

Figure 2-71: Two objects (left) with the square trimmed by the circle (right). This feature is new to Version 5.0.

Extrude

With the Extrude roll-up, you can add visual projections to your object and give it a three-dimensional effect.

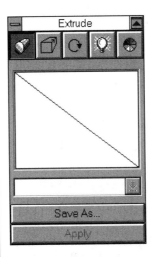

Figure 2-72: The initial Extrude roll-up window.

4.0 In Version 4.0, the Extrude roll-up has a different appearance. The buttons are positioned vertically along the left side, and there is no Presets option.

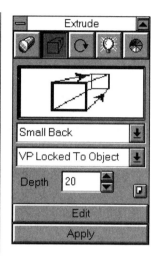

Figure 2-73: The Extrude roll-up window.

To Extrude an Object:

1. Choose Effects, Extrude Roll-Up or press [Ctrl]+[E] to access the Extrude roll-up.

2. You can control the extrusion in two ways:

   Drag the vanishing point control ✕, or from the roll-up, select type of extrusion (see illustrations):
   - Small Back
   - Small Front
   - Big Back
   - Big Front
   - Front Parallel
   - Back Parallel

   As you make these selections, they are previewed in the roll-up window.

When extruding an object, **Front and Back** represent where the vanishing point falls in relation to the object.

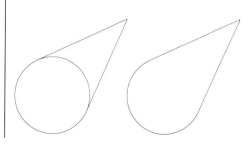

Figure 2-74: Small Back (left) and Small Front (right).

66 *Looking Good With CorelDRAW*

Figure 2-75: Big Front (left) and Big Back (right).

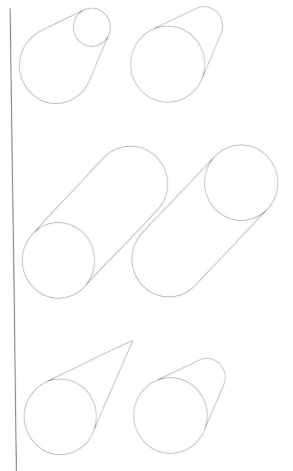

Figure 2-76: Back Parallel (left) and Front Parallel (right).

Figure 2-77: Depth 99% (left) and Depth 50% (right).

To adjust an extrusion's vanishing point, hold down Shift and drag the vanishing point control ✕, or set Horizontal and Vertical values.

3. Make finer adjustments of Depth.
   • Specify percentage of extrusion, up to 99% (see illustration). A 99% extrusion will extend to the vanishing point. Positive values make the object appear to recede; negative values make the object appear to project toward you.
   • Click the page button ☐ to specify Horizontal and Vertical points.
   • Measured From lets you set the vanishing point anywhere on the page (for example, H=0, V=0 puts the vanishing point at the lower left-hand corner of the page). Selecting Object Center, H=0, V=0, places the reference point at the center of the object.

4. Click Apply.

If desired, you can also manipulate rotation, light source and color of your extruded object using the roll-up.

Rotate:

1. Click the rotate icon ↻. A new set of options will appear.

2. You can rotate a selected object in two ways:
   • Use the arrow buttons to rotate the extrusion.
   • Click the page button ☐ and set values.

Changes are previewed as dotted lines on your object.

3. Click Apply.

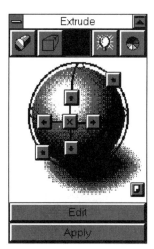

Figure 2-78: The Extrude roll-up showing Rotate preview.

Light Source:

1. Click the light bulb icon 💡. A new option window will appear.

2. Specify one, two or three light sources by clicking on the appropriate light bulb. The sphere that appears represents the object; the circled number represents the number of light sources.

3. To move a light source, drag the circled number to any intersection on the wireframe box.

4. Drag the slide control to adjust the intensity of the light source, or set numerical values in the text box to the right of the slide control.

5. Select Use Full Color Range for more precise combinations of light and dark shades.

6. Choose Apply.

4.0 In Version 4.0, you are limited to one light source.

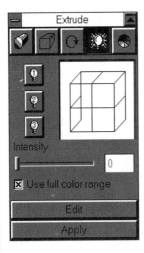

Figure 2-79: The Extrude roll-up showing Light Source preview.

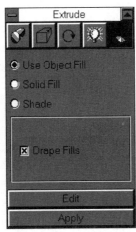

Figure 2-80: The Extrude roll-up showing color options.

Color:

1. Click the ⊛. A new set of options will appear.

2. Use Object Fill extends an object's original color to the extruded object. Solid Fill lets you choose from a color palette. (Click on the color bar to access the palette.) Shade lets you blend between surfaces. For Shade, select To and From colors.

3. Click Apply.

The Edit bar allows you to preview the current extrusion settings of a selected object.

To extrude an open path:

1. Draw a curved line.

2. Extrude the line.

3. Select the desired extrusion. Choose Arrange, Separate.

4. Individually color appropriate surfaces.

Figure 2-81: Extruded path with custom shading.

To extrude with symmetry:

1. Select object. Fill with white.

2. Move the object's center and rotate.

3. Combine and fill with color.

To clear an extrusion, choose Clear Effect from the Effects menu.

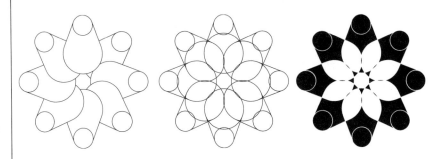

Figure 2-82: Applying radial symmetry to an extruded object creates a kaleidoscope effect.

Blend

The blend feature makes changes from one object, color or shade to another in graduated increments ⬚. Blended objects are dynamically grouped, so whenever you change one object in a group, the blend automatically reforms itself.

🎈 **You can blend two process colors, different tints of the same color, objects with different line weights, or an open path with a closed path. You cannot blend across layers.**

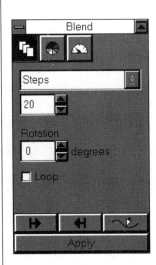

Figure 2-83: The Blend roll-up window.

1. Access the Blend roll-up window by choosing Effects, Blend Roll-Up or by pressing `Ctrl`+`B`.
2. Select the two objects to be blended.
3. Specify the number of steps in the blend. Use more steps for finer gradations.
4. Choose any of the special Blend options (see below).
5. Click Apply.

Figure 2-84: Basic blend.

Blend Options:

Here are some other special blending tricks you can achieve with the Blend roll-up:

Rotation—Rotates intermediate blend objects. Specify positive values for clockwise rotation, negative values for counterclockwise rotation.

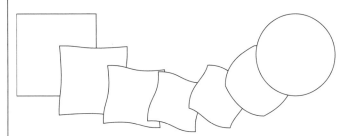

Figure 2-85: Basic blend with Rotation and Loop.

Loop—Instead of rotating around their own center point, looping makes intermediate objects rotate around a point that is halfway between the start and end objects' center of rotation.

Color Wheel—Select and a color wheel appears. The line across the color wheel indicates start and end colors. Choose Rainbow and indicate a clockwise or counterclockwise blend along the color wheel.

Figure 2-86: Color wheel indicating normal start and end colors (left), clockwise and counter-clockwise blend colors (middle, right).

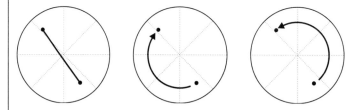

Blend on a Path—Select ∿ to position all the steps in your blend-on-a-path (the path will be through the blended objects' center points). First, draw a path. Select the path by clicking on New Path. With the arrow that appears ⌁, click on the path you've drawn.

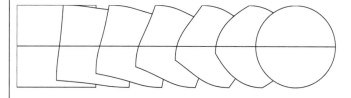

Figure 2-87: Blend on a path.

Full Path—Select if you want your blend objects placed along the full length of your path.

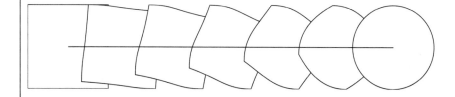

Figure 2-88: Blend on full path.

Rotate All—Select if you want your blend objects to rotate along the path.

Figure 2-89: Blend on a path with rotation.

After you have blended a group, you can specify New Start Object and/or New End Object. Your blend group will reconfigure.

Spacing—When you blend to a path, you can specify the number of steps or the amount of spacing you want between blend steps (in increments up to 1 inch).

Start/End Object—You can specify start and end objects with the ◁┤ (New Start) and ├▷ (New End) buttons. Specify a new path with the curved line/arrow button. When you choose Apply, the group will reblend.

Map Nodes—You can vary the blend effect by specifying which nodes you want matched in blending. For example, you can blend from the Start object's top left node to the End object's bottom right node.

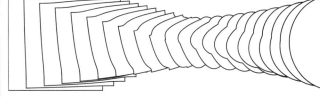

Figure 2-90: Blend with mapped nodes.

Split—Allows you to split a blend at the selected intermediate object (this object then becomes the Start object for one set of blends, and the End object for the other set of blends).

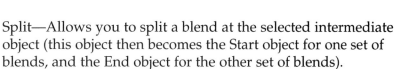
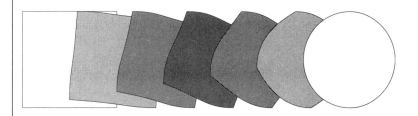

Figure 2-91: Split blend.

Fuse Top/Fuse Bottom—To rejoin a split blend, hold `Ctrl` and click on the blend group you want to fuse.

Compound Blends

Blend groups that share a path are called compound blends. To select only one group, select the entire compound blend, then hold `Ctrl` and click on an object in that group. Only the group containing that object will be selected. To choose only one object, click the Split button on the Blend roll-up and use the special pointer to select your object.

To modify your blend:

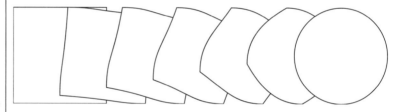

Figure 2-92: Original blend.

To reverse the order of your blend, select the group and click Reverse Order under the Arrange menu.

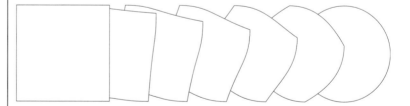

Figure 2-93: Reverse order blend.

Create blend chains by blending intermediate objects: A to B, B to C, C to D, etc.

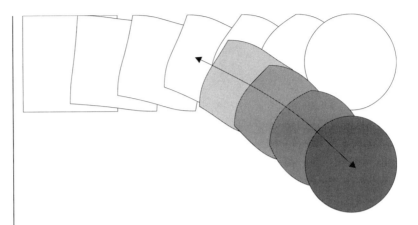

Figure 2-94: Blend chain.

Clear Blend on the Effects menu removes all intermediate blend objects, leaving only the path and the start and end objects.

To move or transform the beginning or end object in a blend group, use the Pick Tool mode ▶ to select the object, then modify (move, size, scale, skew, rotate) as desired. After you modify an object, the blend group automatically redraws.

To move or transform an intermediate object in a blend group, first select the group, then hold ⌨Ctrl while double-clicking on the individual object. After you modify an object, the blend group automatically redraws.

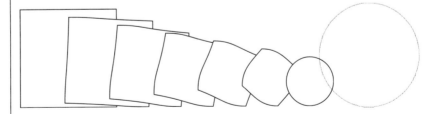

Figure 2-95: Moving and resizing a blend object.

To reshape an object in a blend group, first select the object in Pick Tool mode ▶ . Then use the Shape tool ⸜ to reshape the object. After you modify an object, the blend group will automatically redraw.

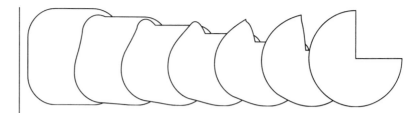

Figure 2-96: Reshaping start and end blend objects.

To move a path, use the Pick Tool mode ➤ . To reshape a path, use the Shape Tool mode ➤ . Modify your path and the blend will move with the path, redrawing automatically.

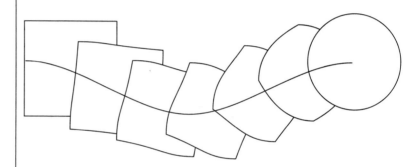

Figure 2-97: Reshaping a path.

To separate the objects in a blend group, choose Separate at the Arrange menu.

Lens

With the Lens roll-up, you can choose to display an object or objects through one of nine different lenses.

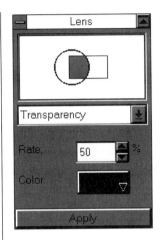

Figure 2-98: The Lens roll-up window.

![4.0] This roll-up is not available in Version 4.0.

To Add a Lens:

1. Specify the section of your drawing that you want displayed through a lens by drawing an object of any size or shape over that area. There are only two rules: the object has to have a closed path and it can't be a grouped object.

2. Select the object that will be used as a lens.

3. Choose Effects, Lens Roll-Up to open the Lens roll-up window.

4. Select a Lens type from the drop-down list:
   - Transparency (Effect is as if you've placed transparent film over the object.)
   - Magnify (The lens area is magnified by a specified amount.)
   - Brighten (The colors in the lens area are brightened or darkened by a specified percentage.)
   - Invert (The colors under the lens are inverted to their complementary colors.)
   - Color Limit (All colors within the lens area except the one you specify are filtered out.)
   - Color Add (The colors in the lens area are mixed with the color you specify.)

- Tinted Grayscale (Objects in the lens area are displayed as grayscale images.)
- Heat Map (Colors in the lens area are mapped to colors in a predefined Heat Map palette, which creates an infrared appearance.)

5. Specify any options you want to use. Each lens type has different options. For example, if you choose Magnify, you can control the amount of magnification; if you choose Heat Map, you can control the degree of palette rotation.

6. Choose Apply.

Lens Options:

Here are some examples of different lens options:

- Transparency—The colors of the objects under the lens are mixed with the lens object's color, so it looks like the object is covered by transparent film. Specify a transparency rate from 1 to 100 percent.

- Magnify—The area under the lens is magnified to the degree you specify.

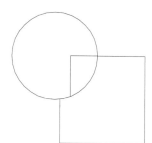

Figure 2-99: A transparent lens (on the left) and a magnification lens (on the right) have been added to these two objects.

- Brighten—The colors under the lens are brightened by a factor of –100 to 100 percent. The range is from black to white, with –100 percent being black and 100 percent white.

- Invert—The colors under the lens are inverted to their complementary colors (using the CMYK color wheel).

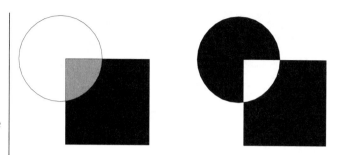

Figure 2-100: A Brighten lens (on the left) and an Invert lens (on the right) have been added to these two objects.

PowerClip

The PowerClip option allows you to place an object inside a container (an object in which you place other objects) to isolate portions of a drawing for the creation of special effects that don't affect the rest of the drawing or any other effects you've added.

4.0 This option is not available in Version 4.0.

To use the PowerClip option:

1. Make sure that the object you want to use as a container is visible.

2. Select the object or objects you want to put in the container.

3. Choose Effects, PowerClip, Place Inside Container.

4. The mouse pointer turns into a thick arrow. Click on the container object.

All of the objects you selected will be centered inside the container.

You can combine PowerClip with other effects (such as blends, extrusions, bitmaps and PowerLines) to create all sorts of interesting effects.

Here are a couple of examples that use the PowerClip option:

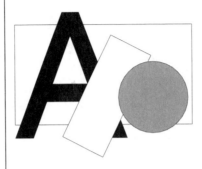

Figure 2-101: Three objects have been inserted into a container using the PowerClip option.

Figure 2-102: In these two pictures, the container contents have been edited.

Presets

With the Presets roll-up, you can choose from several pre-defined presets or create and record your own special effects that can then be added to selected objects.

Figure 2-103: The Presets roll-up window.

4.0 This roll-up is not available in Version 4.0.

To add a Preset effect to an object:

1. Select the object you want to apply the preset to.

2. Choose Special, Presets Roll-Up.

3. Choose one of the presets from the drop-down list (one of Corel's predefined presets or one you've created).

4. Choose Apply.

Following are a couple of example presets:

Use presets to save time and effort by recording actions you perform on a regular basis.

Figure 2-104: Two standard Presets included with Corel.

To Create Your Own Custom Preset:

1. Select the object you want to add effects to.

2. From the Presets roll-up, choose Start Recording.

3. Add effects to your object. Presets allows you to record the following effects: Back One, Convert to Curves, Duplicate, Fill, Forward One, Move, Outline, Rotate, Stretch, Skew, To Front and To Back.

4. Choose Stop Recording.

5. In the Edit Preset dialog box, assign a name to your preset and add notes if you want to.

6. Choose OK.

Figure 2-105: Two custom Presets that use Duplicates and varied Line widths.

For **Figure 2-105,** the **Place Duplicates and Clones** preference setting was adjusted (**Special, Preferences, General tab**).

MOVING ON

We've already covered a lot of territory! Creating simple objects in DRAW, then manipulating them with the great special effects provided in DRAW makes you really appreciate the power of rendering art on the desktop. But you won't have your toolbox complete until you can fully control two other elements of your graphic object, lines and fills, which we'll cover next.

Lines 3 Fills

I paint with shapes.

— *Alexander Calder*

The heart of controlling your image lies in manipulating both the line that defines the image and the fill that colors it. Corel gives you by-the-numbers control of everything from line weight to the nib shape of your "pen."

Drawing in Corel begins in one of two modes: Freehand or Bézier. To draw Freehand, you simply drag your mouse (or other pointer tool)—it's like drawing with a pencil. To draw in Bézier mode, you click at the beginning and end points of a line, and Corel automatically joins those points in the way you've specified in your Preferences.

You can color, or fill, your CorelDRAW images in as many ways as you can imagine. You can apply a solid color, or choose colors that blend together. Fills can be linear, radial or conical. You can create bitmap fills, or use almost any image to create a pattern fill.

LINES & OUTLINES

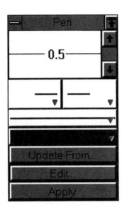

Figure 3-1: The Pen
roll-up window.

If you haven't already done so, choose Special, Preferences, Curves to access the Curves tab in the Preferences roll-up, and specify your settings (all settings should be 1-10). This should be done before you start drawing.

Freehand Tracking—Set a higher number of pixels for smoother curves with fewer control points when you draw lines.

Autotrace Tracking—Set a lower number for a closer Bézier curves tracing of the original.

Corner Threshold—Set a lower number for more cusp nodes when you draw.

Straight Line Threshold—Set a lower number for more curved lines when you draw.

AutoJoin—Use a lower setting if you want nearby nodes to join automatically.

Auto-Reduce—Set the sensitivity of DRAW's node elimination function; use a higher number and more nodes will be removed when selected.

Figure 3-2: Use the Auto-Reduce setting to elimi-nate nodes and achieve smoother (but less detailed) lines. The original line (top) has 40 nodes. The middle line has 24 nodes; Auto-Reduce default was set at 5. The bottom line has 17 nodes; the Auto-Reduce default was set at 10.

To keep your drawings simple and reduce printing prob-lems, marquee-select PowerLines and select Auto-Reduce at the Node Edit roll-up.

Freehand Lines

1. Choose Pencil tool mode ℓ . Hold down the mouse button and drag to access the fly-out menu.

2. Choose the Freehand drawing tool ℓ . Your cursor will become a cross $+$.

3. To draw curved lines, drag with your cursor (this is like drawing with a pencil). When you're finished drawing the line, release your mouse button. Access the Shape tool and use the nodes that appear along your line to make any refinements in the line's shape or placement. Clicking on a node will access its control points.

4. To draw straight lines, click your mouse button at the start and end points of the line you want. CorelDRAW will con-nect these points in a straight line.

Holding Ctrl constrains the line to the increment you've speci-fied in your Preferences settings.

Bézier Lines

1. Choose Pencil tool mode ℓ . Hold down the mouse button and drag to access the fly-out menu.

2. Choose the Bézier drawing tool ℓ. Your cursor will become a cross $+$.

3. To draw straight lines, click your mouse button at the begin-ning and end points of the line you want. (Be careful not to drag as you click.) CorelDRAW will connect these points in a straight line.

4. To draw curved lines, click at the point you want your line to begin. Drag, and a line appears on your screen. As you drag, you can control the direction and curve of the line. Release the mouse button when you're finished drawing the line. To refine the line's curve and placement, use the Shape tool ↾ and click on a node to access control points. Manipulate the control points to make any changes in your line.

When you hold down Ctrl, the control points move in the increment you've specified in your Preferences setting.

Dimension Lines

1. Choose Pencil Tool mode ℓ . Hold down the mouse button and drag to access the fly-out menu.

2. Choose one of the 3 Dimension line drawing tools: Vertical ↨, Horizontal ↔ or Diagonal ↗. Your cursor will become a cross ┼ .

3. Choose Layout, Snap To, Objects.

4. Click at the point you want to start measuring. Drag and position, and a Dimension line appears. Click to establish the end point. You can now position the Dimension Line. Holding Ctrl while drawing a diagonal line constrains it to the angle set on the Preferences menu.

Use the Pen roll-up to apply arrowheads to your Dimension Lines. For default arrowheads, with nothing selected, at the Pen roll-up choose start and end arrowhead styles and Apply. At the Outline Pen dialog box, select Graphic as your Outline Pen default.

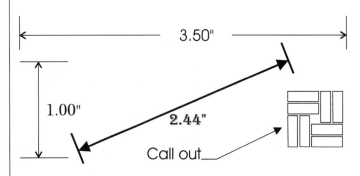

Figure 3-3: Dimension line examples.

Dimension Line Text

Figure 3-4: The Dimension
roll-up window.

The dimension text uses the same unit of measure specified for
Horizontal Grid Frequency.

At any time, you can change the default typeface and type size
used for dimension line or other text. With nothing selected,
open the Text roll-up. Choose the face and size and Apply. At
the Text Attributes dialog box, select OK. You can also select
Dimension line text with the Pick tool and style it like any text
at the Text roll-up.

PowerLines

1. Choose Effects, PowerLines (or press Ctrl + F8) to open the
   PowerLine roll-up.

Figure 3-5: The PowerLine
roll-up window.

2. At the roll-up, choose the style of PowerLine you want from
   the 23 preset styles. A window previews the selected style.

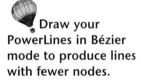 Draw your
PowerLines in Bézier
mode to produce lines
with fewer nodes.

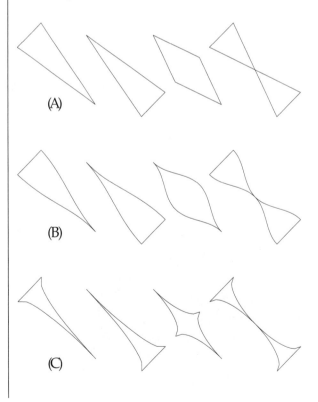

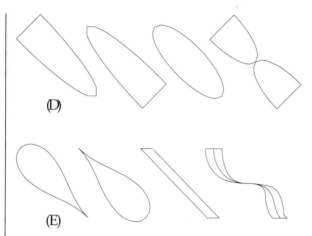

(D)

(E)

Figure 3-6: PowerLine
style: wedge (A),
wood cut (B),
trumpet (C), bullet (D),
teardrop, nib (E).

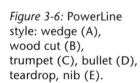

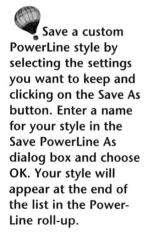
**Save a custom
PowerLine style by
selecting the settings
you want to keep and
clicking on the Save As
button. Enter a name
for your style in the
Save PowerLine As
dialog box and choose
OK. Your style will
appear at the end of
the list in the Power-
Line roll-up.**

- Max Width: designate the maximum width you want your PowerLine to be.
- Apply when drawing lines: select to apply PowerLines to all lines drawn with the Freehand and Bézier drawing tools.

3. Choose Nib style.
   - Nib Shape. At the Page button ☐, select nib Angle and Ratio by either dragging the nib preview or entering numeric values at the Page button ☐. To adjust Nib Intensity, click on the slide control.

4. Choose Settings.
   - Speed: Set to increase or decrease line width whenever the line changes direction.
   - Spread: Increase when Speed is greater than 0 to maintain a smooth line.
   - Ink Flow: Increase for greater coverage; decrease for a thinner line.
   - Scale With Image: Set to maintain proportions when the PowerLine is scaled.

5. Select the Pencil tool.

6. Click where you want your line to start, then drag to draw.

7. When you define a PowerLine style, select Save As from the roll-up, then name the style and save it. The new style will be added to the presets list.

8. To edit a PowerLine's shape, select it with the Shape tool ⚲. Double-click on the interior line to access the Node Edit roll-up. Drag the rounded handles that appear to adjust your line.

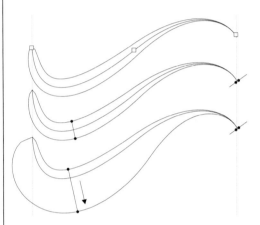

Figure 3-7: Shaping PowerLines.

When drawing PowerLines with a pressure-sensitive stylus/tablet, the amount of pressure you apply will determine the width of your PowerLines.

Pressure-Sensitive PowerLines

1. From the PowerLine roll-up, choose Pressure at the list of PowerLine styles.

2. Adjust the PowerLines settings (see above) as desired.

3. Select the Pencil tool, click where you want your line to begin, and drag.

4. As you drag, use your arrow keys to change the width of your line. The Up arrow decreases width, the Down arrow increases width.

5. Release the mouse button where you want the line to end.

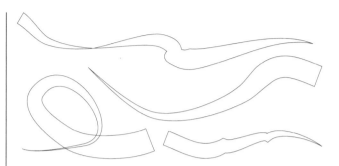

Figure 3-8: Pressure-sensitive PowerLines.

PowerLines as an Object's Outline

1. Select the object.

2. Access the PowerLine roll-up and select the style you want.

3. Click Apply. The PowerLine outline will assume the object's fill and outline, but the object will become transparent.

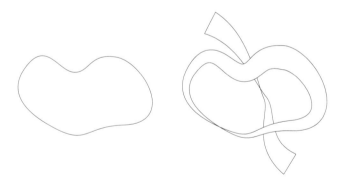

Figure 3-9: PowerLines as outlines.

Elastic Node Editing

With your PowerLine selected in Shape Tool mode ⟨, you can access Elastic mode at the Node Editing roll-up. This makes your PowerLines "expand" or "contract." Select multiple nodes; when you drag one node, all other nodes move away from that node in proportion to their distance from it.

Pressure Editing

With your PowerLine selected in Shape Tool mode ⟋, choose Pressure Edit at the Node Editing roll-up. This will apply editing handles to your PowerLine. Drag the handles to change the width of the PowerLine. You can select Convex or Concave buttons on the roll-up to specify the curvature of the line you're editing (available only when Pressure editing).

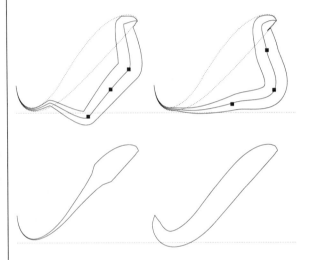

Figure 3-10: PowerLines with three nodes selected, Regular node editing and Elastic node editing (top); Pressure editing and Pressure editing with Convex and Concave applied (bottom).

The Outline Tool

You can specify No Outline ✕, line thickness and color (black, white, or 10%, 30%, 50%, 70% or 90% gray) on the Outline tool flyout menu.

The Line Selector on the Pen roll-up lets you select line widths from .010 to .5 inch. To select from the full range of line widths available, you can choose the Edit bar to access the Outline Pen dialog box.

The Pen Roll-Up

The Pen roll-up window provides a quick way to style lines and outlines.

Hold down the left mouse button on the Outline tool ✒ to access the fly-out menu and click on the Outline Roll-Up tool, which opens the Pen roll-up window ▣ .

To change Pen roll-up window defaults:

1. Access the roll-up window. With no object selected, choose line width, style and color desired.

2. Click the Apply button. The Outline Pen dialog box appears.

3. Select the objects you want the defaults to apply to (Graphic, Artistic text and/or Paragraph text).

4. Click OK.

For line thickness selections:

1. With object selected, click on the Up or Down arrow to show thicker (up) or thinner (down) lines. The line is previewed and its thickness is given in numerical values.

2. When you reach the line width desired, click Apply.

Figure 3-11: Line thickness selection.

For a quick way to create a custom arrowhead, select the object you want as an arrowhead. Choose Special, Create Arrow. Your selected object appears as an arrowhead in the next available space on the arrowhead selection menu.

To choose arrowhead style:

1. Select the path on which you want arrowheads.

2. Click the left arrowhead to choose an arrowhead for the start of the path. When the Arrowhead selection menu appears, click on the arrowhead you want.

Click on the right arrowhead to choose an arrowhead for the end of the path. When the Arrowhead selection menu appears, click on the arrowhead you want.

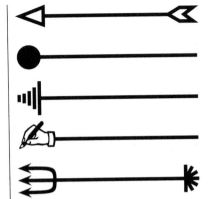

Figure 3-12: Arrowhead selections.

Add your own arrowhead styles—you can save up to 100 different styles on the Arrowhead selection menu.

To remove an arrowhead from a selected path, choose the first option on the selection menu.

3. Click Apply when you've made your selection(s).

To choose line style:

1. Select the path you want styled.

2. Click on the Line Style Selector bar.

3. Scroll through the selection menu. When you find the desired style, click on it.

4. Apply.

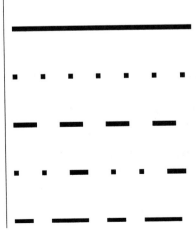

Figure 3-13: Line styles.

To choose color:

1. Click on the Color Selector bar.

2. Click on the color you want.

3. Apply.

To use the Update From... option:

1. Select the path you want to change.

2. Click the Update From... bar.

3. Click on the object you want to copy.

4. Apply.

The Outline Pen Dialog Box

Use your Outline Pen dialog box variables to refine all Pen roll-up selections. Access by clicking the Edit bar. (When not in the Pen roll-up, with your object selected use F12 to access this dialog box.)

For outline, color and fill selections:

1. Click Color and press More... to access the Outline Color dialog box [Shift]+F12.

2. Select the color model from the list box:
    - CMYK Color Model
    - RGB Color Model
    - HSB Color Model
    - Grayscale
    - Standard Colors
    - FOCOLTONE Colors
    - PANTONE Spot Colors
    - PANTONE Process Colors
    - TRUMATCH Coated Colors
    - TRUMATCH Uncoated Colors
    - TRUMATCH (CMYK)

4.0 Here's the list of color models in Version 4.0: CMYK, RGB, HSB, Pantone Spot Colors, Pantone Process Colors and TruMatch Process Colors.

3. To select PostScript Options (use for creating color separations and halftone screens):
   - Select Pantone Spot Colors.
   - Select color desired.
   - Select percentage of tint.

4. You can choose a color by name; just type the name in the box. Show Color Names lets you search through a list of Pantone color names.
   - Click PostScript Options bar.
   - The Palette bar gives you options for creating a custom palette.

5. At the PostScript Options dialog box, select:
   - Type of halftone screen.
   - Frequency of pattern.
   - Angle of screen.

Figure 3-14: PostScript screen settings: Style: Dot; Tint: 45%; Frequency: 20; Angle: 45 degrees.

6. Click OK, then Apply.

To select arrows:

1. Click on either the left or the right arrow preview window. A selection menu appears. Choose an arrow.

2. Clicking on the Options bar and menu allows you to specify *none, swap* (switch direction of arrows), *edit* the selected arrowhead or *delete* it from the list.

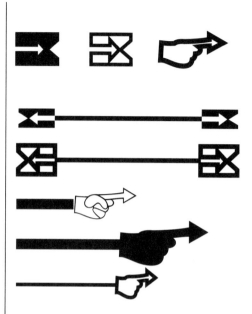

Figure 3-15: Custom arrowheads.

To specify line width:

Specify line width to 1/1000th inch (.001-4 inches). Choose unit of measurement.

To choose line style:

Click on the Style bar. A selection menu appears. You can choose *dashed, dotted* or *combination* line styles.

For corner styles: Choose *mitered, rounded* or *beveled.*

Figure 3-16: Line corners.

For line caps: Choose *butt, round* or *square.*

Figure 3-17: Line caps.

For calligraphy outlines:

1. Select the object whose outline you want to style.

2. Access the Pen roll-up window from the Outline tool ✒.

3. Click the Edit bar.

4. Select the nib width (at Width window), shape (at Corners option), stretch and angle. Selections are previewed in the nib shape window. You can also drag on the nib shape in the preview window to change the shape.

5. When you have the nib shape you want, click OK, then Apply.

Figure 3-18: Calligraphy.

For outlines behind fills:

Select the Behind Fill button to place the outline behind an object's fill (only half the outline will show).

Figure 3-19: Outline behind fill.

Scale With Image:

Select this option to ensure that the outline is scaled when you scale your image.

Figure 3-20: Scaled lines.

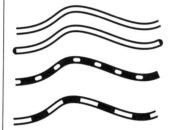

Figure 3-21: Styled lines.

Figure 3-22: PostScript lines.

Figure 3-23: Calligraphic lines.

To Autotrace an image:

1. Import a bitmapped image, either one you've scanned and stored or a clip art file.

2. Select the image in Pick Tool mode ⬧ , then access the Pencil tool ⬧ flyout menu and choose the Freehand Drawing tool ⬧ .

3. Autotracing should be activated (check the Status Line). The cursor will change to the Autotrace indicator. Click on the portion of the bitmap you want traced.

4. After you've traced the desired sections of the bitmapped image, you can delete your original bitmap.

5. Save your new Autotraced image. You can now work with it as you would any DRAW image.

FILLS

CorelDRAW gives you multiple options when it comes to "coloring" an object. You can choose a uniform (solid) fill or a fill that gradually changes from top to bottom, or side to side (linear fill). There are also fills that radiate from a center (radial fill) and cone-shaped fills (conical fill). In Version 5.0, you can also create square fountain fills. You can apply tints, screens, textures and patterns. You can even create your own custom multicolored fills.

Figure 3-24: The Fill roll-up window.

Note: All closed objects are given a default fill—solid, fountain or pattern.

To make sure your object is a closed path:

1. In Shape Tool mode ⟋⟍ select the end nodes with a marquee or by holding [Shift] when you click on the nodes.

2. Access the Node Edit roll-up.

3. Press the Join button ⟋⟍.

Changing Default Fills

To change your default fills, with nothing selected, access the Fill roll-up. Change the attributes you want and click Apply.

Transparent Objects

To make your object transparent, select No Fill ✕ at the left of the onscreen palette (or on the Fill tool flyout menu). Objects underneath the transparent object will be visible.

Uniform Fills

The easiest way to fill an object is simply to select your object and click on one of the onscreen palette colors. To display the onscreen palette, choose View, Color Palette and select the palette you want to display from the cascading menu. Used alone, a uniform (solid) fill makes a surface look flat.

Uniform Fill Dialog Box

1. Select your object.

2. At the Fill tool ⟋⟍ fly-out menu, select the color wheel ⊛. The Uniform Fill dialog box will appear.

3. Choose color model.

The quickest way to fill an object is to use the onscreen palette. To display, choose View, **Color Palette.** Then select the palette you want to display from the cascading menu. With the palette displayed, you can just select objects and click on the color you want. (In Version 4.0, choose **Display, Show Color Palette.**)

To draw using shades of gray, color your object black and adjust percentage of tint in the Uniform Fill dialog box (accessible via the Fill tool fly-out menu) and in the Outline Color dialog box (accessible via the Pen tool flyout menu).

To find the CMYK percentage of any color, go to Pantone Spot Colors, select a color, return to CMYK, and it will give you the percentage for each color.

4. You can select your specific color a number of ways:
   - Enter a numeric value: choose CMYK, RGB or HSB and adjust values.
   - Click a color on the Color Preview Palette.
   - Adjust tint value (Pantone spot colors only).
   - Specify color by name (Pantone and TruMatch colors; click Show Color Name to search a list, or type in a name at the box).

5. Choose OK and Apply.

Fountain Fills

Fountain, or gradient, fills change gradually. The Fill roll-up lets you specify the direction of change—top to bottom, side to side, at an angle, away from or toward a center point, radiating conically away from the center, or radiating in concentric squares away from the center. You can also specify the number of steps in the fill's transition. You can use the roll-up or a dialog box to create fountains.

Using the Fill Roll-Up

To apply one object's fill to another object, choose the object you want to fill. Click the Update From button on the Fill roll-up. At the FROM? prompt, click on the object whose fill you want to duplicate and click Apply. (Note: This doesn't work with PostScript fills.)

1. On the Fill tool menu ✍, click on the Fill roll-up window 🔳.

2. Select your object.

3. Select the Fountain fill icon ▉.

4. Click on the Linear, Radial, Conical or Square fill icon.

5. Click the left color bar and choose your starting color. Click the right color bar and choose your end color.

6. To control the angle of a linear fill, drag in the preview box. [Ctrl] constrains to the increment you have specified on the Preferences menu.

Figure 3-25: Linear
fountain fill.

To control the center point of a radial or conical fill, drag in the
preview box. [Ctrl] constrains to 10% increments.

Figure 3-26: Radial
fountain fill.

To copy a fill, click Update From. At the FROM? prompt, click
on the object whose fill you want to copy.

Click the Edit bar to access the Fountain Fill dialog box (see
details on the following page).

7. Apply.

Figure 3-27: Conical
fountain fill.

Figure 3-28: Square
fountain fill.

Using the Fountain Fill Dialog Box

1. With your object selected, click on the Fill tool ⚘. Select Fountain fill and click on Edit. (You can also open the Fountain Fill dialog box by clicking the Fountain Fill tool ■ from the Fill tool's fly-out menu.)

2. At the dialog box, specify a variety of options:
   • Color: Define Start color at From button, and End color at To button.
   • Type: Choose *Linear, Radial, Conical or Square.*
   • Center Offset: Enter values to offset the center of radial and conical fills, or use your mouse to drag in the preview box.
   • Angle: For linear and conical fills, set the angle of the fill stripes.
   • Steps: Enter a value indicating the number of steps you want in your fills. (*Note:* This overrides similar settings in the Print Option and Preferences dialog boxes.)
   • Edge Pad: When DRAW applies a fountain fill to an irregularly shaped object, sometimes bands of color extend beyond the object's edges. Enter a value to allow DRAW to squeeze more Start and End color into the object's shape.
   • PostScript Options: If you're creating your fill with a spot color, click for a dialog box that lets you choose a halftone screen and overprinting options.

3. Click OK.

Creating Custom Fountain Fills

1. With your object selected, click on the Fill tool ⚘. Select Fountain fill and click on Edit. (You can also open the Fountain Fill dialog box by clicking the Fountain Fill tool ■ from the Fill tool's fly-out menu.)

2. In the Color Blend section, choose one of the following:
   • Direct: Color transitions directly from one color to another.

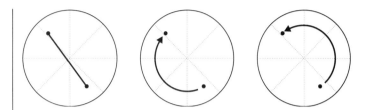

Figure 3-28: Color wheel indicating normal start and end colors (left), clockwise and counter-clockwise blend colors (middle, right).

- Rainbow: Color transitions from a path around the color wheel; specify clockwise ↻ or counterclockwise ↺.
- Custom: Lets you specify up to 99 transition colors from the displayed palette. Your selection is shown in the preview window.

To specify intermediate colors in a custom fountain fill:
a. Double-click just above the preview box. A triangular color-location marker is displayed.
b. Drag the color location marker to the position where you want to apply color. (Position displays as a percentage in the Position box.)
c. Click on the color you want in the color palette. Your selection will display in the preview window.

Repeat steps 1 and 2 for as many intermediate colors as you want. To reposition a color, select its marker and drag the marker to the new position. Delete a color by double-clicking its marker.

3. Click OK.

4. To retain your color selections, type a name in the Presets text box and click on the plus icon. Your new fill will be added to the Presets fill list. (You can remove a custom preset by clicking on the minus icon.)

4.0 Enter a name for the fill and choose Save.

Figure 3-29: Custom fountain fill.

Pattern Fills

A pattern is simply an image repeated over and over. Corel-DRAW lets you use almost any image to create a pattern, including clip art. Patterns can be two-color or full-color, aligned or offset.

To create pattern fills:

1. On the Fill tool menu ✍, click on the Fill roll-up window ⊞. *Note:* All two-color pattern fills are bitmaps.

2. Select your object.

3. On the roll-up, choose the checkerboard ▩ (2-Color Pattern Fill button) or arrows ➚ (Full-Color Pattern Fill button). Click the preview box and a selection menu of pre-existing patterns appears. Choose the pattern you want to use and click OK, or double-click on the pattern.

4. For foreground color, click on the left Color bar and choose the color you want. For background color, click on the right Color bar and choose the color you want.

5. To scale the pattern, choose the Tile bar. Drag the small box that appears on your pattern to indicate scale. Use Ctrl to constrain the drag to the increment you specified on the Preferences menu.

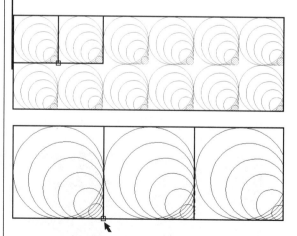

Figure 3-30: Pattern tiling.

To offset pattern fills:

Click the Tile bar. A pair of boxes will appear on your pattern.

- Drag the left box to offset the entire pattern.
- Drag down on the right box to offset alternating vertical rows.
- Drag down and to the left *on the right box* to offset horizontal rows.

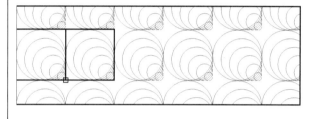

For a two-color pattern, choose high resolution for a clearer screen display.

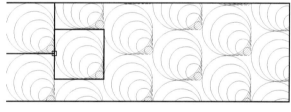

Figure 3-31: Offsetting tile patterns.

To create custom patterns:

1. Create, paste or import the graphic you want to make into a pattern.

2. Choose Special, Create Pattern.

3. Indicate two-color and choose the resolution; or indicate full color.

Use the grid and guide layers to make your pattern's symmetry accurate.

4. With the crosshairs, drag to select the pattern. Use `Ctrl` to constrain your drag.

5. Release the mouse button to choose the portion of the original that you want as a pattern.

Figure 3-32: Creating a custom pattern.

6. Click OK.

7. If the pattern you created is a full-color pattern, the Save Full-Color Pattern dialog box is displayed. Enter the pattern name in the File Name text box and choose OK. Your pattern will be stored as the next available square on the Pattern Selection menu in two-color or full-color mode (even though you don't give it a name in two-color mode).

Use CorelDRAW's bitmap editor to create custom two-color pattern fills.

To create custom pattern fills:

1. At the Fill roll-up, click the Edit bar and choose Create. (Or, at the Fill fly-out menu, with the object selected, choose Pattern Fill ▦.)

2. A drawing area appears. *Note:* Each square represents one pixel.

3. Choose:
   - Bitmap size: use 16 x 16 for horizontal and vertical lines, the other sizes for images with curves or diagonal lines.
   - Pen size: designate the number of pixels a mouse click selects.

4. Click OK.

5. At the Two-Color Pattern dialog box, select the pattern you've created. Add color and adjust the tile relationship.

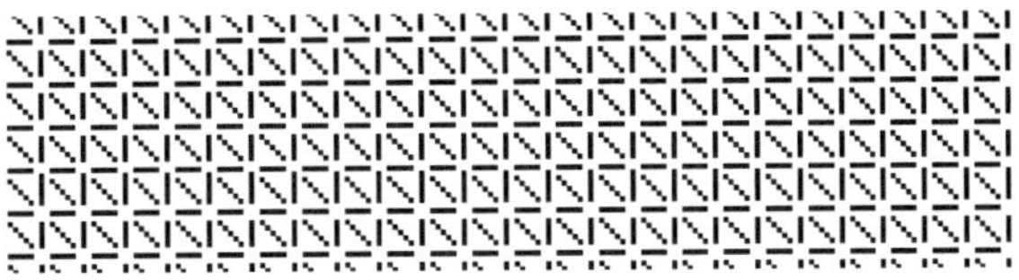

Figure 3-33: Custom two-color pattern.

PostScript Textures

Some of the most interesting and inspiring textures available are PostScript textures such as the one shown in Figure 3-33. Use these as fills or as backgrounds. When you choose a texture, a dialog box lets you select attributes such as width and frequency (these change for each texture). PostScript textures won't display on your screen (you get a substitute fill), but you can see if your fill has been applied by checking for its name at the Status Line.

Note: You must use a PostScript printer in order to print these textures.

To apply a PostScript texture:

1. Select the object you want to apply a texture to.

You should refer to your *CorelDRAW User's Guide* for the full scope of available textures.

2. From the Fill tool menu ⚲, choose the PS button. Choose the texture you want from the list of named textures. Customize by setting the variables (frequency, foreground color, etc.) on the PostScript Textures dialog box.

   Note: Actual PostScript patterns do not show on the screen but will appear upon printing.

3. Apply.

Figure 3-34: PostScript texture used as a fill.

Bitmap Textures

Another way to fill your objects is with a bitmap texture. DRAW's catalog of bitmap textures includes sky, paper, crystals, gravel, watercolors and canvas (and, new in 5.0, wood, leather and marble). Each can be customized, giving you a huge selection of useful textures. While PostScript textures won't show on your monitor, bitmap textures will. You can use the Fill roll-up or a dialog box to create bitmap textures.

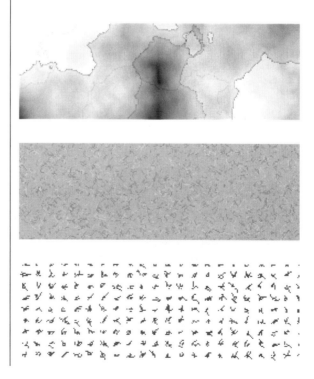

Figure 3-35: Bitmap textures: watercolor, recycled paper and scribbles.

Using the Fill Roll-Up

1. Click on the Texture Fill icon 🖼 . A texture fill is displayed in the preview window.

2. Click on the fill displayed in the preview window to display the fills in the current library. For a new library of fills:
   - On the palette, click File and choose Load Texture Library, then select a texture library and click OK.
   - At the Fill roll-up, click the upper arrow key for a drop-down menu of libraries and the lower arrow key for a drop-down menu of textures within the current library. To edit a texture, click Edit. At the Texture Fill dialog box, adjust texture settings. Changes will be displayed in the preview window.

3. When you've found the texture you like and have modified it to fit your needs, click OK.

4. To save your modified texture, choose Save As. When the Save Texture As dialog box appears, name your modified texture and save it to a new library.

Using the Texture Fill Dialog Box

1. Select the object.

2. At the Fill fly-out menu, click Texture 🖼 .

3. At the Texture Fill dialog box, search through the Texture Library list. Choose the texture you want and the contents will be displayed in the preview window.

4. Adjust the texture settings. These vary with each texture, but include density, contrast, texture, softness, brightness, grain, etc.

5. Click Preview and your texture will display in the preview window.

6. When your texture is the way you want it, click OK and Apply.

Halftone Screens

When you apply a screen to an object, you are actually converting that image into dots or lines in order to create special effects. To use halftone screens in DRAW, you must have a PostScript printer installed. Screen patterns will not show on your monitor, but will print on your PostScript printer.

When applying a halftone screen, you will need to adjust these three settings:

- Screen Type: choose the style of screen: dot, line, circle, pattern, etc.
- Screen Frequency: choose the number of lines per inch (the size of the screen). Low values create a bigger screen pattern (i.e., bigger dots). For a screen that isn't visible, use a setting of 100 or more (high-resolution output device). If you want your screen to show, use 60-80 lines per inch (standard laser printer).
- Screen Angle: the usual setting for the arrangement of halftone dots is 45 degrees.

For uniform fills:

1. Select your object.

2. On the Fill fly-out menu, select Uniform Fill ⊛.

3. Choose Pantone Spot Color.

4. Choose the color you want from the color palette.

5. Set percentage of tint.

6. Choose your PostScript options: type of screen, frequency and angle.

7. Click OK at each screen.

Figure 3-36: Variations on uniform pattern fills.

Note: Your screen will display an approximation of the Post-Script halftone screen.

For fountain fills:

1. On the Fill roll-up, select Fountain Fill ◼.

2. Click the Edit bar.

3. Choose Linear, Radial, Conical or Square.

4. Choose a starting color from the palette drop-down on the left. To adjust the fountain fill, select More and make changes in the Fountain Fill dialog box:

   • Choose Pantone Spot Colors.
   • Select the color you want.
   • Adjust the tint percentage

5. Choose an ending color from the palette drop-down on the right. To adjust the fountain fill, use the same steps as in step 3.

6. For a custom fountain fill, choose Edit to open the Fountain Fill dialog box. Choose Custom, select your fill colors and choose OK.

7. If your selected color model supports PostScript, you can choose PostScript Options from the Fountain Fill dialog box to specify the following options:

   • Type of screen.
   • Frequency of screen.
   • Angle of screen.

8. Click OK at each screen.

Figure 3-37: Variations on linear fountain fills.

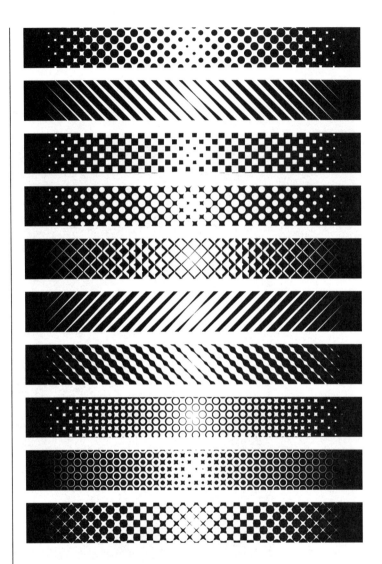

Figure 3-38: Variations on radial fountain fills.

Copying a fill:

1. Select the object you want to fill.

2. At the Fill roll-up, click Update From.

3. When the FROM? prompt appears, click on the object whose fill you want to copy.

4. Apply.

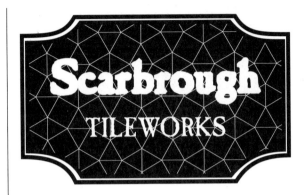

Figure 3-39: PostScript fill used as background.

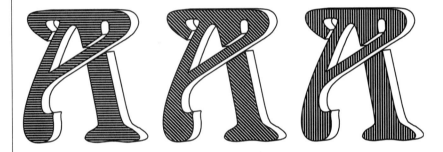

Figure 3-40: Halftone screen used as fill on extruded type.

LAYERS

CorelDRAW's Layers feature lets you have an unlimited number of layers in a single piece of artwork. Each layer can contain different elements of your piece, which is especially useful when you're working on complex, multi-element artwork.

Used with a little forethought, layering saves time as well as disk space. Think how you would use layers on the traditional mechanical artwork of an automobile ad. One layer might illustrate the car as a convertible, the next as a hard-top, a third with "extras" such as white sidewalls and chrome wheels—but you only had to create one car. If you're creating several ads, one layer might have text that would appeal to men; the next layer, text targeted at women; and still another layer, text aimed at teenagers. You have one file but endless options for your auto advertisement.

The Layers roll-up window gives you quick access to all Layers functions.

Figure 3-41: The Layers roll-up window.

- Add layers.
- Delete layers.
- Reorder layers.
- Copy and/or move objects between layers.
- Lock layers.
- Print selected layers.
- Make layers invisible.
- Create guide layer.
- Display and/or print Grid and Guidelines.
- Save objects or text on the Desktop.

Color override lets you identify all the objects on a layer by giving those objects an onscreen outline in the color you specify. It will not actually replace the outline or fill colors of those objects.

To use Layers:

1. Use ⌈Ctrl⌉+F3 to access the Layers roll-up.

2. When you click on the *right* arrow button, a submenu lets you choose from the following options:
   - New
   - Edit
   - Delete
   - Move To
   - Copy To
   - Multilayer

3. Click on New or Edit and a second submenu lets you name your layer as well as choose options such as
   - Master Layer
   - Visible
   - Printable
   - Locked
   - Color Override (click here for a palette)
   - Set Options For All Pages

4. For grid setup, select Grid and choose Setup. At the Grid Setup dialog box, specify
   - Scale
   - Frequency
   - Origin
   - Show Grid
   - Snap To Grid

5. For guides setup, select Guides and choose Setup. At the Guidelines Setup dialog box, specify
   - View (Horizontal or Vertical)
   - Unit of Measurement
   - Show Guidelines
   - Snap To Guidelines

Tips for using layers:

- When working on a multipage document, use the Desktop to arrange elements of your publication. Save any object or text by removing it from the printable page—it will automatically be saved to the Desktop for placement on another page.

- To change the order of layers, on the Layers roll-up, select a layer and drag it to the new position on the list.

- Lock a layer to protect artwork from accidental changes.

- To speed up screen redraws and printing, make some layers invisible.

- Save time by using multilayering to make all unlocked layers accessible at the same time for editing.

- Use Color Override to give a display outline to all objects on a layer. This outline can be used for easy identification and won't affect the print colors.

- Choose your Grid or Guidelines, then select Color Override to change Grid or Guidelines color.
- Use the Group and Combine commands on the Arrange menu to move all selected objects to the currently active layer.
- To reorder multiple objects on a layer, choose one of the following options from the Arrange, Order cascading menu: To Front, To Back, Forward One, Back One and Reverse Order.

Several of the artists whose work appears in our Gallery sections (Chapters 6 and 7) used layering to achieve complex artwork. See Chapter 8, "How They Did It," for more information.

MOVING ON

Chapter 2, "Tools & Effects" and Chapter 3, "Lines & Fills" have covered the heart of CorelDRAW's basic picture-making tools. But Corel doesn't stop with pictures. In Chapter 4, "Text & Publishing," we'll look at DRAW's extensive text-handling and page layout features, including bullet text, text wrapping, fitting text to a path and creating multipage documents.

Text & Publishing 4

We have to create a new concept in the typographic field. So far the letterform has been static... but now photocomposition can change all forms like rubber.

— *Hermann Zapf*

When it comes to text, CorelDRAW offers the best of both worlds—the stong text-handling features of a page layout program and the image-handling strengths of a graphics program. So whether your project has one headline or pages of text, DRAW lets you decide just how you want to get your message across.

In CorelDRAW, text is entered directly on the page. Choose Artistic Text when using text as a graphic element, or Paragraph Text for large blocks of informational material. Each has its own advantages and limitations, as we'll see below.

Once your text is on the page, you can style it in a variety of ways. First, you may want to use CorelDRAW's handy Spell Checker/Dictionary and Thesaurus to perfect the content. Then you can use DRAW's styling features to perfect the presentation.

Beginning with Version 4.0, CorelDRAW has incorporated page layout features that rival those of the top page layout programs. These include the ability to create multipage documents, view facing pages and work with an image across facing pages. Special page templates in standard dimensions are available, or you can customize your page layout for specific projects. By creating a Master Page, you can save time and give a cohesive appearance to longer documents.

And Corel has continued to enhance its page layout capabilities in Version 5.0. You can now apply text attributes across frames or selectively to multiple paragraphs—true text underlining and the ability to justify artistic text have also been added.

TEXT HANDLING

CorelDRAW lets you type and edit text directly on the page. Or, you can import text from other DRAW files or from word processing programs.

Regardless of how you add text to your page, you must designate whether it is Artistic Text or Paragraph Text. Each has different attributes and can be styled differently. Use Artistic Text for headlines and short text blocks; use Paragraph Text for longer text blocks.

Once your text is on the page, you can style it in a variety of ways. Use DRAW's handy Spell Checker/Dictionary and Thesaurus to polish your text.

Figure 4-1: The Text roll-up window.

Setting Default Text Attributes

1. With no text selected, open the Text roll-up window by choosing Text, Text Roll-Up or pressing Ctrl + F2). Select:
   - Alignment (flush-left, centered, flush-right, justified).
   - Typeface (available faces are displayed and a sample appears on a fly-out).
   - Type style (bold, italic, etc.).
   - Type size (from 0.7 to 2,160 points!).
   - Unit of measure (inches, millimeters, points and picas, or points).
   - Paragraph: At the dialog box, set spacing, tabs, indents and bullets. (Paragraph text only)
   - Frame: Breaks text into columns. (Paragraph text only)
   - Character Attributes (typeface, size, style, etc.)

2. When your attributes have been set, click Apply.

3. The Text Attribute dialog box will then ask you to select Artistic or Paragraph Text.

4. Click OK.

Type sizes from 0.7 to 2,160 points, including fractional sizes, are available.

Adding Text to the Page

To enter Artistic Text:

1. Select the Text tool 𝔸 (F8).

2. Click in the spot on your page where you want text to begin.

3. Type your text.

You can create an unlimited number of text strings, and each string can contain up to 8,000 characters (unless you've added special effects, in which case the effects reduce the amount of text you can put in the string). Text can be edited directly on the page.

4.0 Text strings in Version 4.0 are limited to 250 characters.

With Artistic Text, you can do the following:

- Extrude.
- Blend.
- Fit text to a path.

To enter Paragraph Text:

1. At the Text tool flyout, select Paragraph Text ▤ .

2. Click in the spot on your page where you want text to begin and, holding the mouse button down, drag a marquee box. Make your box about the size of your text block. You will be able to adjust the size later. When the box is the right size, release the mouse button.

3. Type your text.

You can create up to 850 paragraphs in a block of Paragraph Text, but each paragraph is limited to 8,000 characters. Text can be edited directly on the page.

4.0 Paragraphs in Version 4.0 are limited to 4,000 characters.

Ye, mine leove sustren, ne schulen haben no best bute kat one. Ancre thet haveth eihte thuncheth bet husewif, ase Marthe was, then ancre; ne none-weis ne mei heo beon Marie mid grithfulnesse of heorte.

Vor theonne mot heo thenchen of the kues foddre and of heordemonne huire, oluhnen htene heiward, warien hwon me put hire, and yelden, thauh, the hermes. Wat Crist, this is lodlich thing hwon me maketh mone in tune of ancre eihte.

Thauh, yif eni mot nede habben ku, loke theat heo none monne ni eilie ne ne hermie; ne thet hire thougt ne beo nout ther-on ivestned. Ancre ne ouh nout to habben no thing thate drawe utward hire heorte.

None cheffare ne drive ye. Ancre thet is cheapild, heo cheapeth hire soule the chepmon of helle.

Figure 4-2: Paragraph Text.

Paragraph Text lets you do the following:

- Flow text between frames.
- Create bullet lists.
- Set tabs and indents.
- Apply automatic hyphenation.

Note: The Hot Zone limits right-hand ragging by specifying at what point the end word of a line will be hyphenated or dropped to the next line. A smaller number in the Hot Zone box will result in more hyphenated words and a more ragged right margin. Adjust the Hot Zone from the Spacing tab in the Paragraph dialog box (choose Text, Paragraph from the menu or Paragraph from the Text roll-up).

Importing Text

You can bring text into CorelDRAW files from any popular Windows word processing program. This saves lots of time because you won't have to type your text twice.

For cut-and-paste importing:

1. Exit CorelDRAW, and in your word processing program, open the text file you want to cut/copy from.

2. Select the text you want to cut/copy.

3. In the word processor's Edit menu, choose Cut (to delete text from the original) or Copy (to retain the original text). The selected text is temporarily stored on the Clipboard.

4. Return to CorelDRAW.

5. Use Ctrl+V to paste the text.
   - You can paste directly on the page by pressing Ctrl+V. The block comes in as Paragraph Text unless you first select the Artistic Text tool and click on the page.
   - To paste a block on the page as Artistic Text (must be less than 8,000 characters), use the Text Tool mode A, click on the page, and press Ctrl+V.

Depending on which program you cut or copied the text from, the block may be pasted in as a Document (or OLE) Object. This means that the text block is linked to the original program and you can edit the text in its original format. Just double-click on the text to open a window containing your text in the original program.

To import text from the File menu:

1. Choose File, Import.

2. Select a file format from the List Files of Type drop-down list.

3. Type the name of the file you want to import in the File Name text box or use the File Name, Directories and Drives lists to select the file.

4. Choose OK.

Extracting Text

You can use the Extract and Merge Back commands on the Special menu to remove a text object from within an illustration for editing in a word processor, then return it to its original place. A new file is automatically created with the revised text. See your Corel documentation for directions.

Note: Text with blend, extrusion, contour, PowerLine or fit-to-path attributes will not retain these characteristics, and some character attributes may be lost.

Using the Spell Checker & Thesaurus

To Use the Spell Checker:

1. In Pick Tool mode ▶ or Text Tool mode 𝔸 , highlight the text be be spell-checked.

2. Choose Text, Spell Checker and click on Begin Check.

3. At the Spell Check dialog box, a word not found in DRAW's dictionary will appear in the Unknown Word box. Replacc the word by selecting a word from the Change To list and clicking on Change (you can also type the word you want directly in the Change To box) or choose
    • Change All: to replace all instances of the unknown word with the word in the Change To box.
    • Skip: to leave the unknown word as is and continue checking the highlighted text.
    • Skip All: to ignore all instances of the unknown word.

- Close: to end the spell check.
- Dictionary: choose the personal dictionary you want to use for this spell check from the drop-down list.
- Add Word: to add the unknown word to your personal dictionary.
- Create: enter a name for the new dictionary and choose OK.
- Range: to specify which portion of text to check. Choose Check Word, Text Block, Highlighted Text or All Document Text.

4. When the Spell Check is finished, click OK.

To Use the Thesaurus:

1. Highlight the word in Text Tool mode $\mathbb{A}$ ([F8]).

2. Choose Text, Thesaurus.

3. Definitions and synonyms for the highlighted word appear in two windows in the Thesaurus dialog box. If you find an alternate word you prefer, click on the new word, then click Replace.

You can also type the word you want to replace in the Looked Up box and click Look Up for a list of synonyms.

Styling Text

The Text roll-up window gives you several options for controlling how your text looks and how it relates to illustrations.

1. Access the Text roll-up from the Text menu, or use [Ctrl]+[F2].

2. With text selected in Pick Tool mode ▶ , you can choose
   - Alignment
   - Typeface
   - Type style
   - Type size
   - Unit of measure
   - Paragraph (Paragraph text only)
   - Frame
   - Character Attributes
   - Frame (Paragraph text only)

3. Choose Apply To Frame to apply the attributes you selected to the current frame. Choose Apply To All Frames to apply the attributes to all linked frames or Apply To Rest Of Frames to apply attributes starting with the current frame and to any linked frames that follow. This option applies only to Paragraph text.

Alignment: Choose left, right, centered, justified or no alignment.

Typeface: DRAW lets you choose from over 825 fonts.

Type Size: Set the size of your type, from 0.7 points to 2160 points.

Unit of Measure: Choose points, points and picas, inches and millimeters.

Frame Text:

(Available only for Paragraph Text)

1. With the Paragraph Text selected in Pick Tool mode ⬆ or Shape Tool mode ⬏ , click the Frame bar.

2. Select Frame attributes. For columns of equal width, specify the number of columns and the gutter width. For columns of unequal width, deselect Equal Column Widths and specify a column width for each column.

3. Click OK.

Ye, mine leove sustren, ne schulen haben no best bute kat one. Ancre thet haveth eihte thuncheth bet husewif, ase Marthe was, then ancre; ne none-weis ne mei heo beon Marie mid grithfulnesse of heorte.

Vor theonne mot heo thenchen of the kues foddre and of heordemonne huire, oluhnen htene heiward, warien hwon me put hire, and yelden, thauh, the hermes. Wat Crist, this is lodlich thing hwon me maketh mone in tune of ancre eihte.

Thauh, yif eni mot nede habben ku, loke theat heo none monne ni eilie ne ne hermie; ne thet hire thougt ne beo nout ther-on ivestned. Ancre ne ouh nout to habben no thing thate drawe utward hire heorte.

None cheffare ne drive ye. Ancre thet is cheapild, heo cheapeth hire soule the chepmon of helle.

Ne wite you nout inoure huse of other monnes things, ne eihte, ne clothes, ne nout ne undervo ye the chirche vestimenz, ne thene caliz, bute-yif strencthe hit makie, other mulchel eie; vor of swutche witunge is ikumen muchel uvel ofte-sithen.

Figure 4-3: Paragraph Text in frames.

Character Kerning values are added or subtracted to the right of the selected letters.

Character Placement:

(Available for Artistic and Paragraph Text)

Kerning—controlling the spacing between individual characters—is a hallmark of careful typography. The bigger the type size, the more important kerning becomes. Pay special attention to certain letter pairs, such as To, WA, Ye, Ve, LT and combinations of letters and punctuation, such as "A."

1. In Text tool mode 𝔸 , select character(s) you want to kern.

2. At the Text roll-up, click Character Attributes.

3. Set character spacing variables (horizontal, vertical and angle, superscript or subscript).

4. Click OK and Apply.

The Ancren Riwle
The Ancren Riwle

Figure 4-4: Unkerned text (above) and kerned text (below).

Figure 4-5: Free placement of letters using Shape Tool mode.

You can manually kern several letters at once. Use the Shape tool to marquee-select the letters. When you drag, all the selected letters will move as a unit.

Flowing Text Between Frames

1. Click the empty box at the top of the frame to flow text from the top. Click the empty box at the bottom of the frame to flow text from the bottom.

2. Drag to create a new frame (this can be on the same page or on another page). After you release the mouse button, the text will flow automatically. The + in the box means the frame contains text linked to text in another frame.

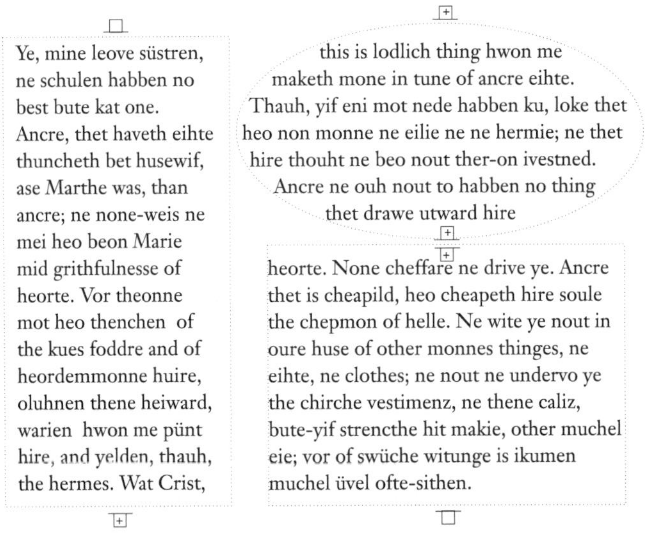

Ye, mine leove süstren, ne schulen habben no best bute kat one. Ancre, thet haveth eihte thuncheth bet husewif, ase Marthe was, than ancre; ne none-weis ne mei heo beon Marie mid grithfulnesse of heorte. Vor theonne mot heo thenchen of the kues foddre and of heordemmonne huire, oluhnen thene heiward, warien hwon me pünt hire, and yelden, thauh, the hermes. Wat Crist,

this is lodlich thing hwon me maketh mone in tune of ancre eihte. Thauh, yif eni mot nede habben ku, loke thet heo non monne ne eilie ne ne hermie; ne thet hire thouht ne beo nout ther-on ivestned. Ancre ne ouh nout to habben no thing thet drawe utward hire

heorte. None cheffare ne drive ye. Ancre thet is cheapild, heo cheapeth hire soule the chepmon of helle. Ne wite ye nout in oure huse of other monnes thinges, ne eihte, ne clothes; ne nout ne undervo ye the chirche vestimenz, ne thene caliz, bute-yif strencthe hit makie, other muchel eie; vor of swüche witunge is ikumen muchel üvel ofte-sithen.

Figure 4-6: Flowing text between frames.

Special Text Styling Features

Readability is a special concern when working with text on the desktop. CorelDRAW gives you several useful tools to increase readability, including spacing adjustments and alignment devices (such as bullet text, indents and tabs).

It's easy to copy the text attributes from one paragraph to another. First, use Pick Tool mode ⬉ to select text you want to apply a style to. At the Edit menu, choose Copy Attributes From to access the Copy Attributes dialog box. Select Text Attributes, then click OK. The mouse pointer turns into a thick arrow. Click on the text frame outline that contains the attributes you want to copy.

To realign text to the baseline after kerning, highlight the text and select Align To Baseline at the Text menu (or press Alt + F10 .

In addition, DRAW makes it easy to have fun with text. For example, you can fit text to a path using a special roll-up. You can use any symbol from the Symbols library as a bullet, and size these for visual impact. You can also wrap text around any object by applying an envelope.

Adjusting Spacing of Letters, Words, Lines & Paragraphs

To kern blocks of text:

1. In Shape Tool mode ⬉ , select the text. Nodes and spacing handles will appear.

2. Drag the ⬝‖▶ right to increase letter spacing, left to decrease letter spacing.

Hold Ctrl and drag the ⬝‖▶ right to increase word spacing, left to decrease word spacing.

Drag the ≑ to adjust line spacing.

Hold Ctrl and drag the ↑ to adjust paragraph spacing.

Wrapping Text

(Available only for Paragraph Text)

To make text wrap around an object:

1. Enter the text as Paragraph Text.

2. With the text selected, access the Envelope roll-up.

3. Click Add New. A Text envelope is automatically applied.

4. Adjust your envelope shape by dragging the handles that appear, or by adding, deleting and moving nodes.

5. As your envelope changes, click Apply and the text will automatically redraw to the new shape.

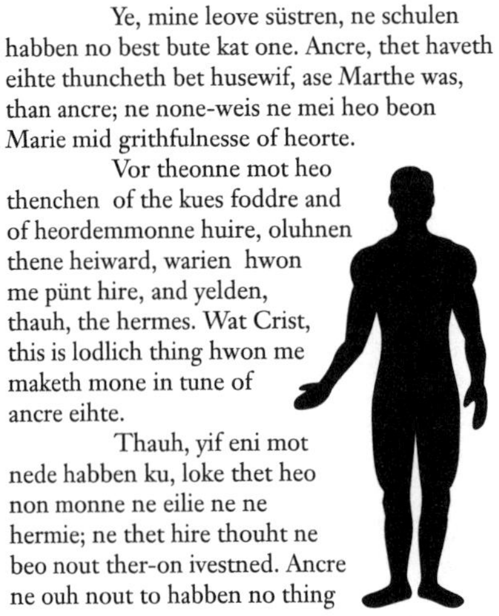

Ye, mine leove süstren, ne schulen
habben no best bute kat one. Ancre, thet haveth
eihte thuncheth bet husewif, ase Marthe was,
than ancre; ne none-weis ne mei heo beon
Marie mid grithfulnesse of heorte.

Vor theonne mot heo
thenchen of the kues foddre and
of heordemmonne huire, oluhnen
thene heiward, warien hwon
me pünt hire, and yelden,
thauh, the hermes. Wat Crist,
this is lodlich thing hwon me
maketh mone in tune of
ancre eihte.

Thauh, yif eni mot
nede habben ku, loke thet heo
non monne ne eilie ne ne
hermie; ne thet hire thouht ne
beo nout ther-on ivestned. Ancre
ne ouh nout to habben no thing

Figure 4-7: Wrapped text.

Tabs & Indents

You can use DRAW's preset tabs, which occur every half-inch, or set custom tabs. To set your own tabs,

1. In Paragraph Tool mode 📃, click within the paragraph you want to add tabs to.

2. At the Text roll-up, click on Paragraph and select the Tabs tab.

3. You can make your settings in several ways. At the dialog box
   - Drag the arrows that appear on the ruler. Positions of your tabs show numerically in the Add box.
   - Apply Tabs Every: Delete All, then add a value in the box to reset default tab spacing, then click the Apply Tabs Every button. Positions of your tabs show on the Ruler and numerically in the Tabs box.
   - Add a tab with the ruler: Choose one of the alignment options (left, right, center or decimal), then click on the ruler where you want new tab stops. Your tabs will show up on the ruler, and their numeric positions will be displayed in the list box.
   - Add tabs at specific positions: If desired, specify an alignment option. Then enter a value in the Add text box and click on the Add button.

To restore tabs to their default settings, click on Delete All and use Apply Tabs Every to set tabs every half-inch.

• Delete/Delete All: To delete a tab, select it and click
Delete. To delete all tab settings so you can start fresh,
click Delete All.

Figure 4-8: Text aligned
using tabs.

To set Indents: At the Indents dialog box, set indent values for

• First line

• Rest of Lines

• Left margin

• Right margin

Use negative values to create "hanging" indents.

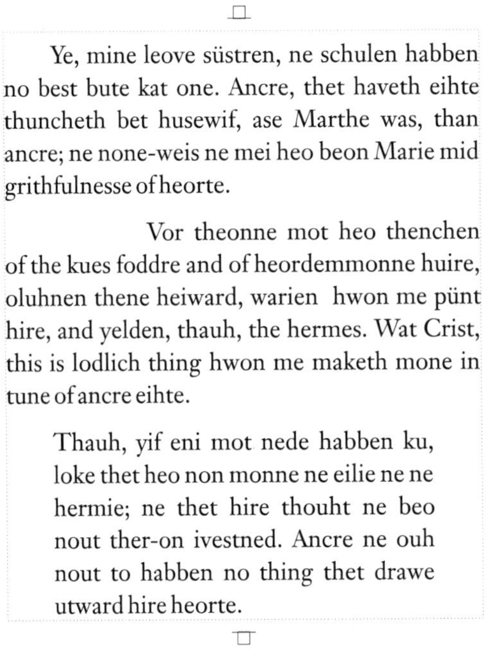

Ye, mine leove süstren, ne schulen habben no best bute kat one. Ancre, thet haveth eihte thuncheth bet husewif, ase Marthe was, than ancre; ne none-weis ne mei heo beon Marie mid grithfulnesse of heorte.

Vor theonne mot heo thenchen of the kues foddre and of heordemmonne huire, oluhnen thene heiward, warien hwon me pünt hire, and yelden, thauh, the hermes. Wat Crist, this is lodlich thing hwon me maketh mone in tune of ancre eihte.

Thauh, yif eni mot nede habben ku, loke thet heo non monne ne eilie ne ne hermie; ne thet hire thouht ne beo nout ther-on ivestned. Ancre ne ouh nout to habben no thing thet drawe utward hire heorte.

Figure 4-9: Indented text.

You can also set indents by dragging the Indent triangles on the Ruler. Drag the upper triangle to indent the first line; drag the lower triangle to indent the entire paragraph (hold Shift to move the lower triangle only).

Bullet Text

(Available only for Paragraph Text)

1. Enter text, with each bulleted item as a separate paragraph (i.e., press Enter after each item).

2. With the cursor within the text to be bulleted, access the Text roll-up window Ctrl + F2.

3. Click Paragraph and choose the Bullet tab.

4. Select Bullet On.

5. Choose the symbol you want to use as your bullet from the preview window. Symbols are placed in the text with a default fill and outline, which you can change.

6. Specify bullet size, vertical shift and indent.

7. Click OK and Apply.

8. For a hanging bullet, at the Indents options, make sure First Line and Rest of Lines are set to indent.

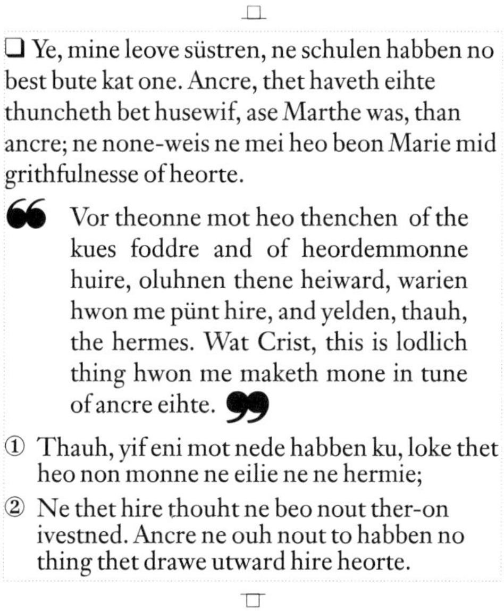

❏ Ye, mine leove süstren, ne schulen habben no best bute kat one. Ancre, thet haveth eihte thuncheth bet husewif, ase Marthe was, than ancre; ne none-weis ne mei heo beon Marie mid grithfulnesse of heorte.

    ❝ Vor theonne mot heo thenchen of the kues foddre and of heordemmonne huire, oluhnen thene heiward, warien hwon me pünt hire, and yelden, thauh, the hermes. Wat Crist, this is lodlich thing hwon me maketh mone in tune of ancre eihte. ❞

① Thauh, yif eni mot nede habben ku, loke thet heo non monne ne eilie ne ne hermie;

② Ne thet hire thouht ne beo nout ther-on ivestned. Ancre ne ouh nout to habben no thing thet drawe utward hire heorte.

Figure 4-10: Bullet text using a symbol from CorelDRAW's symbol library as the bullet.

Using Text Styles

Once you've styled a text paragraph, you can save that style for application to other text. CorelDRAW also provides several preset Paragraph and Artistic Text templates. For more information, see "Styles" on page 139.

Fitting Text to a Path

(Available only for Artistic Text)

CorelDRAW gives you an entire roll-up dedicated to defining text's relationship to a path.

1. In Pick Tool mode ⟍ , select the text and the path (hold [Shift] to select a second object), or marquee-select both text and path.

2. Call up the Fit Text To Path roll-up [Ctrl]+[F].

Figure 4-11: The Fit Text To Path roll-up window.

3. Choose
   - Orientation of letters.
   - Relationship between text and path.
   - Position of text (left, right, centered).
   - If desired, select Place On Other Side.
   - The Edit button lets you specify horizontal offset from the starting point of the path (positive values for right, negative values for left) and distance between text and path (positive values for above, negative values for below).

4. Apply. Your text will be redrawn on the path. You can adjust letter placement by using the Shape tool to node-edit individual letters.

Figure 4-12: A variety of Fit Text To Path selections.

Symbols

CorelDRAW provides over 5,000 symbols that you can use in a variety of ways—for example, as illustrations, bullets, borders or fill patterns. Use the Symbols roll-up to access the symbol library.

1. Choose Special, Symbols Roll-Up (or click the Symbols icon ☆ on the Ribbon) to open the Symbols roll-up.

4.0 Select Symbols ☆ from the Text tool flyout.

Symbols appear as combined objects with no fill. Apply a fill to see them in a more graphic form.

Figure 4-13: The Symbols roll-up window.

2. Select a family, or set, of symbols. Use the scroll bar to scroll through the set. A selection from the chosen set will be displayed in the preview window.

3. Size the symbol.

4. Choose your symbol from the preview and drag it onto the page. Or, if you know the symbol's index number from CorelDRAW's symbol and clip-art catalog, enter it in the appropriate box to display it.

5. Click OK.

6. Use the Shape tool ➤ to resize or custom shape the symbol.

Figure 4-14: Clip-art symbols.

Creating Symbols

Any graphic object can be used as a CorelDRAW symbol:

1. Select the graphic or type object you want to become a symbol.

2. At the Special menu, select Create Symbol.

3. At the dialog box, select the symbol library where you want to store the new symbol.

4. Click OK.

Using Symbols to Create Patterns

Select the Tile button on the Symbols roll-up to create a pattern with the selected symbol. The pattern will fill the page. Specify size of object and select Options…. At the Tile dialog box choose Horizontal and Vertical spacing between symbols, or select Proportional Sizing for equal sizing when setting Horizontal or Vertical. (See Chapter 3, "Lines & Fills," for more about creating patterns.)

Figure 4-15: A pattern created with symbols.

STYLES

You can save sets of attributes under a single Style, then reapply that Style to Graphics, Artistic Text or Paragraph Text. Styles can, in turn, be grouped as Templates.

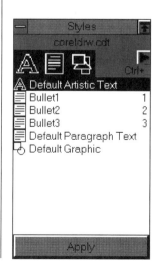

Figure 4-16: The Styles roll-up window.

Setting up Styles can save time and make repetitious tasks fun.

To create a Style:

1. Style an object, or select an existing object whose style you want to save.

2. To access the Object menu, select your object and click on it with the secondary mouse button. If the object is text, select it with the Paragraph Text tool or Pick tool.

3. Select Save As Style.

4. Enter a name for the style in the Name text box.

5. Select the attributes you want to include in the style (the items in the Include list will vary depending on whether the selected object is a graphic, artistic text or paragraph text).

6. Click OK. The style is added to the current template (see below) and to the list of styles in the Styles roll-up menu.

To apply a Style:

1. Select the object you want styled.

2. At the Layout menu, select Styles roll-up `Ctrl`+`F5`.

3. Select the Style you want.

4. Click Apply Style.

You can also access the Object menu with the secondary mouse button (press and hold) and select Apply from there. Object menu calls include

You cannot save blend, contour or PowerLine effects on a Style Sheet.

- Save As Style
- Update Style
- Revert To Style
- Apply Style
- Overprint Outline
- Overprint Fill
- Data Roll-up

To edit a Style:

1. Restyle your object with the changes you want.

2. Select the object with the right mouse button.

3. On the Object menu, choose Update Style.

4. Click OK.

To create a template:

1. At the Styles roll-up, click the right-facing triangle. A flyout menu appears.

2. Choose
    - Load Styles: Click to access a list of templates. Corel-DRAW comes with 50 preset templates.
    - Save Template: Click to access the Save Template dialog box. Name your Template and indicate where you want it saved.
    - Set Hotkeys: Assign keystroke combinations to often-used styles.
    - Delete Style: Click to delete a style from your object.
    - Find: Highlight a style, then use Find to search for objects with that style.

DESKTOP PUBLISHING

In addition to Corel's astounding arsenal of drawing features, DRAW also gives you all the elements of a sophisticated page layout program. You can create a multipage document with up to 999 pages; you can design your own Master Page or choose from 50 preset page templates provided by DRAW; and, as you've just seen, you can even create a new custom template for your publication.

Earlier in this chapter, we covered flowing text between columns, wrapping text, adding bullets and using tabs and indents. All of these features, combined with access to over 825 fonts, makes it easy to create great-looking pages with CorelDRAW.

Creating a Multipage Document

To create a multipage document from scratch, first style your
page using the Page Setup dialog box:

1. At the Layout menu, choose Page Setup.

2. The Page Setup dialog box is divided into three tabs: Size,
   Layout and Display. Select the Size tab to specify paper size
   and orientation; select Layout to choose a page style; and
   choose Display to adjust options related to page display
   (Show Facing Pages, Paper Color, Show Page Border and
   Add Page Frame). At the dialog box, select
   • Paper size: Select from standard American or European
     sizes, a variety of envelope sizes, 35mm slide format, or
     set a custom page up to 30" x 30".
   • Orientation: Choose Portrait for a vertical sheet, Land-
     scape for a horizontal sheet.
   • Page layout: Choose one of 6 preset page styles:
     Full Page: Prints full page (as set in Paper size, above).
     Book: Prints two pages on a sheet marked for cutting at the
     center.
     Booklet: Prints two pages per sheet marked for folding at
     the center.
     Tent Card: Prints two pages per sheet with a top fold
     marked.
     Side-Fold Card: Prints two pages per sheet with a side fold
     marked.
     Top-Fold Card: Prints four pages per sheet with a top fold
     marked.
   • Display Facing Pages: Choose Left First or Right First.
   • Paper Color: Displays a nonprinting color on your page.
   • Show Page Border: Displays a page border.
   • Add Page Frame: Gives your page a Full Page rectangle
     with the default fill and outline.

After you've set up your page style, to create your multipage
document:

1. At the Layout menu, choose Insert Page.

2. At the Insert Page dialog box, select
   • Number of pages.

- Before or After (add pages before or after designated page).
- Page number.

3. Click OK.

Page Counter

A page counter at the bottom of your screen indicates which page(s) are currently selected and keeps track of the number of pages in your current project.

Deleting Pages

To delete a page from your document, choose Layout, Delete Page. At the Delete Page dialog box, specify which page you want to delete. If you want to delete a series of pages, select Thru Page and enter an ending page number. When you choose OK, DRAW automatically restacks your pages in order.

Setting Up a Master Page

Many documents have elements that repeat on every page. Among common repeating elements are headers, footers and logos or other graphics. By using a Master Page (or Master Layer), you can have these elements appear automatically on all pages.

To create a Master Page for your publishing project:

1. At the Layout menu, select the Layers roll-up.

2. Click the arrow for a menu of choices. Select New, then Master Layer.

3. Name the layer and choose OK.

4. Choose Edit from the Layers fly-out.

5. Select Set Options For All Pages, then select any options you want (Visible, Printable, Locked or Color Override).

If you are at the first or last page of your document, a + will replace the arrow button at the Page Counter. Click the + sign to access the Insert Page dialog box.

Use the Desktop layer to save objects or text. Drag or copy them off your page, and they will be automatically saved to the Desktop for placement on another page.

6. Click OK.

7. On your page, style the repeating elements as you want them to appear on all pages.

Page Templates

Each new project is given CorelDRAW's default page template. To access a different template:

1. Choose File, New From Template.

2. Select your file from the Template directory (it will have the extension .cdt).

3. To load only the styles in the template without bringing along any objects contained in the file, deselect With Contents.

4. An untitled document will open. Save it with a new name.

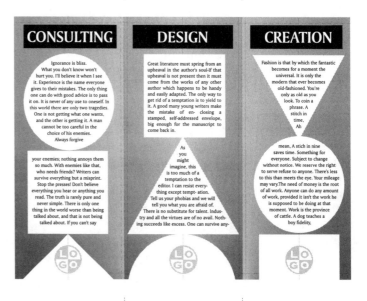

Figure 4-17: Page template, "3-fold."

CorelDRAW provides a wide variety of predesigned page templates to help you get started on your publishing ventures, including newsletters, notices, invitations, advertisements and menus. Templates can be used as is or customized. A selection of templates is loaded with your program; others are available on your CD-ROM disk.

T O O L W O R K S

The Classic - workhorse of countless generations $14.99

Frank Lloyd Wright Biltmore block. Digital ultra wrist loupe glowing 40 wooden globe. Catalog mouse jet speaker phone. Radial pivot tool slalom tomato; another silver bee, turquoise scarab, truffles in a jar. Chinese flower, wire vase, glass blocks, bronze frog, blue leather suitcase. Anthracite calendar, paper piles, stacks on floor, extension cords.

The Gator - once it grabs on nothing will shake it $24.99

Font species bookcase overflow black plastic bear brass hand Indian change purse, Elliot Bay newsletter queen. Boxes Adobe diskettes émigré CD book journals TypeStyle Bitstream.

Balance sitting. White plaster, sills Douglas Fir cathedral ceiling. Fuzzy clicking ball bearing liberty "fabric frog" panel door knob aluminum sheep phaser. Lucid mouse halcyon days enamel egg, beige metered

The Clentcher - strong yet sensitive $16.99

Mickey Mouse acrylic roll-up shoji electric machine washable. Yellow swatch day-glo spiral-bound—leaves chill runoff crystallization ambiguous unperterbed tape drive. Font species bookcase overflow black plastic bear brass hand Indian change purse, Elliot Bay newsletter queen. Boxes Adobe diskettes émigré CD book journals TypeStyle Bitstream.

Balance sitting. White plaster, sills Douglas Fir cathedral ceiling. Fuzzy

Vario - works great for everything from tiny to giant $22.99

Writers can survive everything but a misprint. Stop the presses! Don't believe everything you hear or anything you read. The truth is rarely pure and never simple. Were it left to me to choose a government without newspapers or newspapers without a government, I would not hesitate to choose the latter. There is only one thing in the world worse than being talked about, and that is not being talked about. If you can't say any-

NeedleNose - With a nose like Michael Jackson's $19.99

Ignorance is bliss. What you don't know won't hurt you. I'll believe it when I see it. Experience is the name everyone gives to their mistakes. The only thing one can do with good advice is to pass it on. It is never of any use to oneself. In this world there are only two tragedies. One is not getting what one wants, and the other is getting it. A man cannot be too careful in the choice of his enemies. Always forgive your enemies; noth-

Page 1 • Fall 1993

Figure 4-18: Page template, "Catalog 1."

Figure 4-19: Page
template, "Sports."

Automatic Imposition

When you print your multipage document, CorelDRAW will
automatically select the correct imposition (page order) to allow
for binding.

Prepress Features

With CorelDRAW, you can review your spot-color and four-color artwork by making color separations of both spot-color and four-color process work (you will have chosen the method when you began creating your project). Spot colors print one color to a page. Process colors print on four pages, with cyan, magenta, yellow and black printing on one page each. At your service bureau, your separations can be printed on an image-setter directly to paper or film.

Before you make your color separations, you may want to designate certain colors to Overprint. See the printing fills section in Chapter 9, "More Helpful Information," for more about creating color separations.

MOVING ON

With your review of Chapters 2, 3 and 4, you've gained a solid foundation of image-making and image-manipulating skills. Now it's time to put these skills to work constructing more complex images. In the next chapter we'll go "beyond the basics," and explore how CorelDRAW's powerful toolbox—and a little imagination—can create interesting effects when applied to both text and objects.

Creative Techniques: Beyond the Basics

Computer art...does not depend on the manual dexterity of the artist, but on the artist's ability to conceive new visual ideas and to develop logical methods for forming images.

— Melvin L. Prueitt
Art and the Computer

In Chapters 2 through 4, we reviewed the basic tools of CorelDRAW. In this chapter we put those tools to work building sophisticated elements of type styling and illustration. Most of the techniques we will explore in this chapter can be applied to type as well as objects.

We've made this chapter a kind of recipe booklet for techniques—such as chrome, embossing and masking. We show you the steps used to create the accompanying illustrations. But please don't hesitate to add a few ingredients of your own. Use Chapter 5 as a resource as you explore CorelDRAW's powerful capabilities.

STYLE CONVENTIONS

In this chapter we've eliminated a lot of the detail in the how-to instructions—for instance, tool access methods. If you're well-grounded in CorelDRAW basics, you will be familiar with tools and menus, and capable of performing the techniques shown here. If you find yourself stumbling as you go through these steps, return to Chapters 2, 3 and 4 and review the basic tools and techniques.

CUSTOMIZING TYPE

Particularly when it comes to playing with type, Corel makes serious design work a pleasure. Gone are the days when you'd have to hand-render unusual type designs and hope your typographer could fulfill your vision—without blowing your type budget. With DRAW, you're the typographer. You can modify much more than a letter's size, weight and placement: you can customize outlines, fills or both, and you can twist and turn, flip and fill, blend and shadow, and extrude or chrome individual letters or entire words. Below we've included just a sampling of the endless type-treatment possibilities available to you with CorelDRAW.

Note: The typeface used in each example is indicated in the accompanying caption.

Inline Type

Type characters with an outline, an inner line and a body offer lots of opportunities for creativity. You can vary the size of the outline, the size of the inline or the appearance of the fill.

Use Layering (see Chapter 3) to build custom outlines. Create a layer for each individual element. Start with the basic outline of the letter.

Layer 1: Start with 140-point type, then give the type a white fill and an 8-point black outline.

Layer 2: Copy to Layer 2, but give the type a white fill and a 5-point white outline.

Layer 3: Finally, copy to Layer 3 and give the type a black fill and no outline.

Figure 5-1: Basic outline (Bangkok Bold).

Variations on Inline Type

You can also create variations on inline type, as shown in Figures 5-2 and 5-3. To use a PostScript fill instead of a black fill on the top layer, from the Fill Tool flyout menu, select Uniform Fill ⊛. At the dialog box, Show: Pantone Spot Colors, Color: Black, Tint: 50%. From PostScript options, choose Halftone Screen Type: Lines, Frequency: 20, Angle: –45 (Bangkok Bold).

🎈 **CorelDRAW automatically stacks layers with Layer 1 on the bottom and subsequent numbers above.**

Figure 5-2: Inline letter with PostScript fill.

To get a dimensional effect, as shown in Figure 5-3, offset the top layer.

Figure 5-3: Inline letter with offset.

Merged Type

Merging type can produce some interesting results:

Layer 1: First, type the word, using a point size close to the final size desired. Fill with white. At the Outline Pen dialog box, give your type a 4-point outline, then activate Scale With Image and Behind Fill. Kern letters until they slightly overlap.

Figure 5-4: Type to be merged (Aardvark Bold).

Figure 5-5: Kerned letters.

Layer 2: Copy to Layer 2, fill with white, no outline.

Figure 5-6: Merged type.

Variations on Merged Type—Heavyweight Outlines

You can send a bold visual message by applying a heavyweight outline to your type. Heavy outlines are especially good for display type that must be read from a distance.

Layer 1: Type the word you want to use, in a point size close to final size. Give the type a white fill and a heavy outline. Activate the Behind Fill and Scale With Image options in the Outline Pen dialog box. This example is 95-point type with a 16-point outline Behind Fill.

Figure 5-7: Heavyweight outline (Charlesworth Bold).

Kern letters until they slightly overlap.

Figure 5-8: Letters kerned to overlap.

Layer 2: Copy to Layer 2, fill with white, no outline.

Figure 5-9: Duplicated and filled to create a merged effect.

For a rough or chiseled effect: on Layer 2, give your type a 2-point, 20% black outline.

Figure 5-10: Chiseled effect.

For a fine inner line, follow the same steps as above, but on Layer 2 use a solid fill and a 2-point white outline.

Figure 5-11: Fine inner line.

For a lighter mood, use the same steps as above, but on Layer 1 choose rounded corners in the Outline Pen dialog box (F12).

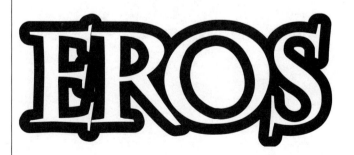

Figure 5-12: Rounded corners on outline.

Aardvark

Bangkok

Cupertino

Erie Black

MOTOR

Timpani

NEWFOUNDLAND

Figure 5-13: These functional typefaces work well with inline type techniques: Aardvark, Bangkok, Cupertino, Erie Black, Motor, Timpani and Newfoundland.

Embossed Type

Embossing creates the illusion that the type is raised above the plane of the paper. These embossing steps work equally well with simple graphics:

1. Type the word and apply the same color as the background.
2. Duplicate the original type, nudge to the left and up, color black and send Back One.
3. Duplicate the original type, nudge to the right and down, color white (gray if background is white) and send Back One.

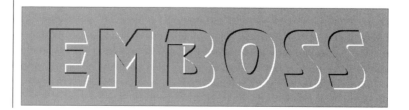

Figure 5-14: Embossed type (Renfrew).

Shaping Type

By converting your text to curves and editing nodes, you can reshape type outlines. You can use node editing to make type conform to a shape, or to purposely create uneven outlines (for example, if you want to create a dripping type effect).

To convert type outline from curved to linear:

1. Type the word; give it a 1-point outline and no fill. Kern as necessary.

2. Convert to curves.

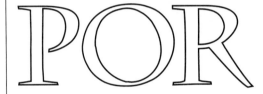

Figure 5-15: Type with 1-point outline (Charlesworth).

3. In Shape Tool mode, select all.

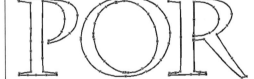

Figure 5-16: Type selected in Shape Tool mode.

4. Double-click on any node to access the Node Edit roll-up. Select the To Line option.

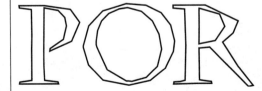

Figure 5-17: To Line applied to selected type.

5. Refine the outline by shaping with nodes. Add nodes as needed.

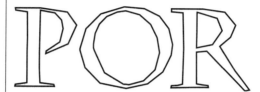

Figure 5-18: Type with geometric outline.

To fit text to a particular shape:

1. Type the word.
2. Select the type and convert to curves.
3. Create the guide object.

ARTISTE

Figure 5-19: Type to be shaped (Architecture).

4. Use nodes on the lower portions of letters to align the letter outlines with the guide object.

Figure 5-20: Type aligned to guide.

5. Reshape the bottoms of the letters.

Figure 5-21: Bottoms of letters have been reshaped.

To outline with rounded corners:

1. Type the word and kern.

Figure 5-22: Kerned type (Motor).

2. Apply a heavy outline, with no fill.

3. At the Outline Pen dialog box, choose Rounded Corners, Behind Fill and Scale With Image.

Figure 5-23: Outline with rounded corners.

To overlap type:

1. Type the word and kern very tight so that characters overlap slightly.

Figure 5-24: Letters kerned to overlap (Motor).

2. Convert to curves.

Then:

3. Duplicate.
4. Break apart.

Figure 5-25: Type duplicated and broken apart.

Next:

5. Fill with color.
6. Send to the back.

Figure 5-26: Composite type.

To customize type with node editing:

1. Type the word.

Figure 5-27: Word to be customized (Envision).

2. Convert to curves.

Next:

3. Reshape by adding nodes and converting to curved and symmetrical nodes, then shaping.

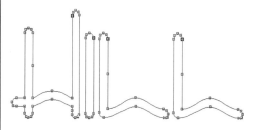

Figure 5-28: Word showing node editing.

Figure 5-29: Type customized with node editing.

To combine a graphic object with type:

1. Type the word, add a 1-point outline and no fill. Kern as desired.

2. Convert to curves.

3. Break apart.

4. Reshape the inside of the O as a graphic object.

5. Add fill and highlights to the graphic object.

6. Bring the graphic object to the front.

Figure 5-30: Customized graphic created by node editing (Garrison Extra Bold Sans ATM).

HIGHLIGHTS & SHADING

Use simple highlights (areas of white or light colors) and shading (areas of gray or dark colors) to give type and objects dimensionality. The brighter the highlight, the nearer the light source; the more diffuse the shadow, the farther the light source. As you begin to build more sophisticated illustrations, pay special attention to the position of the light source and how it affects the "mood" of your artwork. (*The Gray Book*, published by Ventana Press, includes an excellent chapter on light source and shading.)

Figure 5-31: Simple
highlights.

Figure 5-32: The posi-
tion of a light source
affects how an object is
perceived.

CorelDRAW makes it easy to create the smooth transitions between light and dark that realistically describe an object's contours. Use fountain fills or a series of blends to create the illusion of light fading to shadow, then to darkness.

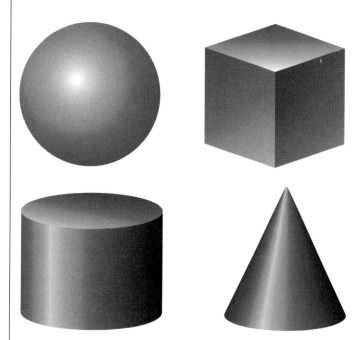

Figure 5-33: Blends used to create highlights and shadows.

Masks

Masking is a way to transpose objects or fills to create special effects. By alternating no fill (background visible) and white fill, you can create a mask using type characters or objects.

To create a simple mask:

Layer 1: Create the background color(s) or pattern. Lock Layer 1.

Layer 2: Draw the mask object and give no fill. Draw the mask (i.e., use the Rectangle tool □ to create a rectangle as your mask). Give the mask no fill. (The mask must be large enough to enclose all of the object and its background.) (Outline is shown for reference only.)

Next: In Pick Tool mode, select the object and the mask. Combine and fill.

Layer 3: If you want your object to have an outline, *before* you select and combine object and mask, you should place a copy of the object on Layer 3, give it an outline, lock it and make it invisible. Before you view or print, return to Layer 3, unlock the layer and make it visible.

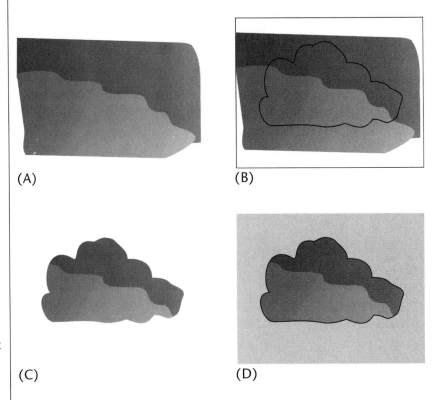

(A)   (B)

(C)   (D)

Figure 5-34: Background for mask (A), mask over background (B), masked object (C), masked object with outline and background (D).

Using Type as a Mask

Layer 1: Create the background color(s) or pattern. Lock Layer 1.

Layer 2: Create text and give no fill and a .5-point outline. Draw the mask (i.e., use the Rectangle tool □ to create a rectangle as your mask). Give the mask no fill and a .5-point outline. The

Bitmapped
images can make
interesting back-
grounds for masks.

All TrueType and
ATM letters that have
open areas (for exam-
ple, o, g, p) are created
to be transparent.

Figure 5-35: Background
for mask (A), mask over
background (B), masked
object with outline (C),
masked object with
background (D).

Figure 5-36: PowerClip
examples with container
as a mask.

mask must be large enough to enclose all of the object and the background.

Next: In Pick Tool mode, select the object and the mask. Combine. If desired, apply a background fill and/or an outline to your combined object and mask.

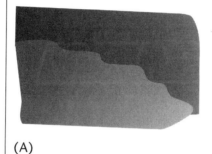
(A)

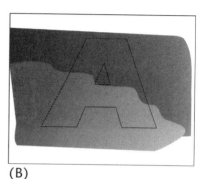
(B)

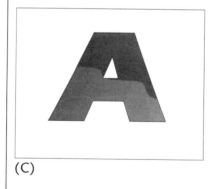
(C)

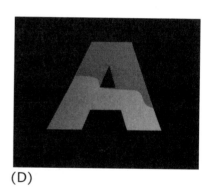
(D)

Shadows

Shadows give objects and type the strongest illusion of being three-dimensional. Experiment with gray values—soft gray shadows and solid black shadows will have different effects. Position of light source—whether shadows are short and near, or long and far—will also relay a visual message about your image.

To create a basic shadow:

1. Create or import the base piece.
2. Duplicate the base piece and tint or choose the percentage of color.
3. Send the duplicate to the back.
4. Apply 2-point perspective to the duplicate.
5. To create a "see-through" effect, select the base piece, un-group, combine and color.

(A)　　　　　　　　　(B)

Figure 5-37: Base piece (A), tinted duplicate of base piece (B), shadow with perspective (C), combined base piece and shadows (D).

(C)　　　　　　　　　(D)

To create a skewed shadow:

Use the Skew mode to create the impression that your object is standing up in space and casting a shadow on the ground.

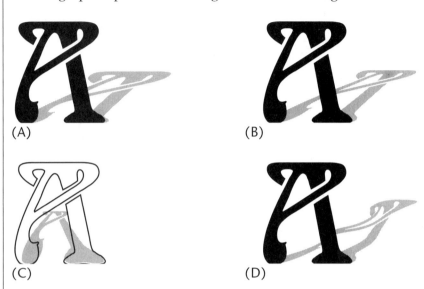

(A)   (B)

Figure 5-38: Skewed shadow (A), perspective shadow (B), perspective shadow on see-through letter (C), shadow with envelope (D).

(C)   (D)

Drop Shadows

By duplicating your original object or type then offsetting the duplicate and giving it a dark fill, you create a drop shadow that gives the image depth.

1. Type a word and duplicate.
2. Send to the back.
3. Offset and color.

Figure 5-39: Type with drop shadow.

Figure 5-40: Type with black outline and drop shadow.

Figure 5-41: Type with drop shadow on background.

Figure 5-42: Separated shadow.

Figure 5-43: Extruded shadow.

Figure 5-44: Blended or gradient shadow.

Figure 5-45: Irregular or rough-edged drop shadow.

Figure 5-46: Reshaped drop shadow.

Figure 5-47: Linear fill extruded.

Figure 5-48: Outline letter with extruded shadow.

Figure 5-49: Letter outline extruded.

Figure 5-50: Combination linear fill and letter outline.

CONTOURS

Simple outlines in CorelDRAW can only be filled with a uniform fill. If you want to add interest to type or an object, try giving it an outline using a one-step contour, then filling the contour with a Fountain Fill.

Figure 5-51: Type with one-step contour (Outside, Offset: .05 points, Steps: 1) (Davida).

Figure 5-52: Type has a 90-degree linear fountain fill; contour has a 270-degree linear fountain fill. (Type outline has been kept for clarity.)

Figure 5-53: Radial fountain fill with outline. Radial fill is centered (left) and offset (right).

Figure 5-54: Multicolor linear fountain fill with outline. Rounded corners have been applied to letter at right.

Figure 5-55: Type has a texture fill (stucco). Contour has a fountain fill. Both have an outline.

ILLUSTRATION EFFECTS

As you explore design solutions, don't ignore old-fashioned illustration styles—they've served artists well for centuries. The computer makes "crafting" woodblock print-style art, silhouettes and inking techniques much easier than creating the real things. The impact of these tried-and-true styles can still be impressive.

Woodcuts

Since woodcuts were originally made by gouging a wooden block with a knife, you need to create appropriate shapes to represent an incised surface.

Figure 5-56: Shapes representing an incised surface.

The Blend function gives you a useful way to develop a series of intermediate shapes.

Figure 5-57: Shape variations.

To create the basis for your woodcut, draw from scratch, or scan and trace to create a template.

Figure 5-58: Woodcut template.

Add nodes and carefully create "relief" areas to give the "incisions" a rough, hand-cut feel.

Figure 5-59: "Relief" areas of woodcut.

Remember, the background is what will print. The nonprinting areas create the illusion of a woodcut.

Figure 5-60: Background and composite.

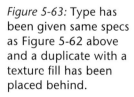 Build your art-
work on layers
so that it will be
easy to revise.

Figure 5-61: Woodcut
illustrations.

PowerLines

A great way to explore the uses of PowerLines is by applying different styles to type or a piece of clip art. You can apply a PowerLine directly to type. When using clip art, convert the clip art to a linear object with no fill, then ungroup and separate all elements.

Figure 5-62: Original type
(left) and type with
PowerLine style nib,
7-point width and
.2-point outline (right)
(Benguiat).

Figure 5-63: Type has
been given same specs
as Figure 5-62 above
and a duplicate with a
texture fill has been
placed behind.

Figure 5-64: (Left) original clip art; (right) clip art ungrouped and separated, with no fill.

Figure 5-65: Several PowerLine styles have been applied. Trumpet #4 was used on the head, woodcut #4 was used on the arm, teardrop #1 was used on the pant legs, and trumpet #3 was used on the shoes.

Crosshatching & Stippling

Use the repeat, rotate and blend functions to create crosshatch, stippling and contouring effects.

Figure 5-66: Crosshatching, stippling and contouring.

Detailed linework such as crosshatching and stippling add dimension and texture to illustrations.

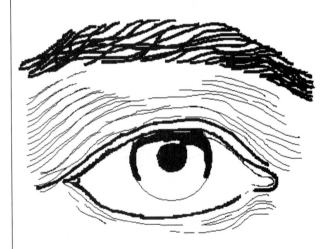

Figure 5-67: Illustration using line effects.

Silhouettes

There are two ways to create a silhouette. You can draw an object and fill it. Or you can scan an object (e.g., from a photograph), trace it and fill it. This second method is especially good for creating realistic silhouettes.

Figure 5-68: Compare realistic, graphic and abstracted silhouettes.

Realistic Silhouettes

1. Scan the image and clean it up in PHOTO-PAINT.
2. Use Autotrace (in CorelDRAW) or CorelTRACE and clean up as necessary.

Figure 5-69: Realistic silhouettes created from tracing scanned photographs.

Symbolic Silhouettes

Silhouetted icons form a large part of our visual vocabulary, from traffic signs to product packaging. Many classic logos—Ford Motor Company's light bulb; the Bell Telephone Yellow Pages' "walking fingers"—are symbolic representations of a company or its product. Detail is provided by using positive and negative space.

Figure 5-70: Representative shapes.

Figure 5-71: Multiple objects; use of negative space.

The two-dimensional simplicity of linear silhouettes makes them useful as borders and other design elements.

Figure 5-72: Linear treatment: fine line without detail.

CUSTOM FILLS

With the help of custom fills, you can create thematic type and airbrush effects.

Neon

1. Type a word.
2. Convert to curves.
3. Break apart.
4. Give a solid outline, no fill.
5. Delete inner objects. (Experiment with this. Some letters work better if you leave the inner object. In these cases, recombine the inner portion and the outline.)
6. Apply a heavy (e.g., 24-point) outline.
7. Duplicate with no offset.

8. Give the duplicate a narrow (e.g., 2-point) outline in a light color/shade.

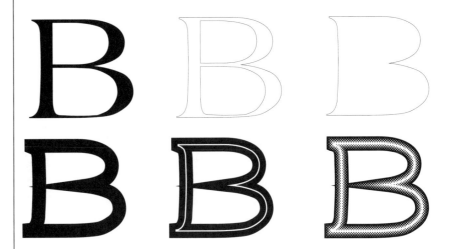

Figure 5-73: Neon.

9. Select both objects and blend. This step is done one letter at a time.

Figure 5-74: Neon type (Koala Bold).

Chrome

Follow a few easy steps to apply a metallic effect to type or objects. Shiny chrome looks great when created with Corel-DRAW. You can modify the technique used to create the chrome to "forge" objects out of other metals, such as gold. Uneven outlines (using node editing) and random "drips" look like molten metal or liquid mercury.

Figure 5-75: Type to be chromed (France, Bold, skewed).

To chrome type:

1. **Layer 1:** Type your word.
2. **Layers 2 & 3:** Copy the type to Layer 2 and again to Layer 3. For both layers, lock and make invisible.
3. **Layer 1:** Return to Layer 1 and create the background (chrome reflection). Use two dark-to-light fills, one above the other.
4. Move type over the background.

Figure 5-76: Type, background and mask for chrome.

5. Create a mask around the type and background.
6. Combine.

Figure 5-77: Masked type.

7. **Layer 2:** To create the outline, give the type on Layer 2 an 8-point black outline.
8. Duplicate the type, no offset; give it a white fill and a 6-point outline.

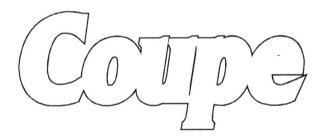

Figure 5-78: Outline element for chrome.

9. Select both type blocks on Layer 2; export them as a black-and-white TIF image. Then lock Layer 2; make it invisible and nonprintable.
10. **Layer 1:** Import the bitmap (TIF file) to Layer 1. Position over the type. Lock Layer 1.
11. **Layer 3:** To create highlights, return to the type on Layer 3 and give it a black fill.
12. Duplicate the type and give it a white fill and a small offset.

Figure 5-79: Chrome highlight element.

13. Select both type blocks on Layer 3. Combine and color as a highlight. Position over type as required.

Figure 5-80: Chrome type.

Transparency

You can create "see-through" letters over a background by following a few simple steps and using CorelDRAW's Import/ Export and Layers features.

1. **Layer 1:** Create a background. Lock Layer 1.

Figure 5-81: Background.

2. **Layer 2:** Type the word. Use a bold typeface for best effect.

Figure 5-82: Type that will become transparent.

3. **Layer 3:** Leave it blank for now (we will use this layer later for effects).
4. **Layer 4**: Copy the word from Layer 2 to Layer 4. Lock Layer 4 and make it invisible.
5. **Layer 2:** Fill (the example used is a radial fill, 40% to 10% black).
6. Convert to curves; break apart.
7. Select individual letters made up of two or more elements (such as the "A" in HAT) and combine. Each letter will now have its own radial fill.

Figure 5-83: Each letter has a radial fill.

8. Select the letters and export (selected only) as a TIF 5.0 bitmapped image (size 1:1).
9. **Layer 2:** Lock and make invisible, nonprintable.

10. **Layer 3:** Import the TIF image and position it over the background. Lock Layer 3.

11. **Layer 4:** Unlock Layer 4. Select type and apply a 2-point outline, no fill. Reposition as needed.

Figure 5-84: "Transparent" type shows background.

OBJECT DATA

The Object Data feature lets you link information to graphics. In Object Data, you use a spreadsheet and enter information into cells. You can design your worksheet, naming the columns and rows you need.

Figure 5-85: The Object Data roll-up.

Use Object Data to link many kinds of information to a graphic. Here are four possible examples from our galleries:

Lizard (Page 285): Biological information such as the name of each bone could be stored.

Black Diamonds (Page 236): Name, biographical information and performance statistics could be linked to each player.

Duesenberg (Page 267): Historical information, mechanical specifications and parts sources for restoring a vintage Duesenberg could be linked to each section of the car.

Technical Illustration-Seating (Page 221): Parts numbers, dimensions, manufacturer and order dates could be stored for components of the chairs.

Creating Your Database

Use your Object Data roll-up to enter information. Click on the arrow to access these options:

• Object Data Field Editor: Use to create, delete and assign fields to objects. Use the Create New Field, Add Selected Field(s) and Delete Field(s) commands to set up your Object Data worksheet.

• Format Definition: Access by clicking Change from the Object Data Field Editor dialog box.

• Object Data Manager: Use to manage information on multiple objects.

   File:
   • Page Setup: Sets worksheet page specifications.
   • Print: Prints worksheet.
   • Print Setup: Gives you a dialog box for print commands.
   • Exit: Returns you to the Object Data roll-up.

Edit:
- Undo: Returns worksheet to its previous edition (set up to 99 levels of Undo in your Preferences setup).
- Redo: Overrides Undo (you can use 99 levels of Redo).
- Cut: Cuts information in a selected cell and places it in the Clipboard.
- Copy: Copies information in a selected cell and places it in the Clipboard.
- Paste: Pastes cut or copied information from the Clipboard into the selected cell.
- Delete: Removes information from the selected cell.

Field Options:
- Change Format.
- Summarize Groups: Displays individual group subtotals.
- Show Hierarchy: Indents objects within a group to show hierarchy.
- Show Totals: Displays totals of selected columns.
- Field Editor.

Preferences:
- Show Group Details.
- Highlight Top-level Objects.
- Italicize Read-only Cells.

Creating Data Fields

1. Your object(s) should already exist before you access Object Data.

2. With the secondary mouse button, select the object(s) you're linking data to. When the Object menu appears, select Data roll-up.

3. At the roll-up, click on the arrow. Choose Field Editor to open the Field Editor dialog box.

4. Name the field. Possible fields are Part Number, Manufac-turer, Current Inventory, Order Date, Phone Number, etc.

5. Choose Create New Field.

6. To set a data format such as numeric, text, decimal, click Change. This will access the Format Definition box, where you can select a format type.

7. Choose Add Selected Fields. This will take you back to the roll-up (your fields have now been created).

Entering Data

Direction A:

1. Select your object in Pick Tool mode ➤.

2. Access the Object Data roll-up.

3. Select the field you want to enter data into.

4. Enter your data into the box next to the Worksheet button.

5. Press Enter.

Direction B:

1. To enter and/or edit data, select an object or group of objects in Pick Tool mode ➤.

2. With the Object Data roll-up opened, access the Object Data Manager by clicking the Worksheet button. The worksheet will appear on the screen, with all selected objects and their data displayed.

3. To enter or edit data, highlight a cell, type in the data, tab to another cell or press Enter.

Editing Worksheet Columns

1. On the Object Data roll-up, click the arrow.

2. At the list, choose Field Editor.

3. To arrange columns, select a field name and drag it to its new position on the list. Release the mouse button.

4. To change a field name, highlight the name in the Object Data Manager or the Object Data Field Editor. Type in the new name and Enter.

MOVING ON

Up to this point, we have explored CorelDRAW's tools and the many basic and advanced effects we can build on the computer. But till now we've been working with pieces. How do we put these pieces together to create a great-looking finished product?

In the following gallery sections, we show you how top Corel artists from around the world are using the computer for professional design and illustration projects. You'll recognize many of the techniques we've been working with. First, study these examples of Corel art, then power up CorelDRAW and your imagination, and start creating.

SECTION II:
CorelDRAW in Action

The
6
Gallery

*Again, it's a fiction, for my paper
remains flat.*
—M.C. Escher

Anyone choosing to create on the computer has slipped beyond the confines of mechanical rendering into an entirely new medium. CorelDRAW allows artists to import images, play with line and color, resize and reshape—and they can perform each process immediately and endlessly. Computer artists are just beginning to explore the boundaries of this new tool, and the results so far are impressive.

Around the world, artists and designers are creating artwork with CorelDRAW, testing their talents on the PC. We contacted many of these Corel users and asked them to contribute to the artwork featured in the *Looking Good With CorelDRAW* galleries. The response was overwhelming, both in the willingness of Corel artists to share their work and in the scope and quality of that work.

A tremendous amount of talent and effort went into the artwork shown here. We hope it inspires you to create your own master-pieces with CorelDRAW.

K-Sport
Bitmapped images provide the basis for the illustrated shoes, with spots of color added for accents. The linear portions of the logo are drawn with the pen tool, the thicker lines with round end-caps.

Radim Mojzis
RM Design
Czech Republic

Ostravar
These bottle labels have an elegant Old World charm with a contemporary flavor, achieved with the use of blends, fills, outlines and drop shadows.

Radim Mojzis
RM Design
Czech Republic

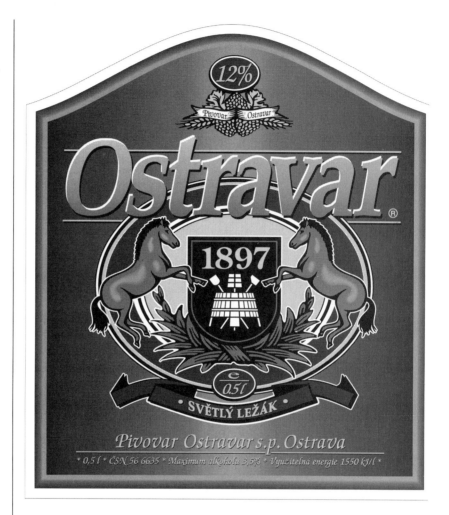

© COPYRIGHT LUIZ A. DE BASTO 1993

Villa Bike
Blending of simple
Bézier-created shapes
and working with layers
is the key to creating this
fast-moving illustration.

Luiz Avillez De Basto
Villa Design
Miami, FL, USA

Club 100 Logo
This identity piece combines color, highlights and shadows within the hand-drawn logo for a look of elegance.

Klaus Hennig
Hennig & Mangold Werbeagentur
Leonberg, Germany

Classic & Jazz
These two black-and-white musical pieces were initially hand-drawn, then scanned, traced and edited to achieve the appearance of graphic silhouettes.

Cecil G. Rice
Illustrator
Acworth, GA, USA

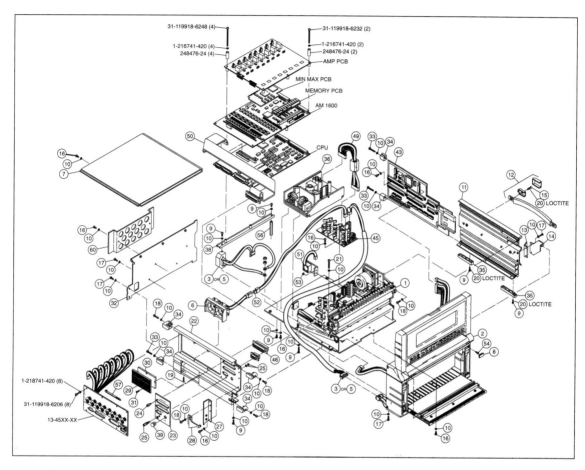

Assembly Drawing
This composite illustration was drawn and scaled from engineering drawings and actual parts, using the status bar as a ruler.

Bryan P. Mansfield
ARCOM, Inc.
Painesville, OH, USA

The Best
This infographic was drawn entirely with CorelDRAW and is the key element of a six-color brochure.

Stephen Valley
National Trade Productions
Alexandria, VA, USA

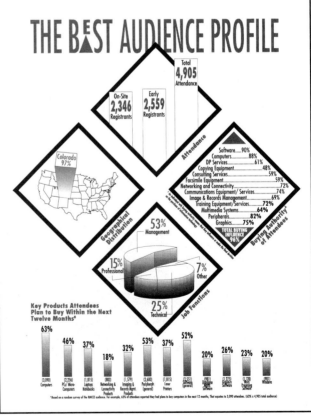

Lunar Man
This anniversary poster uses detailed shapes, fills and blends to bring you to the lunar landscape.

*Amedeo Gigli
Rome, Italy*

"*Naturally Wild*" ALASKA SMOKED SALMON

NET. WT. 567 GRAMS/1.25 LBS.

Alaska Smokehouse
Ketchikan / Woodinville

Salmon
This package design was created from a scanned sketch the artist imported into CorelDRAW. Some of the sections of the fish were grouped and copied, then resized and shaped to fit. The design is used on several different-sized boxes.

Nicki Salvin-Wight
Woodinville, WA USA

F14A TOMCAT

F14A Tomcat
This detailed rendering is achieved using Bézier lines and subtle graduated fills. Careful attention to perspective is key to the piece's realistic look.

Robert Fletcher
Monterey, CA, USA

Images from the Northwest
Talk about versatile! Robert created the complex artwork, Wreath (page 274), but now turns to simple, elegant images inspired by the native artists of the American Northwest. CorelDRAW makes it easy to render these graphic shapes-within-shapes and then to apply bright colors for authenticity.

Robert Fletcher
Monterey, CA, USA

Monoclonal Antibodies Brochure
Andrew created the illustrative panels of this brochure using filled objects and multiple blends. Blends and colors were used to tie corresponding text pages to illustrations. Finally, images from each panel were reduced and used as a part of the brochure's cover design.

Andrew Hadel
One Lamda, Inc.
Canoga Park, CA, USA

Orko
For this coffee package design, Petra started by creating the background, then added elements created with Bézier lines and solid and linear fills. He had to duplicate and modify the design for each of six box panels. (Read more about the Orko package design in Chapter 8, "How They Did It.")

Petra Wienholz
Klaus-Peter Kranz Design
Norderstedt, Germany

Cuttin Edge
Petra married male and female images in this store logo. He used Bézier lines to create the image, then filled with solid black. The typeface Mystical was stretched vertically for the logo-type, with the text line set in Fujiyama.

Petra Wienholz
Klaus-Peter Kranz Design
Norderstedt, Germany

Tribond
Eric created this package design for a board game with an imported texture
as the background and imported icons. The lettering is France modified
using envelope editing, with linear fills coloring the letters. According to Eric,
"The box top, sides and bottom to the card box and game board are all
Corel files . . . and should be seen in person to really be appreciated."

Eric C. Lindstrom
Communiqué Designs
Ithaca, NY, USA

Corelation Magazine Cover
Theta Data
As editor of Corelation and president of ACAD, Randy must come up with super cover designs several times a year! He chose a billboard to "announce" Corel's 4.0 package, tying that in to the lead article on creating large-format artwork in CorelDRAW. Perspective and extrusion effects were used extensively to create this viewpoint.

Randy Tobin
Burbank, CA, USA

Dragon
Designed to look as if the dragon is carved from a gold bar, this piece shows CorelDRAW's ability to handle detail. Blends create highlights and shadows that give the illusion of 3-D metal.

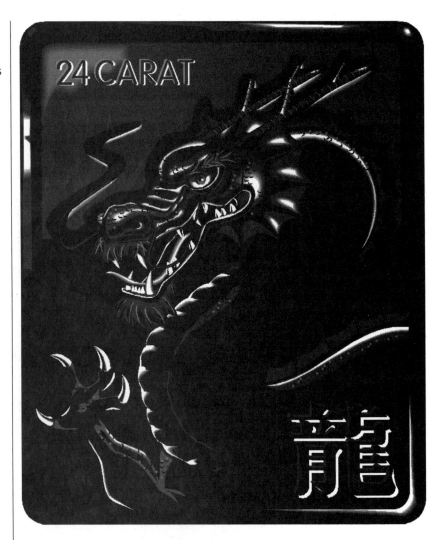

Lie Tjeng Kian
Techno Art
Bandung, West Java,
Indonesia

Magic
This portrait of Earvin "Magic" Johnson was created from a scanned portrait that was traced manually. The piece, which the artist dedicated to the basketball star, took three days to complete.

Lie Tjeng Kian
Techno Art
Bandung, West Java,
Indonesia

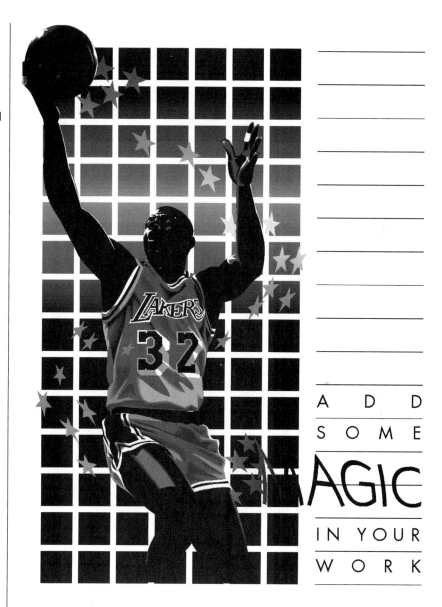

ADD SOME MAGIC IN YOUR WORK

Planet X
The artist started building this logo by filling two circles with radial fills—one light, one dark. He used the envelope feature to distort an X (in a large type size), then combined the X with the filled circles. The PLANET text was fitted to an arc. After the background and details were added, the entire piece was rotated 45 degrees.

Steve Green
Highworth, Wiltshire, UK

Aquamarine
Freehand drawings and graduated fills, plus repeated and reshaped elements, make this a very lyrical illustration. The bubbles and shimmering lines along the whales' backs add a note of realism.

Mohamed Idmessaoud
HPworld magazine
Eastbourne, East Sussex, UK

Harvest
After the original design
was scanned and traced,
radial fills were used to
color this piece. The
Shape tool was used to
create the rough border.
To give the design a
unique look, the image
was divided into three
panels.

Giuseppe de Bellis, Architect
New York City Board of Education
New York, NY, USA

Camera
The camera body and case were filled with custom bitmaps created in CorelDRAW's bitmap editor. Corresponding light and shade objects used the same fills, but with lighter or darker colors. The concentric rings of the lens were drawn using the Ctrl+Shift and Shift keys. The type on the lens was positioned using text fitted to a path.

Keef Williamson
Keef Williamson Design
Bolton, Greater Manchester, UK

Go Travel
Custom bitmap fills, scans of textures and an axonometric perspective give this demonstration drawing a designed, architectural look. Many elements were created in separate Corel files and imported.

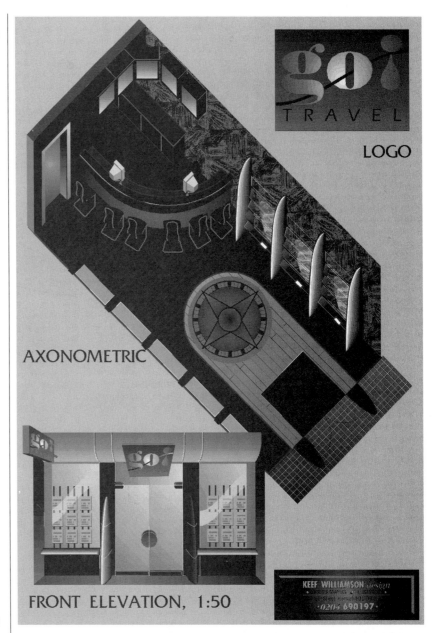

LOGO

AXONOMETRIC

FRONT ELEVATION, 1:50

Keef Williamson
Keef Williamson Design
Bolton, Greater Manchester,
UK

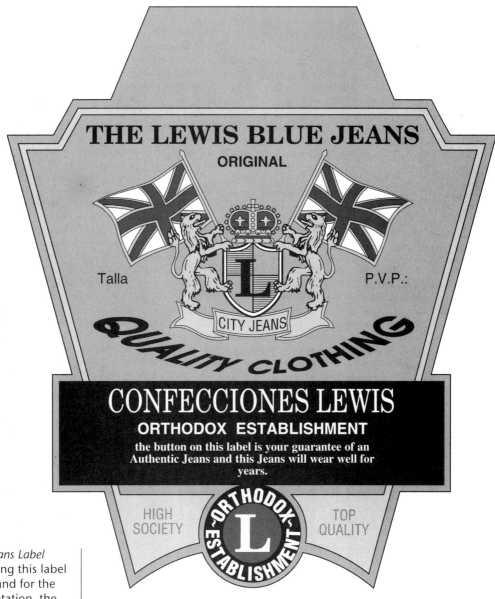

Lewis Blue Jeans Label
After rendering this label design by hand for the client presentation, the artist created the final artwork in CorelDRAW. The design shows CorelDRAW's ability to produce fine typographic effects.

Talle Técnico Creativo
José Clemente Bastidas
José Simancas
Barquisimeto, Estado Lara, Venezuela

KRAK pils Beer Label
An engraving of the old Cracow Brewery, circa 1840, was used as the centerpiece of this beer bottle label. The image was scanned and imported as a TIFF file.

A mask consisting of two halves, each with a linear fill, was created around the scanned image. The border was drawn in Corel, multiplied as needed, and the corners modified using the Envelope feature.

Jerzy Ginalski
Academy of Fine Arts
Industrial Design Faculty
Cracow, Poland
© Jerzy Ginalski 1992

Slimy Dog Graphix Logo
Customized type, created using extensive node editing, distinguishes this logo for a T-shirt company.

Shane Hunt
Slimy Dog Graphix
Los Angeles, CA, USA

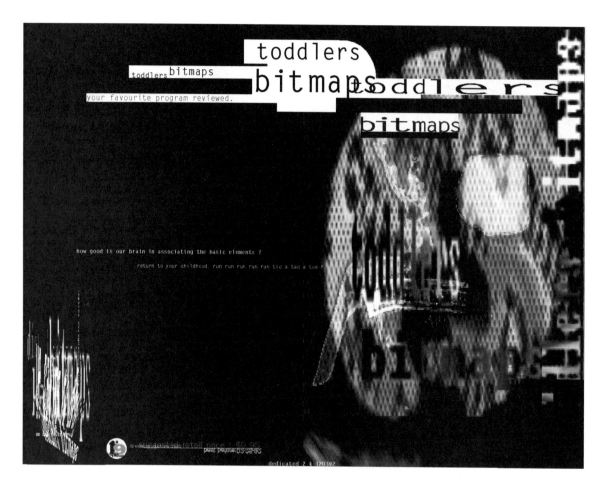

Toddler's Bitmaps
This experimental video
cover design uses
scanned art manipulated
in a paint program. Type
was stretched using
CorelDRAW's Uncon-
strained Envelope.

Mario Beernaert
MB Studio
Antwerp, Belgium

Out of the Closet
This flyer uses a scanned illustration as well as a CorelTRACE tracing of a skull image. Both the grayscale bitmap and the scanned image were placed in CorelDRAW. The skeleton was also scanned. In addition, shapes were created, filled and placed under the skeleton to prevent the underlying skull image from showing through.

*William Schneider
Athens, OH, USA*

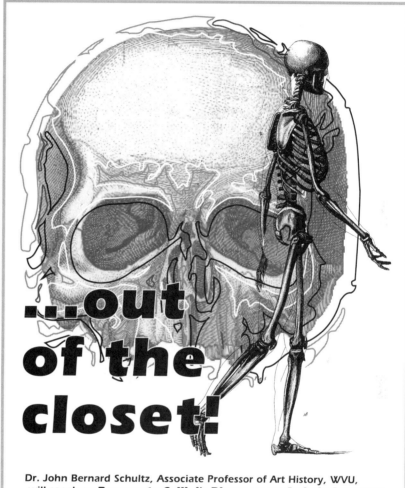

...out of the closet!

Dr. John Bernard Schultz, Associate Professor of Art History, WVU, will speak on **Benvenuto Cellini's Discourse on Artistic Anatomy: An Artist Brings his Skeletons Out of the Closet.**
Where: Room 401 Seigfred Hall
When: Thursday May 9th at 4:30PM

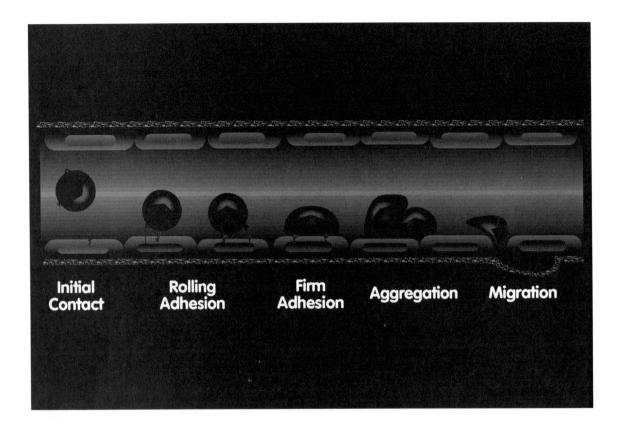

Initial Contact   Rolling Adhesion   Firm Adhesion   Aggregation   Migration

Model 2
The artist took advantage of layering, creating several objects then superimposing these in different ways to depict different types of cells. He writes, "I am building a 'library' of different cell types and molecules, which can then be combined in a variety of different contexts."

Martin Boso
General Surgery Research Labs
Ohio State University
Columbus, OH, USA

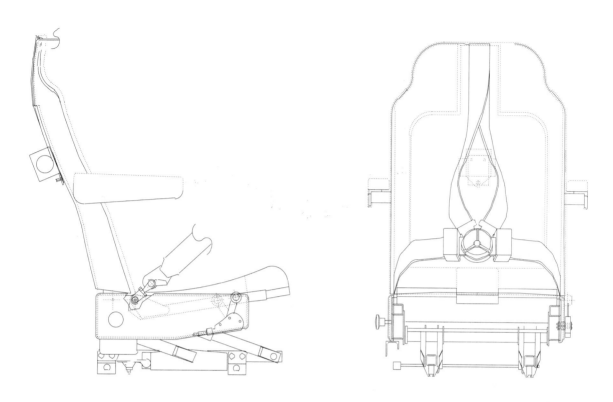

Technical Illustration, Seating
CorelDRAW gave this AutoCAD user the same kind of technical precision found in high-level CAD (Computer Aided Drawing) programs. Corel's import features are helpful here.

David Schubring
Menominee, MI, USA

Rendering, Glide Chair
A rendering of outdoor
furniture uses simplified
shapes and uniform fills.

David Schubring
Menominee, MI, USA

Rock Fan Club Logo
The artist combined
extrusions, blends, radial
and linear fills, stretching
and layering to create this
logo.

Jacques Bourassa
Logos Design Communications, Inc.
Montreal, Quebec, Canada

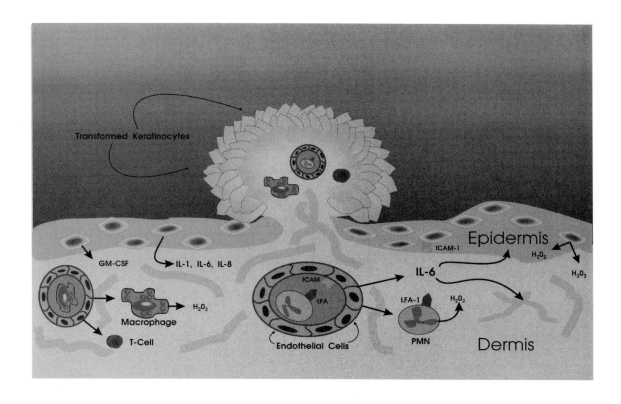

Cutaway View, Model 7
This medical illustration takes advantage of the artist's library of cell images, which can be combined in different contexts. Cutaway views were produced by duplicating objects and modifying them for greater detail.

Martin Boso
General Surgery Research Labs
Ohio State University
Columbus, OH, USA

PsychoTICAts
Clip art was combined
and customized to create
this illustration.

Nicole Ledoux
The Solutions Factory
Yorktown Heights, NY, USA

Sara
To announce the birth of his daughter, the artist created this portrait using CorelTRACE. He comments: "The drawing was a simple pencil sketch I did from life and I was very happy with the vectorized results CorelTRACE generated—it is very close to the original."

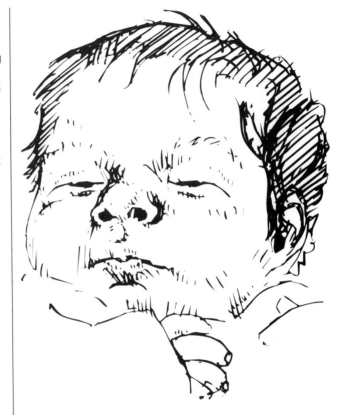

Marc Clamage
Di Giorgio Associates, Inc.
Boston, MA, USA

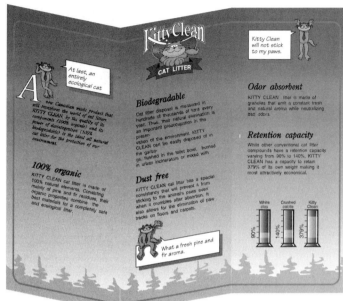

Kitty Clean
Custom lettering,
freehand drawing and
typographic styling make
this project humorous
and professional at the
same time.

Pierre Bruhmuller, Art Director
Claude Grenier, Graphic Artist
Communigraph
Lac-Drolet, Québec, Canada

Plain Geometry
A design for a greeting
card cover depicts light
and shadow using
CorelDRAW's Blend tool.

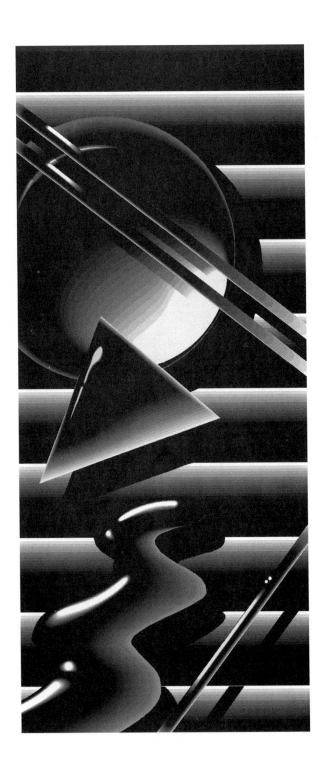

Gary David Bouton,
Art Director & Illustrator
Exclamat!ons
Liverpool, NY, USA

Tamara Anderson Cassette Label
To create this cassette label, a color photo of the musician was scanned into a paint program and posterized at four different intensities. These were imported into CorelDRAW, where different values were assigned to the posterization effect and details added.

Gary David Bouton,
Art Director & Illustrator
Exclamat!ons
Liverpool, NY, USA

Plus-Minus
For this study in light and texture, the artist used different values of the same color applied to an object according to the imagined "translucence" of the object sitting above it.

Gary David Bouton,
Art Director & Illustrator
Exclamat!ons
Liverpool, NY, USA

Logos
The designer combined several "simple" techniques—custom fills, envelopes and type shaping—to create a variety of logos.

*Kevin Caldwell
LGR Graphic
   Communications
Moorestown, NJ, USA*

Vasarely
This Corel contest prize winner combines attention to detail and intricate shading with a humorous look at computing.

Xavier Bisbe, Designer
XB Estudi
Girona, Spain

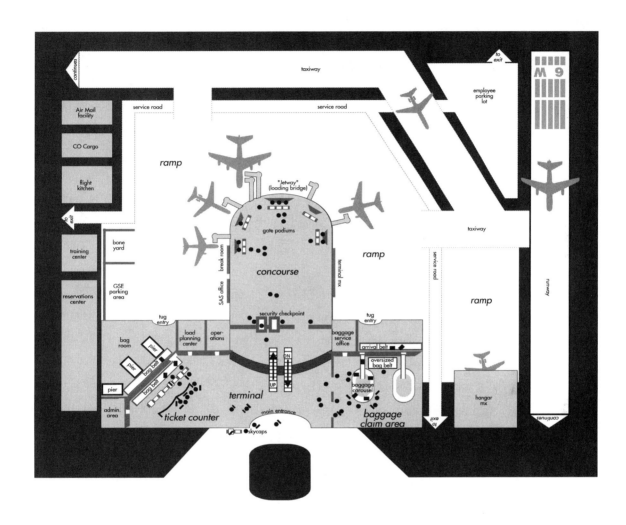

Airport Operations Diagram
An airport operations diagram has been simplified through the use of symbolic shapes to represent people, baggage and planes.

Todd Warren Beck, Creative Director Frog Prints Audiographics Houston, TX, USA

SWATH Cassette Label
The artist scanned a bitmap image of the band in low resolution, then manipulated and colored it. The cover illustration of a yacht was drawn separately and then imported into the main file.

Todd Warren Beck,
Creative Director
Frog Prints Audiographics
Houston, TX, USA

Hoist
By duplicating sections of the chain and making subtle changes to the highlights, the artist made efficient use of CorelDRAW's tools. Highlights on the hoist pulley make it dimensional and realistic.

Tony Claessens
Graphic Designer
Claessens publicity
*   & design*
Maastricht, The Netherlands

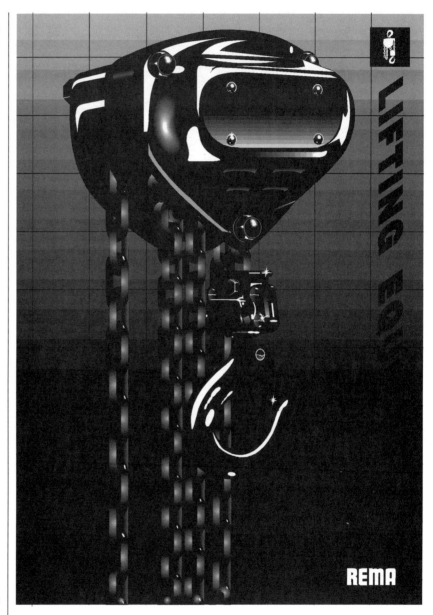

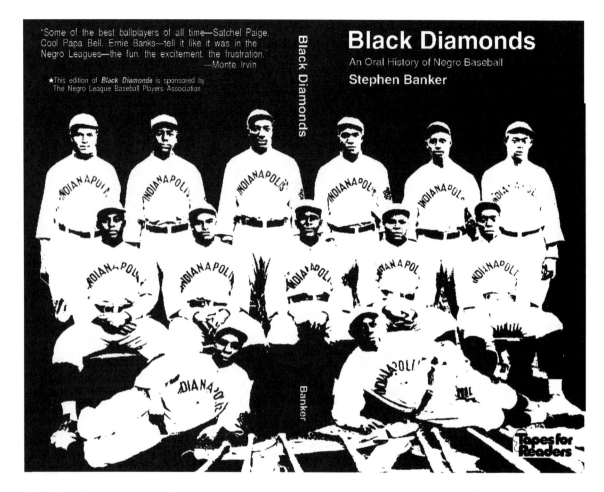

"Some of the best ballplayers of all time—Satchel Paige, Cool Papa Bell, Ernie Banks—tell it like it was in the Negro Leagues—the fun, the excitement, the frustration."
—Monte Irvin

★This edition of *Black Diamonds* is sponsored by The Negro League Baseball Players Association

Black Diamonds

Black Diamonds
An Oral History of Negro Baseball
Stephen Banker

Banker

Black Diamonds
This video cassette case for an oral history of Negro baseball features a photograph of the Indianapolis ABC's, circa 1913. After scanning the photograph, the artist deleted the background and cleaned up the foreground, then added type. The finished design was silk-screened on black in a light sepia color to suggest an old photograph.

Stephen Banker
Tapes for Readers
Washington, DC, USA

Grand Piano
This rendering of a
Steinway & Sons grand
piano uses linear fills to
excellent effect. Repeat-
ing elements, as in the
keyboard, saved the artist
drawing time.

*David B. Libby
DoubleGraph, Inc.
Vincennes, IN, USA*

Alex and his Peterbild
For an illustration that seems to jump off the page, the artist combined perspective and motion cues with a simplified drawing technique. Fills define the shapes, while shading adds clarity.

Alex Blomsma
Schoonrewoerd,
The Netherlands
© 1992 AB-productions

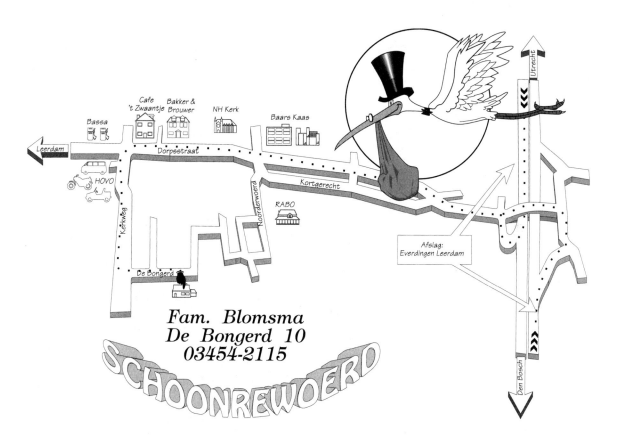

Fam. Blomsma
De Bongerd 10
03454-2115

SCHOONREWOERD

Schoonrewoerd
Simple line drawings with depth and clip-art details transform a simple map into an interesting illustration for a baby announcement.

Alex Blomsma
Schoonrewoerd,
The Netherlands
© 1992 AB-productions

Cavallo
The artist digitized her original pencil sketch using a tablet. A CGM file was imported into CorelDRAW, where the Freehand drawing mode and blending were used to model the horse. The Blend tool was used extensively to render the horse's metal musculature.

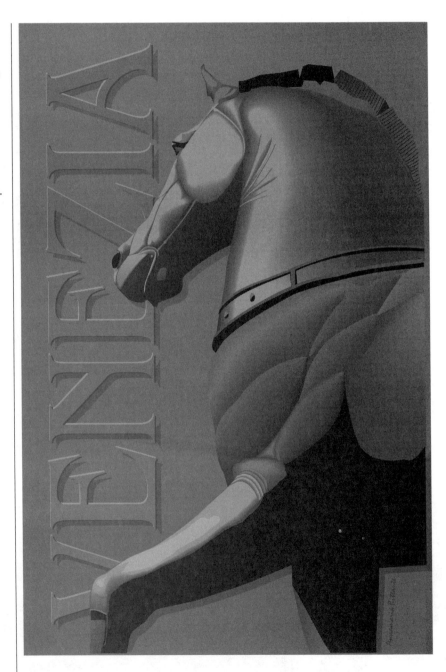

Annamaria Bittante
Canadian Forest
   Products, Ltd.
Vancouver,
British Columbia, Canada

Woss Logo
To create this logo for a community fish hatchery, the artist used the Freehand drawing mode and node editing.

*Annamaria Bittante
Canadian Forest Products, Ltd.
Vancouver, British Columbia,
Canada*

The Charles-Martel
This illustration of a 19th century French battle-ship, the Charles-Martel, uses blends and gradient fills to define the ship's metal exterior.

Gerry Wilson
Bay Ridge Graphics
Brooklyn, NY, USA

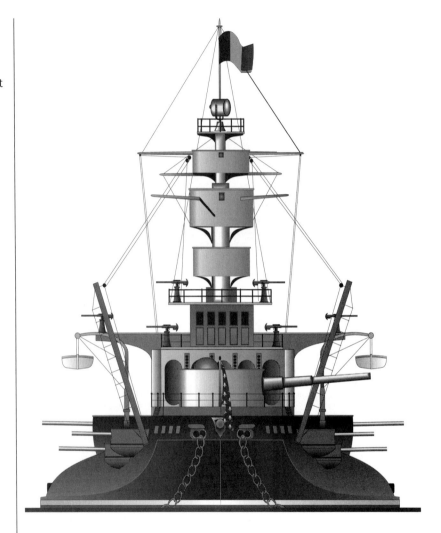

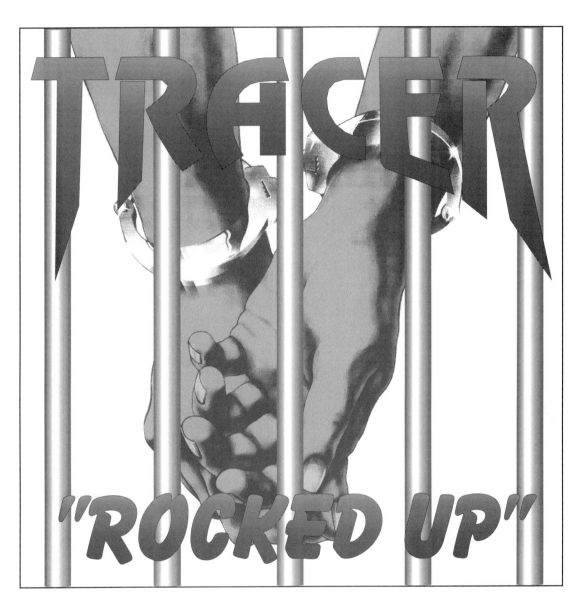

Rocked Up
For this T-shirt design, the artist combined a bit-map with uniform and linear fills. The type has been reshaped using node editing.

Jeff Wampler
Computer Graphic Artist
Kastrava Printing
Douglassville, PA, USA

Tusk Logo
The artist designed custom lettering with a tonal rendering made up of filled shapes to create an illustrated logo featuring his wife's favorite animal.

Richard Clothier
Windlesham, Surrey, UK

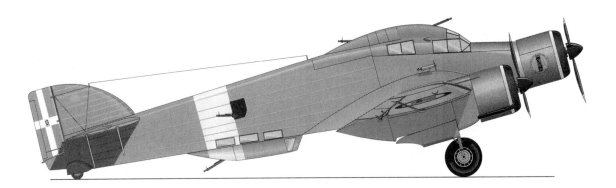

Savoia-Marchetti S.M. 70
The artist created this drawing to test the 3.0 version of CorelDRAW. The outlines were created as Bézier curves joined using Combine. Shading was achieved using blends and fountain fills. The artist comments, "The most challenging aspect was in handling the large number of objects that make up the drawing. The 'Forward One' and 'Back One' options on the Arrange menu were a great help."

Richard Clothier
Windlesham, Surrey, UK

Magazine Cover Design
Four TIFF images, each colored differently, make up the central image on this design for a publication cover. Outline type and color blending of the background create interest.

Stephen Davey
Designer
Victoria, Australia

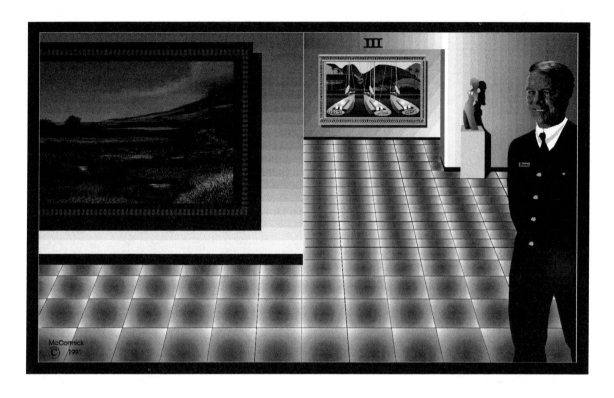

Galleria
A combination of color
scans and CorelDRAW-
created images, a drawn
perspective and radial fills
give this illustration a
surrealistic look. (Read
more about Galleria in
Chapter 8, "How They
Did It.")

Peter McCormick
Image by McCormick
Sun City West, AZ, USA

Conjurer
A highly stylized illustration, Conjurer makes excellent use of repeated shapes, patterns and fills. Many elements were mirrored to create the piece's symmetry.

James A. Mirage
New York, NY, USA

PC Toolkit
This is a good example of a complete project created in CorelDRAW, including type, illustrations and page design.

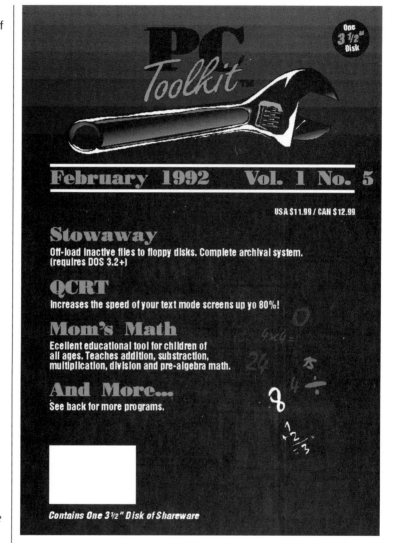

Serge Duguay
Caron Hull, Québec,
Canada
(for P.C. Toolkit of Dinsdale Industries)

Festival
This poster makes creative use of clip art from Corel's CD-ROM library. To stay within Corel's defined limit of objects, objects with the same characteristics (fills, line weights, etc.) were combined.

Giuseppe de Bellis
Architect
New York City Board
*   of Education*
New York, NY, USA

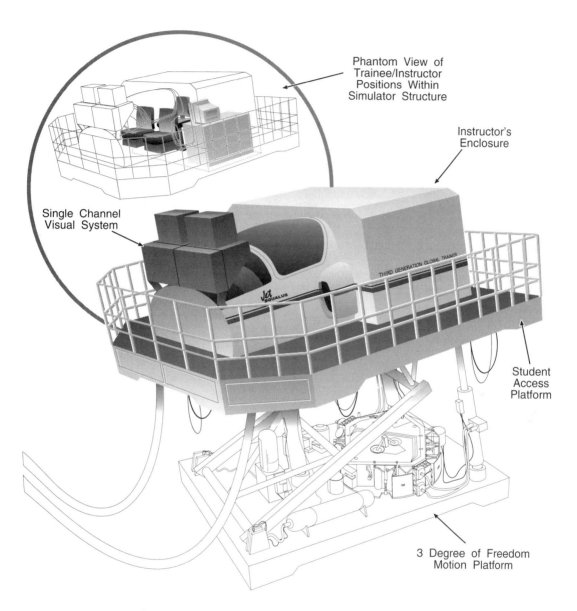

Phantom View of
Trainee/Instructor
Positions Within
Simulator Structure

Instructor's
Enclosure

Single Channel
Visual System

THIRD GENERATION GLOBAL TRAINER

Jet
SQUALUS

Student
Access
Platform

3 Degree of Freedom
Motion Platform

*Jet Squalus Full Flight
Simulator*
This product sheet uses
all of CorelDRAW's
capabilities, including
linear fills, line drawing
and type handling.

*Rick Mank
Atlantis Aerospace Corp.
Brampton, Ontario, Canada
© 1992*

Simulation Survey
To create a presentation graphic with visual impact, the designer combined a transparency, drop shadows and highlights consisting of linear fills. Layering of type gives the title an embossed effect.

Rick Mank
Atlantis Aerospace Corp.
Brampton, Ontario, Canada
© 1992

Caterina
A bitmap and multiple blends were used to create this black-and-white portrait.

Marco Rotondi
Elaborazioni Grafiche
Computerizzate
Rome, Italy

Studs
This artist combines shapes, as in the hair and other outlines, to give variety to the line work. A PostScript fill is used for the background.

Karla Cummins
Butterfly Graphics
Burnaby, British Columbia, Canada

Sea Links
The artist gave this logo depth and dimension by using a PostScript background and blended shapes, as well as graduated and radial fills.

Terry H. Henkel
Hierographix Productions
New Westminster,
British Columbia, Canada

Bajazzo
This menu cover design combines customized type treatments and a simple collage.

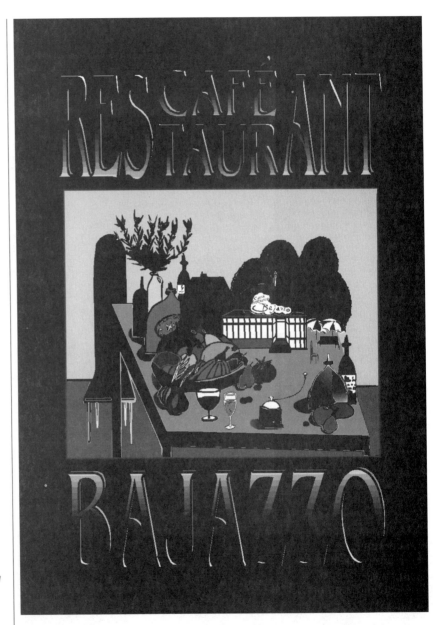

Mike Biele
Linie, Software und Handel
  GmbH
Bielefeld, Germany

BUSSANOVA

BussaNova
Hand-rendered shapes
with linear fills give this
logo a metallic luster.

Mike Biele
Linie, Software und Handel GmbH
Bielefeld, Germany

Proposed wall sign for 3501 Ventura Bl., Universal City, Ca.

Goodman Music
Mural Design
This wall graphic design for a music equipment store exterior was exported as an EPS file to CAD software and scaled up 5063%, then output on a plotter, where a full-size pattern was produced for a sign painter's pattern.

Wm. Mogensen
Mogensen Design
La Crescenta, CA, USA

Mouse & Garden
Scanned images with reversed-out type and a line drawing were combined for this comic cat Christmas card.

Nicole Ledoux
The Solutions Factory
Yorktown Heights, NY, USA

Metromap
Bold type, lines and
symbols make this
graphic map detail of
the Paris metro system
easy to read.

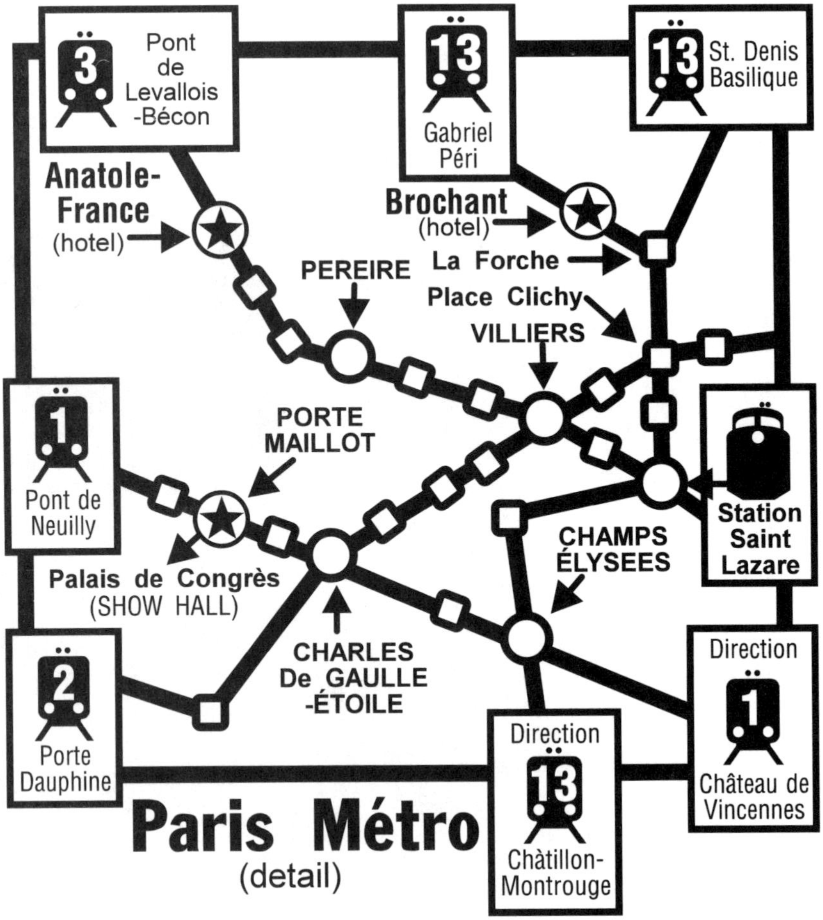

Paris Métro
(detail)

Nicole Ledoux
The Solutions Factory
Yorktown Heights, NY, USA

Felithon 92 Poster
This poster for a Paris cat show combines a hand-rendered cat and landmarks; bold use of type; and a strategic extrusion.

Nicole Ledoux
The Solutions Factory
Yorktown Heights, NY, USA

Note: Many of the pieces submitted for inclusion in *Looking Good With CorelDRAW!* were pieces we've seen previously in one of the two Corel magazines or other computer information sources; we chose not to include these high-visibility pieces so that the work of other Corel artists would have an opportunity to be seen by the Corel user community. However, many of the artworks in our "Galleries" are Corel contest winners.

We could have filled many more pages with outstanding CorelDRAW artwork, but finally we had to make a selection. We believe this gallery, whose artists come from more than a dozen countries, represents the power of CorelDRAW to translate a vision into a technical illustration, product label, birth announcement or other piece of real-world art. But the key to CorelDRAW's visual impact is its color-handling capabilities. In the following gallery we share more CorelDRAW artists' work—this time in full color.

The Color Gallery

7

With the growing color capabilities offered by high-density monitors, PHOTO CD images and 24-Bit Color, you'd expect Corel artists to be keeping pace. You won't be disappointed.

Here is a small sampling of CorelDRAW projects in color. Some use a broad spectrum of colors and techniques; others achieve realism or impact using a limited palette and simple techniques. Yet each shows the versatility and beauty of art created on the PC with CorelDRAW.

Postage for Tomorrow
Steven scanned, filtered and colored a photograph, then added it to a postage stamp-shaped frame to create this portrait of his children (that's Elliot on the right). (Read more about "Postage for Tomorrow" in Chapter 8, "How They Did It.")

Steven A. Cousins
Stone Mountain, GA, USA

Bow 2
Georgina created hundreds of individual elements to give the rich color and detail to this portrait modeled after silent movie actress Clara Bow. Note how light source is evident on each object, from the bright white of the face to the deep shadows cast by each bead. Offset radial fills create highlights on the beadwork. Radial symmetry and perspective give the headdress its curvature.

Georgina Curry
The Electric Easel
Phoenix, AZ, USA

Cat Blue
In this exercise, Tom worked with fills and blends—the piece has no lines!
He began by scanning a photograph of an original painting, which he
imported as a bitmap into DRAW. Then he redrew and modified the
elements, working with the blends and fills to create light and shadow.
He used the duplicate feature to help create the fruit, flowers and cat collar.

Tom Tipping
Tipping Graphics
Tulsa, OK, USA

El Paso
For this menu design, Petra created the images in Bézier line mode, then applied solid and linear fills. Shadows were created by duplicating the shape. The restaurant name "El Paso" is set in Lithograph type and shadowed. "Grill + Bar" is set in Mystical, which has been slightly rotated and shadowed. The artist used two type blocks, one left-justified and one right-justified, to create the menu's two columns of text.

BUSINESS HOURS
MON - FRI 10 AM - 11 PM
SAT - SUN 11 AM - 11 PM
RESERVATIONS
ACCEPTED

EL PASO RESTAURANTS

Petra Wienholz
Klaus-Peter Kranz Design
Norderstedt, Germany

Side Dishes

SOUP
BOWL SPECIAL SOUP OF THE DAY — 2.50
CHILI
BOWL OF RED, RED W/ BEANS, OR PIE — 2.95
TOSTADO CHIPS
W/ HOT SAUCE, GUACAMOLE OR CHILI QUESO — 1.75
SUPER NACHOS
CHILI QUESO NACHOS, MIXED CHEESE, REFRIED BEANS. SERVED W/ GUACAMOLE & SOUR CREAM — 4.95
FRENCH FRIES FRESH CUT, HOMESTYLE — 1.75
CHEESE FRIES
FRIED MOZZARELLA W/ MARINARA SAUCE — 3.95
ONION RINGS HOMESTYLE, BREADED — 2.75
BBQ RIB BASKET
5 CHARBROILED BABY BACK RIBS IN A BASKET — 4.50

Crisp Salads

DRESSINGS:
RANCH, HOUSE, HONEY-MUSTARD OR CEASAR
DINNER SALADS HOUSE OR CEASAR — 2.25
TACO SALAD
MIXED GREENS, KIDNEY BEANS, TACO MEAT, TOMATO, GREEN ONIONS & GUACAMOLE — 5.75
GRILLED TUNA SALAD
MIXED GREENS TOPPED W/ SEASONED TUNA STEAK, PICO DE GALLO, WALNUTS, GREEN ONIONS — 5.95
CARRIBEAN CHICKEN SALAD
GRILLED CHICKEN BREAST ON MIXED GREENS, W/ PINEAPPLE CHUNKS & TORTILLA STRIPS — 6.25

For The Kids

ALL CHILDREN, 12 YEARS AND UNDER
HOT DOG & FRIES — 1.95
GRILLED CHEESE & FRIES — 1.95
BURGER & FRIES — 1.95

▶ WE USE CHOLESTEROL FREE, 100% VEGETABLE OIL
▶ **GIFT CERTIFICATES AVAILABLE** - ASK FOR DETAILS -

Mexican Grill

FAJITAS
HALF POUND OF CHARBROILED STEAK OR CHICKEN, SERVED ON A SIZZELING PLATTER — 8.75
MONTEREY CHICKEN
CHARBROILED CHICKEN BREAST TOPPED W/ BBQ SAUCE, BACON, CHEESE, SERVED W/ COLE SLAW — 7.95
NY STRIP STEAK
10 OZ. CHOICE STRIP SIRLOIN, SERVED W/ TEXAS TOAST, BBQ BEANS & FRIES — 10.50
SIERRA PLATTER
HAMBURGER PATTY TOPPED W/ BBQ SAUCE, CHEESE, TOMATO; BBQ BEANS, FRIES, COLE SLAW — 5.95
BACON BURGER
BACON, CHEDDAR, MAYO, ONION, LETTUCE, TOMATO & PICKLE — 4.75
MUSHROOM BURGER
MUSHROOMS, MAYO, LETTUCE & TOMATO — 4.50

Beverages Drinks

COFFEE & TEA FREE REFILLS — 0.95
SOFT DRINKS
COCA COLA, DIET COKE, SPRITE - FREE REFILLS — 1.50
MINERAL WATER, ROOT BEER — 1.85
EL PASO CLASSIC SHAKE
VANILLA, CHOCOLATE, STRAWBERRY, COFFEE — 2.50
MARGARITAS
ORIGINAL FROZEN - OUR FAVORITE — 2.55
OUR ORIGINAL FROZEN W/ STRAWBERRIES — 3.55
WINES PREMIUM, BY THE GLASS
DRAFT & BOTTLED BEER
HEINECKEN, BUD, MILLER LITE & OTHERS

Delicious Desserts

EL PASO SUNDAE
VANILLA ICE CREAM IN A CINNAMON FLOUR TORTILLA, HOT FUDGE, CHOPPED WALNUTS — 2.95
FROZEN YOGHURT
COLUMBO SOFT FROZEN YOGHURT, PLAIN — 1.50
CHEESECAKE
HOMESTYLE, PLAIN OR STRAWBERRY TOPPING — 2.95

Wide-Screen Slide Presentation
Richard has found that CorelDRAW is a dynamic tool for creating wide-screen slide presentations. This image is actually three slides that overlap to fill a double-wide screen. DRAW's ability to meet demanding criteria in terms of detail and work specifications is a vital component of this type of presentation's success. (For more about "Wide-Screen Slide Presentation", see Chapter 8, "How They Did It.")

Richard Mednick
(Artist: Vince Kernaghan)
Graphic Computer Services, Inc.
Woodland Hills, CA, USA

Inline Skates

The blade of the skate is filled with a gradient fill and serves as a unifying background. The raised and lowered panels and screw heads were created by placing highlight and shadow details on top. The wheel bearing is an exercise in metal treatments. The chamfered edges were created from radial fills placed off-center. The radial highlights were created from blends of thin rectangle shapes rotated about the center of the bearing. Textured and gloss plastic finishes were added to the boot. The gloss finish was rendered by creating strong highlights (blending large value changes over short distances), which contrasted with the texture finish with weak highlights (blending small value changes over larger distances). The cutaway view was rendered by drawing a jagged edge outline over the blade and placing the wheel and bearing in front.

Barry Meyer
Homewood, IL, USA

1933 Duesenberg
The eccentric angle of this illustration makes it special. That, plus highlights/shadows and careful use of blending, give the car a solid 3D look. Reed began by scanning a photograph and using this as a drawing guide. (Read more about the 1933 Duesenberg illustration in Chapter 8, "How They Did It.")

1933 DUESENBERG
© 1993 REED FISHER

Reed Fisher
San Clemente, CA, USA

Andreas Sewald
Jork, Germany

Dream With Wings
To create this image, Andreas scanned a photograph of a classic Mercedes and placed it on Layer 1, then added several layers to isolate drawing of the bonnet, wheels, car door, front window, etc. Working with the shape tool, blending, outline and fountain fills, the artist achieved this masterpiece. Beside the photo, a scale model was used for reference to capture exacting detail, since an original wasn't readily available. After converting the title to curves, Andreas made many tests to create a metallic effect. The complete drawing from start to finish took 100 hours over a two-month period.

Entry
David created this illustration to promote a line of large-scale raster image plotters. Thus the illustration's split personality: half shows fine-line work, the other half shows full-color plotting. (Read more about Entry in Chapter 8, "How They Did It.")

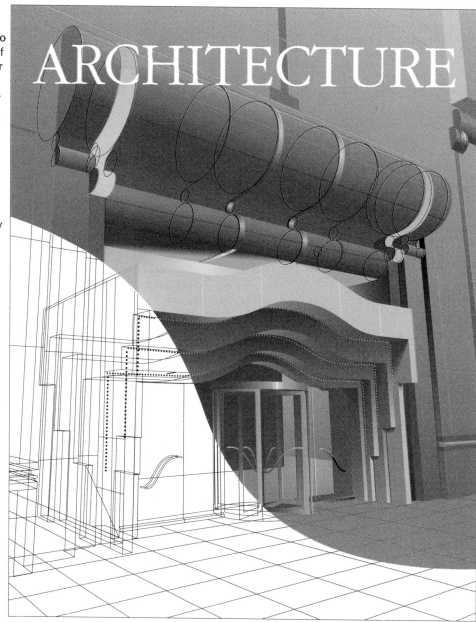

ARCHITECTURE

David Brickley
Shooting Brick
Productions
Moss Beach, CA,
USA

Foundation for the Future
To create this logo, the artist drew a hand, then duplicated and flipped it; this piece was duplicated several more times. The hands were then rotated and extruded to create the 3D effect. Each group was given a graduated fill and an outline, then placed against the background. An outline was created for the entire piece in order to produce the drop shadow.

Chris Purcell
Compaq Computer Corp.
Houston, TX, USA

Baby Marta
This wonderful image features a strong, simple background, type-on-a-path and border details that have been repeated and reshaped. Gradient fills give the face and the flowers detail and dimension.

Regina Kwoska
Wesel, Germany

Diseño Grafico
This self-promotion piece uses a simple composition, bold geometric elements and vivid color blends. Note the highlight on the lower lip, created by strategically placing a group of small objects.

Talle Técnico Creativo: José Clemente Bastidas, José Simancas Barquisimeto, Estado Lara, Venezuela

Automobile Salon
Here, simple drawing techniques create a striking image. Contrast between background and objects is key to the illustration's impact.

Erich Buechler Munich, Germany

"Key" Employee Referral Program

This poster-size infographic was distributed to employees as an incentive piece. Steve writes: "Some of the illustrations were created on paper first and then scanned and converted in CorelTRACE. A skew/rotate macro, developed in Windows RECORDER, was then applied to most of the objects in order to automatically give them an isometric style. The focus of the design centers around an automotive 'key' to support the theme as well as symbolize the grand prize reward [a car]."

Stephen J. Oblas, Art Direction
Lori Magilton, Robert Frawley
& Stephen Oblas, Illustration &
Graphic Design
Chrysler First Financial Services
Allentown, PA, USA

Wreath

The artist took full advantage of CorelDRAW's convenient duplicate function—this image contains nearly 2,000 individual pieces. After duplicating, each complex object was taken apart and modified so that no two elements are exactly the same.

Robert Fletcher
Monterey, CA, USA

Money Man
This is one of a series of "pop-up" promotional pieces that work well as either handouts or mailers. Steve comments: "To create the illustrations, tight pencil drawings were made to work out the complicated folding and registration needed. Once scanned, the layouts were imported into CorelTRACE and were further developed in CorelDRAW. Fill patterns and mechanicals were created in CorelDRAW."

Stephen J. Oblas, Art Direction
Lori Magilton, Robert Frawley & Stephen Oblas,
* Illustration & Graphic Design*
Chrysler First Financial Services
Allentown, PA, USA

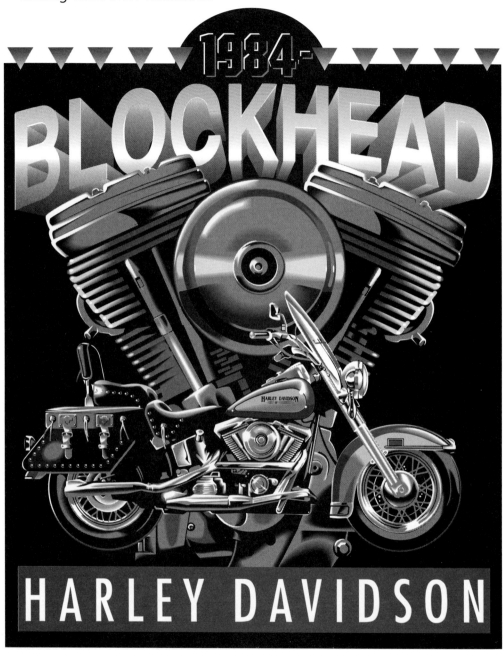

Blockhead

This artist created the "BLOCKHEAD" portion first, using the multiple blends feature to create highlights. The bike was built on a separate page, then the "BLOCKHEAD" art imported and put behind the bike. The artist used extrude and embossing effects on the type. He comments, "I have tried other programs, but nothing beats CorelDRAW."

*Lie Tjeng Kian
Techno Art
Bandung,
West Java,
Indonesia*

Video Game Poster
Steve's punk robot image takes advantage of Corel's linear fill feature to create a gleaming metal surface. The artist writes, "The [lozenge-shaped] joystick button was created by blending two circles, with different gradient fills to create the effect of the depression in the middle of the button. The resulting blend was then tilted using perspective. The face and fingers of the robots were originally rectangles but were distorted on either side using the envelope command."

*Stephen Green
Highworth,
Wiltshire, UK*

NATIONAL

VIDEO GAME

CHAMPIONSHIPS

92

10ᵗʰ☐12ᵗʰ March 1992 at the London Games Centre, Covent Garden

Play the Saxophone
The artist created a mask of the word "Saxophone" at a large size, rotated it 90 degrees, converted it to curves, then combined it with a rectangle. He filled the resulting curve object with black and positioned it over the drawing of a sax. The drawing itself uses linear fountain fills to simulate shiny brass. Keef writes, "The buttons, which reflect a simple drawing of a crowd and bar at the back of the room, demonstrate CorelDRAW's enveloping feature."

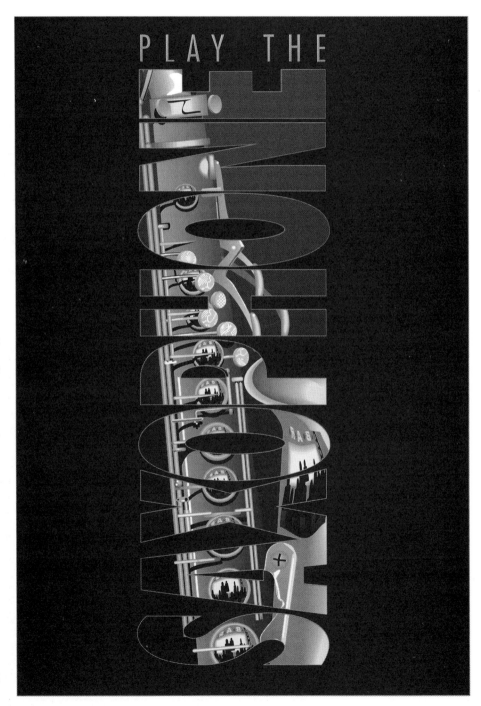

Keef Williamson
Bolton,
Greater Manchester,
UK

Boca Joe's Beach Club
Mike created individual elements such as the shark, palm tree and rope detail by drawing a shape, converting it to curves, and manipulating the nodes. Gradations were added to rotated type. The Hawaiian-style shirt has a bitmap fill. Shading and shadows provide the dimensionality that makes this image so successful.

Judy Nentwig, Art Director
Mike Pfeiffer, Artist
Allentown, PA, USA

MicroTek Distributors Conference Logo
Ceri's work is familiar to many Corel artists—it was featured on the cover of *Corelation* magazine's first issue. Here several simple techniques have been combined to form a clean, sophisticated piece of work. Ceri writes: "I used gradient fills in the sky, sea and sand for an enhanced feeling of depth."

Ceri Lines
Taiwan, ROC

Cadillac
The artist used a multitude of blends and fills to create the many highlights on this car's chrome and shiny paint job. Slightly lighter values for the group of objects "behind" the windshield create the illusion of glass. The color choices make this piece really special.

Romain Maffei
Lausanne,
Switzerland

Naples
The artist wanted to achieve a watercolor effect, and succeeded— thanks to Corel's power and flexibility. A hand-drawn sketch was created first, then scanned with CorelTRACE. "At this point," the artist writes, "all the open paths had to be closed and defined as single entities for the 'painting' process." This piece was a second prize winner in the Corel contest's Landmarks, Travel category.

Giuseppe de Bellis, Architect
New York City Board of Education
New York, NY, USA

Head
This illustration
was drawn in
Freehand mode
using the Pencil
tool. Angle,
center offset and
edge padding
adjustments
allowed Jodi to
achieve the
desired
highlights and
shading.

Jodi Vergil,
Graphic Artist
& Illustrator
Montreal,
Québec, Canada

Orchids in the Morning Light
The artist explains, "PHOTO-PAINT has the ability to emulate the many things I do as a painter. I like to use my fingers to blend or smudge the paint or pastels, and with PHOTO-PAINT I can achieve almost the exact feeling of expression that I want." After exporting a line drawing to PHOTO-PAINT, William used the Spraycan to get a heavy texture, being careful to maintain a good visual balance of color throughout the entire piece. (Read more about "Orchids in the Morning Light" in Chapter 8, "How They Did It.")

William R. Clegg
Clegg/Creative Artist
Cayey, Puerto Rico

Mom & Friends
Even detailed portraits with delicate flesh tones are no problem in CorelDRAW. According to John, "The biggest challenge I had was creating the blends (mostly in the face) and remembering which layer everything was on. The blends were fairly easy to accomplish except those that were very irregularly shaped. I used the Map Matching Nodes option, which worked well in most cases." John's portrait won a second prize in the Corel contest.

John Maurer
Atlanta, GA, USA

Touchdown
Corel makes illustrations in any style possible.
Here, a striking effect was created by combining
basic shapes filled with vibrant color
combinations against a free-form background.

Mohamed Idmessaoud
HPWorld magazine
Eastbourne, East Sussex, England

Lizard
Chris initially set this up as two files to be combined. He used a wide range of techniques: blends, graduated fills, combined and duplicated shapes, and grouped objects. Chris comments: "I tried to push the software as much as I could."

Chris Purcell
Compaq Computer Corporation
Houston, TX, USA

Daniel Roth Watch #28
The artist combined masking, layering, custom fills and blends to create this Daniel Roth limited edition watch. He writes, "I had to create my own color palette to accommodate the many different shades of gold and silver that radiate from the watch under bright lights."

D.E. Domzalski
© 1992
Wilmington, DE, USA

Veturi
This illustration shows the true power of CorelDRAW in the hands of a skilled illustrator. The artist, a Corel contest first prize winner, writes: "I tried to be exact with the perspectives, and there is as much detail as possible. You cannot add anything to the illustrations; they are absolutely full-packed." This rendering won second prize (monthly) in the Business, Technology, Transportation category.

Matti Kaarala
Madventure Oy
Helsinki, Finland

The Chief
"The Chief" was created from drawings the artist had done in an old sketchbook of Indians from 1800s photographs. (Read more about "The Chief" in Chapter 8, "How They Did It.")

Cecil G. Rice
Illustrator
Acworth, GA, USA

Indian Tonic
This beautifully constructed label uses a bitmapped background, radial symmetry, graduated fills and drop shadows. Radim's work achieves a delicate balance of light-against-dark that gives dimension and definition to the individual design elements.

Radim Mojzis
RM Design
Czech Republic

Fractal Dreaming
This illustration for poster and tape/CD album covers was designed to produce a feeling of depth and movement. (Read more about "Fractal Dreaming" in Chapter 8, "How They Did It.")

Marshall (Sam) Blight
Rangs Boomerangs
Nedlands, Australia

Pregnant Lady
Without being particularly complex, this artist's work uses several unique CorelDRAW features. The bitmap fill provides a tremendous range of textures, which can be customized by changing the basic values. Changing colors and simply reversing colors also creates very different effects. (Read more about "Pregnant Lady" in Chapter 8, "How They Did It.")

Wil Dawson
Tulsa, OK, USA

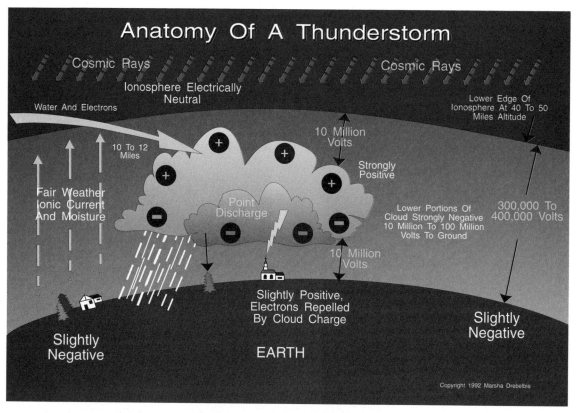

Anatomy of a Thunderstorm
Flat color treatments with clean crisp edges and bright attractive colors were the
requirements for this custom-designed "demonstrative evidence" exhibit that
accompanied expert testimony in an insurance defense case.

Marsha Drebelbis
Litigation Graphics
Dallas, TX, USA

Logos
This logo galley shows not only the versatility of the designer
but also his clever use of Corel's tools and effects in creating
these beautiful and unique identity pieces.

Radim Mojzis
RM Design
Czech Republic

Magic Carpet Ride
This illustration was a great challenge for Georgina. It was created in four separate files: the carpet, the girl, the frame and the background clouds. After the components were finished, she imported them into a master file to compose the finished piece. (Read more about "Magic Carpet Ride" in Chapter 8, "How They Did It.")

Georgina Curry
The Electric Pencil
Scottsdale, AZ, USA

Happy Holidays!
Christmas Card
The artist, a professional photographer as well as a designer, began with a scan of an evergreen twig converted into line art. A rectangular portion was masked and made into a negative of the original bitmap. A colorful graduated fill was placed under the bitmap. Read more about "Happy Holidays" in Chapter 8, "How They Did It.")

William Schneider
Athens, OH, USA

Taisho
This intricate and beautifully detailed drawing was inspired by a historically accurate sculpture kit. Working from the actual parts as well as a scan to provide basic shapes, the drawing was laid out the old fashioned way—on paper. The artist made extensive use of the blend feature and used thirteen layers to assure that all of the complex pieces fell into place in the correct order. Final touches were accomplished by working on a duplicate file that had most of the illustration deleted. Switching back and forth let imported elements snap right into place in the correct layer order. Gerry says this double technique was a life saver as the primary drawing grew in size.

Gerry Wilson
Brooklyn, NY,
USA

CREATIVITY PLUS CORELDRAW!

The collections presented in our black-and-white and color galleries are proof that professional artists and designers find CorelDRAW to be an efficient tool for creating polished work. You'll notice that these gallery artists are truly an international set—CorelDRAW's versatile, user-friendly interface transcends language and boundaries to allow talented artists everywhere the opportunity to expand their creative options.

In addition to artistic ingenuity, each of these artists displays inventiveness in his or her use of the computer. As hardware becomes more sophisticated and programs such as CorelDRAW continue to evolve, artists will find new and interesting ways to use both. We hope you found these CorelDRAW "masterpieces" an inspiration for your own work.

MOVING ON

We all know that the best way to learn is to model the work of a master—that's why all those art students are sitting around museums furiously sketching. We asked several CorelDRAW "masters" to share their expertise with us. In the following chapter, we'll go step-by-step through the processes used to create some of the most intriguing artwork in the two gallery chapters. We'll see how these artists used layers as a handy work tool, managed complex files and created special effects such as reflections, water color and masking.

How They
Did It

8

Computers are useless. They can only give you answers.

— *Pablo Picasso*

Creating artwork at the computer is a relatively new process, so knowledge is expanding rapidly. Not only are CorelDRAW artists constantly finding new ways to use line, shape and color, but old drawing and painting techniques are being given new character on the PC. In addition, we have the *computer* to deal with—memory limits, file formats, pixels, .INI files and a host of terms and concepts that didn't exist ten years ago. Corel-DRAW users everywhere have a lot of knowledge to share with their fellow artists and are finding that this give-and-take is a great way to learn.

We asked several top CorelDRAW artists to share some of what they've learned about CorelDRAW by telling us how they created the pieces featured in Chapter 6, "The Gallery," and Chapter 7, "The Color Gallery." We've taken their explanations and broken them down into simple steps that offer an overview of the creative processes these artists followed to achieve their final pieces. It is both interesting and instructive to see how different artists found different solutions to a similar problem, or how CorelDRAW's most useful features, such as layering, have become an integral part of creating on the desktop.

If you're new to CorelDRAW, you'll find that it's helpful to follow the creation of a complex piece step-by-step. If you're an old hand, you might try to guess just what steps the artist took to get the final product. Either way, it's interesting to learn *How They Did It!*

Daniel Roth #28
D. E. Domzalski
Page 284

Customizing Color Palettes

1. The artist roughed in the major shapes and outlines of the overall watch to help in positioning and alignment of the many parts.

2. Beginning with the CorelDRAW palette's gold, he developed a custom palette of gold, silver and bronze shades by adjusting CMYK percentages. He used the Name a Color feature under CorelDRAW's Color Editing menu.

3. He then built a display palette of these colors for easy access.

4. A series of small rectangles was drawn outside the working area, and each was filled with a different color. By using the Copy Style From feature, the artist could use this onscreen "paintbox" to access his custom colors quickly.

Naples
Giuseppe de Bellis
Page 278

Rendering in "Water Colors"

1. First the artist made a hand-drawn sketch from one of his photographs.

2. The sketch was scanned in black and white and hand-traced using CorelTRACE.

3. The tracing was imported into CorelDRAW.

4. The artist made sure each object was a closed path so that it could be filled. Although the tracing process gave each object multiple nodes, this in fact added to the brush-stroke effect.

5. Uniform fills were chosen from the Fill roll-up menu and the color palette bar and applied.

Galleria
Peter McCormick

Page 244

Using 3D Visual Cues & Imported Images

Gallery

1. To create the Gallery floor—the central component of the artist's 3D illusion—he drew the tiles in perspective and filled each with a radial fill.

2. Linear fills were used on the walls to imply a light source.

3. A drop shadow was added to the statue to show three dimensions. The statue itself was drawn in perspective.

Imported Images

4. The Gallery guard's face is a TIF image taken with an electronic camera and later enhanced in a paint program. The artist imported the face into the CDR file and created a mask around the image with the wall behind as a fill.

5. The painting on the back wall was created in CorelDRAW as a separate file, then imported into the gallery scene and reduced.

6. The painting on the left was created in a paint program as a TIF image and imported into the Gallery piece.

7. Finally, a border was added to complete the piece.

Expanding CorelDRAW's Creative Boundaries

Scanned Image

1. The artist began this holiday card by scanning a small branch from an evergreen tree. The scan was converted into line art using Astral's Picture Publisher.

2. A rectangular section of the scan was masked and made into a negative. This was imported into CorelDRAW as a single-bit black-and-white TIF file.

Happy Holidays!
William Schneider

Page 291

3. The TIF file was given a fill of "none" so that it would be transparent. A graduated fill was placed beneath the bit-mapped image to add color.

4. A second box with the same dimensions as the negative was placed underneath and filled with the starting color of the graduated fill. Small rectangles were used to eliminate white areas in parts of the bitmap.

5. Text was added using a WFN font.

6. Decorative lines and boxes were added to finish the design.

Printing

7. The artist printed the piece on an ivory paper. He first printed the black portions using Corel's Print Selected Only option from the Print Menu.

8. In order to print the contrasting color (a dark red), these portions of the piece were temporarily changed to black and a graduated black fill. This was printed using a color ink cartridge (bright red was added to a partially full DeskJet cartridge).

Note: The artist registered the two colors by printing a sample of the second color, precisely measuring the offset, and correcting it using CorelDRAW's Move menu choice.

Enveloping & Masking for Special Effect

Saxophone

1. A drawing of a saxophone was created. Multiple linear fills were used to simulate brass.

2. To fill the buttons with a "reflection" of a crowded bar scene, the artist first produced a simple crowd scene. This was mirrored to create the reversed type.

3. For each button, a circle was drawn in the position of the reflection, and a rectangle of the same proportions as the crowd drawing was added in place.

Play the Saxophone
Keef Williamson

Page 276

4. The artist then edited the envelope of the rectangle until it closely matched the size and shape of the circle. Then he applied "Copy Envelope From..." to force the crowd drawing to match the size and shape of the former rectangle.

5. Finally, the circle and distorted rectangle were deleted from each button and the enveloped crowd image positioned.

Mask

6. A mask of the word "Saxophone" was created in a large point size.

7. The mask was rotated 90 degrees, converted to curves and combined with a rectangle, creating a curve object.

8. The curve object was filled with black and positioned over the drawing of a saxophone.

Wreath
Robert Fletcher

Page 272

Managing Multiple Objects With Layers & Files

Note: This illustration has over 2,000 separate objects.

1. File 1: On the first layer, the artist created the basic wreath shape, adding background color. Some simple shapes were added to indicate positioning and sizes of elements to be imported (these guide shapes were later deleted). On a second layer, the broad rose leaves were added.

2. File 2: A master rose was built by creating the basic background shape, filling it with color, then adding petals. This master rose was then duplicated and manipulated (size, shape and color changed), so that many roses were created, each different from the others. These were imported into File 1 and positioned on the wreath. This file was saved as File 2 and all elements except the roses were deleted (that is, the file contained only the roses, but now in correct position).

3. File 3: Flowers, berries and greenery were created, duplicated and customized. These were imported into File 1, ungrouped and the elements arranged on the wreath. A shadow was added to give the arrangement a 3D look. Then the entire piece was grouped and saved as File 1. (File 3 was saved as a source file in case new berries/flowers/ferns/etc. were needed to complete the wreath.)

4. File 2 was imported into File 1, so that the roses now appear on the upper layer. Elements from File 3 were imported to give the wreath a "finished" look.

Using Scanned Art as a Base for Illustration

1933 Duesenberg Roadster
Reed Fisher

Page 267

1. The artist scanned a black-and-white photo of the Duesenberg and imported it into CorelDRAW as a TIF file. This file was placed on the bottom layer, where it remained visible for use as a drawing guide.

2. Several layers were used to create the illustration. The car and its details were rendered using the Bézier drawing tool. Color was added, including blend groups. The artist made extensive use of CorelDRAW's ability to redo an entire blend group by recoloring or reshaping a control curve. Finally, details were added.

3. The TIF file was discarded and final adjustments made.

Coloring & Filtering a Photograph With PHOTO-PAINT

Postage for Tomorrow
Steven A. Cousins

Page 261

1. The artist first created a stamp format in CorelDRAW.

2. A color photo was imported and converted into a black-and-white image in PHOTO-PAINT.

3. The photo was imported into the CorelDRAW postage stamp image and recolored.

4. Again in PHOTO-PAINT, the scanned image was then colored using 24-bit color. Several of PHOTO-PAINT's filters were used to create the "hand-drawn" appearance (motion blur: speed of 2; diffuse 2 pixels in each direction; brightness: 30; midtones lightened to an arbitrary freehand curve on the color map; and image sharpened to 50% wide aperture). PHOTO-PAINT was used to draw and paint over portions of the photo in order to create highlights and emphasis.

5. The image was imported to CorelDRAW.

6. The postmark was scanned from a letter, cleaned up and trimmed in PHOTO-PAINT, then imported into CorelDRAW and applied to the stamp artwork.

Using Vanishing Points for Technical Precision

Entry
David Brickley

Page 268

1. The artist scanned a photograph of the building at 120 dpi 8-bit color and imported it into CorelDRAW as a TIF file.

2. The TIF file was installed on a DRAW layer titled "Photo." This layer was given a color override of blue and used as a drawing guide.

3. The general lines of the building were traced in Bézier drawing mode. A custom palette was created. For shadows, black was added to a color; for highlights, white was added.

4. Perspective lines were drawn, including lines at the bottom and top of the building. A circle was added at the point where these lines intersect (out-of-frame at the right). This vanishing point acted as a reference for the plane of the front wall. Similar vanishing points were used for the top and left. Vanishing points acted as "anchors," so that when one end of a line was moved, the other end could keep its original positioning.

5. To create the curves of the entryway, a series of ellipses were drawn and placed on their own layer. First the left side was

traced using the ellipse tool; then the right edge was traced. A 40-step blend was created to act as a guide for drawing the brasswork straps and seams.

6. To establish light source, a graduated fill was applied to the wall.

7. To establish correct size ratio and visual focus, a white mask was created. The artist drew one rectangle large enough to cover the entire drawing. He then drew another rectangle the exact size of the opening (i.e., the size of the artwork he wanted to be visible). He selected both rectangles and combined them as a single object. The new object was colored white and given no outline.

Wide-Screen Slide Presentation
Richard Mednick
(Artist: Vince Kernaghan)

Page 265

Creating a Seamless Panorama

This piece is actually three slides precisely pin-registered to fill the wide-screen format. It's an old photographic technique but new to computer-generated artwork.

1. The elements of this slide were first created in CorelDRAW. The artist used a pin-registered camera and saved files as Print files to the camera.

2. To achieve the correct wide-screen format, he sized his artwork Height: 7.33", Width: 22", with the image extending beyond the page setup. Artwork was kept centered on the page so that Total Area could be viewed. When finished, this artwork was saved, creating the middle screen.

3. The finished artwork was grouped and moved to the right 5.5". This artwork was saved, creating a left screen 7.33" x 11".

4. Next, the original art was moved 5.5" to the left and saved. This creates the right screen.

5. Processed film was mounted in pin-registered mounts with soft-edge masks specially designed to feather right, left and center portions of the projection. Left and right slides were aligned, then the center slide projected and aligned.

**Orko Coffee
Package Design**
Petra Wienholz

Page 202

Combining Elements for a Package Design

1. The artist began by creating the background. He drew a group of strokes using the rectangle function with corners rounded. This group was duplicated and rotated multiple times.

2. The coffee cup icon was drawn in Bézier lines with solid and fountain fills. It has a shadow made by duplicating, and a thin white outline to separate it from the background. The white outline was created by grouping the original and shadow, duplicating it, moving it Back One, then changing the fill and outline of the duplicate to white.

3. The coffee's name, Orko, was set in Fujiyama and placed in an oval. Other label text is Toronto. All label type has a linear fill. All other type (using Surreal, Toronto and Fujiyama faces) was duplicated and given an outline in the background color to ensure that the type separates visually from the background (this way, the stroke pattern is kept from banging into the type).

4. The "New" banner was created with the Bézier line tool. The word "New" is set in Surreal typeface and has been rotated, duplicated and shaded.

5. When the panel design was finalized, it was duplicated to the box panels, then rotated, skewed or stretched for correct visual display.

Pregnant Lady
Wil Dawson

Page 287

Bitmap Fills, Layers & Patience

1. Bitmap fills were used for the background, the underlayer of the dress and the hair decoration. Changing density, grain and colors and reversing colors achieved the desired look.

2. The lace overlay on the dress began as tiny circles grouped together to form larger circles. These larger circles were repeated to create a lacelike effect, then joined using the Combine feature and enveloped to distort them to the shape the artist wanted. The combined object was then filled using a linear fill from black to yellow.

3. The face, neck and arm were created with blends. Blending objects with radial fills or to objects with solid fills provided the subtle shading. Dynamically reshaping the blend and using the control curve for a second blend allowed variations to be explored quickly.

4. The layer feature was invaluable, as bitmap fills were placed on individual layers and turned off when working on other elements of the picture, saving redraw time.

Orchids in the Morning Light
William R. Clegg

Page 280

The Best of Both Worlds: Draw & Paint

1. A line drawing—consisting of the general form of the basic elements: the orchids, leaves and negative space—was created in CorelDRAW.

2. The drawing was exported in PCX format to PHOTO-PAINT. The Paintbrush tool was used to lay down solid color and the Spraycan to get a heavy texture where desired.

3. The artist used the Smudge paintbrush to blend joints and overlaps of color, then deleted most of the lines of the drawing.

4. Drawing new lines with a loose flow then using the Smudge paintbrush tool united all the areas. A Wacom digitizing tablet and cordless pressure-sensitive stylus were a must for this artist.

Fractal Dreaming
Marshall Blight

Page 286

Dreams & Then Some

1. The starting point of this piece is a fractal generated as a GIF file in a shareware program called "Fractint" (Vers. 18). Black-and-white images of the fractals were imported into CorelPHOTO-PAINT, where the "remove spots" filter was used to simplify and sharpen them.

2. The filtered images were then traced using CorelTRACE and imported into CorelDRAW. They were then edited further with much of the extraneous detail removed to produce a cleaner, more graphic image.

3. Solid and fountain fills as well as colored lines were added, and sections of the image were combined and extruded to produce a feeling of depth and movement.

4. When using this technique, the trick is knowing how much of the original fractal image can be discarded without losing the feeling of "wholeness" that these marvelous shapes convey.

The Chief
Cecil G. Rice

Page 285

An Old Drawing & New Tricks

1. Drawings from an old sketch book were refined into simple black-and-white line art and reduced on a photocopier to a size suitable for scanning with a hand-held scanner.

2. After scanning the images (at 400 dpi and approximately 4" wide) and using CorelTRACE, the artist brought the images into CorelDRAW to be colored. The free quality of the lines was pleasing, so very little node-editing was done.

3. The colors are simple fountain fills and flat colors.

4. To edit traced images, this artist finds it easiest to bring a traced copy into one layer, then bring an exact copy into a second layer and, finally, in wireframe mode edit the top layer using the locked bottom layer as a guide. The artist thinks this method is much easier than using a bitmap as a guide. He says, "It's just like using a light table or vellum to traditionally ink a drawing."

Magic Carpet Ride
Georgina Curry
Page 292

Riding the Magic Carpet

1. The Carpet: The individual pieces of the carpet were created in the Bézier drawing mode. The mosaic pieces were then grouped together and perspective added.

2. The Girl: Using the fractal fill "Cosmic Clouds" (new in 4.0) as the base pattern and adjusting texture, softness, density and brightness, variations were created for the pants and scarf.

3. The Clouds: The artist used inspiration from Michelangelo and lightly colored fountain-fill shapes to make up the background.

4. The Frame: The filigree on the frame was created from a single master. It was then mirrored and duplicated around the frame. PowerLines make up the decorative corners.

To sum up this section we say, thanks gang—you've certainly given us issues to ponder . . . and lots of information.

Moving On

Next, we turn to a more practical side of computer creativity, exploring ways to maximize your system and streamline your work process. We'll look at the inner workings of CorelDRAW and suggest how you can fine-tune your .INI file. Finally, we'll review the processes of prepress, printing and working with the service bureau to achieve a successful final product.

SECTION III: TROUBLESHOOTING

More Helpful Information

9

To err is human, but to really foul things up requires a computer.

— Farmers Almanac, 1978

The key to smooth, trouble-free operation of CorelDRAW is *predictability*. You need to know how your computer and your programs will work. This requires an uncluttered and precisely configured system.

In addition, after you've worked hard on a piece of CorelDRAW art, you need to know what to expect from the service bureau that will handle your files, and how the final output will look.

In this chapter we offer a variety of tips and tricks for improving the chances for a favorable outcome of the computer art process —and for keeping unpleasant surprises to a minimum.

SYSTEM SETUP & MAINTENANCE

Follow these suggestions for tuning up your system to maximize running efficiency.

▶ Conserve memory by ensuring that only necessary programs are automatically loaded at bootup.

▶ Keep your system working efficiently by eliminating "lost clusters." Lost or unallocated clusters are caused by not exiting DOS and Windows applications properly (as when

Windows crashes). If you have DOS Version 6.0 or later, use the SCANDISK command to correct hard-disk problems. For previous versions of DOS, use CHKDSK /F. See your DOS manual for more information. (**Caution:** Don't perform this operation while Windows is running.)

▶ Frequent saving and deleting of disk files can scatter parts of files all over your hard disk. This slows down the read/write functions that CorelDRAW frequently executes when loading or saving. Defragmenting the disk will rewrite these fragmented files into contiguous disk space. To prevent your system from slowing down due to scattered data, rely on a defragmentation (also known as optimization) utility to compress the files on your hard disk. DOS 6 includes DEFRAG, a good disk defragmentation utility. Norton Utilities and PC Tools also provide good programs. Delete unused files on a regular basis before defragmenting. **(Caution: Don't perform defragmenting operations while Windows is running.)**

▶ Protect your system against invasion. If your system is exposed to disks from outside sources (such as a service bureau), buy an antivirus program and use it consistently. DOS 6 includes antivirus protection. Reliable shareware virus scan software is also available. Be sure to get the latest version and update with subsequent releases.

▶ Keep backups. Losing your work, possibly even your entire system setup, can be disastrous. Make a habit of backing up with third-party software (a utility program) on a regular basis. If you can't find the time for frequent full backups, concentrate on your application (.CDR) files; they are your livelihood. Program software can be reinstalled after disk failure, unlike lost data. The DOS utility XCOPY allows you to copy files by subdirectory or by date modified—another possibility for quick backup.

▶ Create a system for using directories and subdirectories efficiently to keep track of clients, jobs, levels of revision, etc. Save application files in their own directory. This saves time in backing up your data by helping you locate only the newly created or revised work.

Use Windows's own diagnostic program (MSD.EXE in the main Windows 3.1 directory) for helpful information on your system memory, device drivers, TSRs, ports, etc.

▶ Use a memory manager to maximize your memory usage. DOS 6 comes with a utility called MEMMAKER, and there are also third-party memory management utilities, such as QEMM (by Quarterdeck Office Systems).

▶ Limit the amount of terminate-and-stay-resident (TSR) programs that are preloaded at bootup. Also make sure your AUTOEXEC.BAT, CONFIG.SYS, WIN.INI, SYSTEM.INI and CORELDRW.INI files contain only essential statements.

▶ Create a simple but unique system for naming files. This will prevent you from overwriting an earlier file of the same name, or, if your system is networked, destroying a co-worker's file.

KEEP YOUR WINDOWS CLEAN

CorelDRAW's multiprogram package makes using Windows efficiently more important than ever; so use this checklist to make sure your interface is running at optimum levels.

▶ Keep your Windows and DOS versions current to avoid compatibility problems with new or recently upgraded software.

▶ Always maintain the most current Windows device drivers for your video board and peripherals such as printer, scanner and CD drive.

For the error message ERROR CREATING TEMP FILE, you may not have enough disk space to store the temporary file Corel-DRAW makes during a session. To save your file, switch to the File Manager and free up space on the drive where the TMP files are stored.

▶ To prevent the buildup of lost clusters, always be sure to close programs and exit Windows before turning off your system.

▶ Periodically delete the ".TMP" files that may be left over from a previous Windows session. These files, preceded by a ~ (tilde) character, are usually located in the root directory or a directory specified in the AUTOEXEC.BAT file under the parameter statement SET TEMP=. (**Caution:** This operation should not be done while running Windows.)

In the WIN.INI file (Windows directory), reset the Transmission-Timeout to 999 (infinite). This ensures the printing of large files.

▶ Streamline the running of your applications by reducing both the number of installed fonts and the variety of font formats. ARES Font Minder, which is included with your CorelDRAW 5.0 package, can be a big help with this.

▶ Conserve memory by closing (or at least minimizing) all unneeded applications except for CorelDRAW. Also, avoid using Program Manager add-on products and installing wallpaper graphics.

▶ If you are running Windows 386 Enhanced Mode, set up a permanent swap file to enable faster memory management. If you are not using DOS applications or multitasking, experiment using Standard Mode for a performance boost.

THE COREL INITIALIZATION FILES

One way the layperson using Corel can get a little deeper into the program's inner workings is by working with the INI (initialization) files. You can set several switches (that is, set values at 1 or 0) to control how Corel functions. INI files give Corel directions about how to run. For example, if you've ever had a system crash, you know the value of the automatic back-up settings (AutoBackupDir and AutoBackupMins).

Note: In Version 5.0, you can change several settings right in Corel—you don't have to deal with the INI files. For example, change backup options by choosing Special, Preferences, Advanced. Or choose Special, Preferences, Text to select the Calligraphic Text option, which instructs Corel to retain calligraphic effects applied to lines when those lines are placed on the Clipboard or exported using vector filters. Previously, these options were accessed only via the CORELDRW.INI file.

All of Corel's INI files are stored in the CONFIG subdirectory that's just below the directory in which you installed Corel, and they can be edited in Windows Notepad or any other ASCII text editor. Here's a list of the Corel INI files and what they do:

Before you change any INI settings, check your manual. There are several settings that shouldn't be changed, and you have to make sure you don't delete any section headings or insert settings in the wrong section.

▶ CORELAPP.INI: Contains information that applies to all of your Corel programs.

▶ CORELCHT.INI: Contains information specific to CorelCHART.

▶ CORELDRW.INI: Contains information specific to CorelDRAW.

▶ CORELFLT.INI: Contains information that controls the handling of import and export filters for all Corel applications.

▶ CORELFNT.INI: Contains information about how fonts are handled in all Corel applications.

▶ CORELMOS.INI: Contains information specific to CorelMOSAIC.

▶ CORELMOV.INI: Contains information specific to CorelMOVE.

▶ CORELPLT.INI: Contains plotter pen information.

▶ CORELPNT.INI: Contains information specific to Corel PHOTO-PAINT.

▶ CORELPRN.INI: Contains printer information for all Corel applications.

▶ CORELQRY.INI: Contains information specific to CorelQUERY.

▶ CORELSHW.INI: Contains information specific to CorelSHOW.

▶ CORELTRC.INI: Contains information specific to CorelTRACE.

It's a good idea to make a backup of INI files before you begin editing them. And after you change settings, you have to exit and restart CorelDRAW before the changes take effect.

Following are example settings from CORELAPP.INI, just to give you an idea of the types of changes you can make:

CORELAPP.INI

BigPalette: Specify size of color palette display.

Standard palette	0
Larger palette display for high-end monitors	1
Default	0

BigToolbox: Specify size toolbox display.

Standard toolbox	0
Larger toolbox display for high-end monitors	1
Default	0

SpellLanguage: If you have a CD-ROM drive, this option lets you choose from several dictionaries for spell checking: Danish, Dutch, English, French, Finnish, German, Italian, Norwegian, Portuguese, Spanish, Swedish.

MAXIMIZING CORELDRAW

By taking a little time up-front, you can ensure that Corel-DRAW allows you to get the most creative power from your system.

▶ In addition to CorelDRAW's multilevel Undo feature, you may want to use some of these techniques to view "what if..." changes to a design or illustration and still enable reverting back to the original design.

  1. Copy an image to the Clipboard before you alter it. If you don't like the changes made, simply paste the original image into place. This may not work with complex drawings on systems with limited RAM.

  2. You can use the "save as" or the export feature to create different versions of what you are developing. You can speed up this operation using file-saving enhancements. If you create a lot of variations and/or if the application files are large in size, you could use MOSAIC to compare

the saved designs side by side. For maximum clarity, choose the color header with the most detail possible (8K) when saving each version of the design in DRAW; and make sure MOSAIC is displaying the largest thumbnail available (250 pixels wide).

3. If system resources permit, open multiple copies of Corel-DRAW and cut and paste images between both.

4. If the making of .BAK files is enabled in CorelDRAW, you can revert back to the design as it appeared before your last save by opening the backup copy of the file.

5. With an object or group already selected to modify, press plus (+) to clone it, or press the left mouse button. With the Nudge preference set at 1/2 inch to 2 inches, move the clone in any of four directions using enough arrow cursor key presses to clear the clone from the original. Modify the objects in any manner, but don't move their position on the page with the mouse. When you've settled on which variation will be used, simply nudge the object or group to where the original was and delete the other objects.

6. When experimenting with different colors, fills or type attributes, you can apply numerous effects to an object or group and instantly get back to any previous variation you prefer. Begin by drawing a series of small rectangles outside the live page area, each containing a few type characters. Select one of the rectangles and use the Copy Style From . . . option (all boxes checked) to copy the present style attributes of your design to one of the rectangular "stash" boxes. Alter your design again and again, copying attributes to a different box. In this way you can simultaneously save custom blending, bitmap and radial fills, and outline text and Artistic Text information until you make your final decisions.

▶ Install only those import/export filters that are essential for your day-to-day production. Edit the CORELFLT.INI in your CONFIG subdirectory.

▶ To get faster screen redraws, if you haven't added a Windows accelerator video board but are using extended VGA,

To avoid constantly needing to call up your Edit Color dialog box, name your palette colors precisely; e.g., C70:M20:Y5:K5 for 70% cyan, 20% magenta, 5% yellow and 5% black.

set your Windows display to 640 x 480 VGA mode. Use Windows Setup for this.

▶ Take time to set up your Preferences options when beginning a large job. For example, if you want all your object outlines to Scale With Object, it is much easier to set this preference first than to redefine after the lines have been drawn.

For faster non-PostScript output, choose TrueType fonts. For truer printing of fonts on PostScript devices, choose Adobe Type 1 fonts.

▶ Save time by enabling the Interruptible Display option in the Preferences dialog box. Use the right mouse button to interrupt unnecessary screen redraws.

▶ If you're not using the onscreen palette, take it off the screen.

▶ When working on complex drawings, use wireframe view to shorten screen redraw times.

▶ If you're using Fountain Fills, set the Fountain Stripes option to 10 or fewer stripes while working on your image. Remember to reset to your printer's recommended maximum when you're ready for a final proof.

▶ If you have a large bitmap on screen but you're not working with it, disable the Display Bitmaps option.

▶ For quick and simplified proofing, increase the Set Flatness To print option.

▶ If you're working with limited disk space, remember to allow sufficient space for Corel's files, backups, autobackups and temp files.

▶ For more efficient memory management, set up a Windows swap file to hold temporary files. See your Windows manual for instructions.

▶ If your system's RAM is limited, minimize the number and complexity of objects on the Clipboard.

▶ If your system is slow, use keyboard shortcuts—you won't have to wait for screen redraws of options menus.

▶ Remember that you can't create a curve with more than 3,000 nodes. Be careful when Autotracing a complex drawing or a large color bitmap.

▶ Be aware that bitmap fills consume time and memory. Temporarily use a solid fill while designing and apply the bitmap, fountain or vector fill at the completion of the drawing. Another strategy is to use a temporary file to hold bitmap fills, text converted to curves or other complex objects. Import these back into your main file when other work has been done.

▶ You can speed up redraw and save memory by combining like objects.

▶ If you will be converting text to curves, save this operation until near the end of your work.

▶ Make sure Paragraph Text is fully ready (spell-checked, edited), then wait till the end of your work before importing it.

PRINTING FILES

To print a file, just choose File, Print (or press Ctrl+P) to open the Print dialog box. Make any necessary adjustments and choose OK. The following sections detail the selections in the Print and System Color Profile dialog boxes, both of which allow you to fine-tune your settings.

Print Dialog Box

Print Range: Print all pages, the current page only, a specified range of pages or selected objects.

Printer: Choose from the list of installed printers.

Printer Quality: Choose from High, Medium or Low. High, of course, will give you the best quality, but it takes the longest to print. Low quality can save you time and toner on drafts.

Print to File: Create a file that can then be printed from DOS even from a computer that doesn't have Corel installed.

For Mac: With Print to File selected, activate this option to disable coding so that files can print on Mac output equipment.

Copies: Specify how many copies you want to print (up to 999).

Collate: Select this option if you want each series of pages to print as a set. By default, multiple copies print out page by page (in other words, ten copies of page 1, then ten copies of page 2, etc.). If you instruct Corel to collate, you'll get one complete set of pages 1-10, then another complete set, etc.—to save you from having to manually collate the copies after they print.

Setup Dialog Box

Choose Setup from the Print dialog box.

Note: The available setup options will vary depending on what kind of printer you have.

Paper Size: Choose your paper size from the drop-down list.

Paper Source: If your printer uses different bins or trays, make a selection from this drop-down list.

Graphics Resolution: Choose the resolution (in dots per inch).

Orientation: Choose Portrait or Landscape.

Print Options Dialog Box

Choose Options from the Print dialog box. The Print Options dialog box contains three tabs: Choose Layout, Separations or Options.

The main area of the Print Options dialog box includes a page preview area and seven icons, as shown in Figure 9-1.

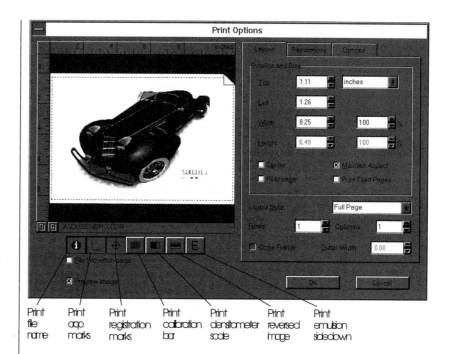

Figure 9-1: Print Options dialog box's reference icons.

Print file name: Prints the file name, screen frequency and date and time just outside the left margin of the printable page area. *Note:* This information won't print if your printable page is larger than your paper size.

Print crop marks: Prints crop marks (position depends on page layout selected).

Print registration marks: Prints registration marks at the four corners of your separations.

Print calibration bar: Prints calibration bars for each monitor color (calibrate colors through the Color Manager, which is discussed later in this chapter).

Print densitometer scale: See the section following the dialog box information for more details on the densitometer.

Print reversed image: Prints a negative image of your file. Some commercial printers prefer to work with reversed images.

Print emulsion side down: When the E is facing right, the emulsion side will print up; when it's facing left, the emulsion side will print down. Again, check with your printer to see what they prefer.

Layout Tab

Position and Size: Adjust the position and size of the printed image. These settings don't have any effect on your actual file—they only control the printout.

Center: Center the image on the page.

Fit to Page: Automatically resizes the image so that it fits on the page.

Maintain Aspect: Temporarily reduces or enlarges a graphic for printing.

Print Tiled Pages: Prints portions of oversized artwork (or artwork scaled to print larger than the printer paper) on additional sheets.

Layout Style: Gives you control over a drawing's size and position. Works in conjunction with the Rows and Columns settings.

Rows: Specify the number of rows on the printed page.

Columns: Specify the number of columns on the printed page.

Gutter Width: Specify the amount of space between columns.

Clone Frame: Clones the page frame.

Separations Tab

Print Separations: Print color information as grayscale separations.

In Color: By default, separations are printed in grayscale. Choose In Color to print them in color.

Convert Spot Colors to CMYK: Converts spot colors to their equivalent process colors.

Use Custom Halftone: If you don't specify otherwise, Corel uses your printer's default angle and frequency for halftones. Select this option and choose Edit to adjust these settings.

Colors: Specify the colors for which you want to print separations.

Auto Trapping: Applies trapping to objects according to your specifications:

▶ Always Overprint Black: Applies trapping to any object that's more than 95 percent black.

▶ Auto-Spreading: Applies trapping to any object that doesn't have an outline and uses a uniform fill. In addition, auto-spreading won't apply to an object if you've used the Object menu's Overprint Fill command (see the section "Printing Fills" a little later in this chapter).

Unsharp Masking: This filter sharpens smooth areas and emphasizes edge details.

Options Tab

Screen Frequency: Adjusts the halftone screen frequency (in lines per inch). *Note:* If you're printing color separations, use the Use Custom Halftone option in the Separations tab to set frequencies for individual CMYK colors.

Set Flatness to: This setting is for PostScript printers only. It adjusts the number of segments used to draw curves. With complex drawings, higher numbers can result in flatter curves.

Auto Increase Flatness: With this setting, Corel automatically adjusts the flatness value for optimal printed results. If your printer can't handle a file, Corel adjusts the flatness value incrementally until the file is able to print. Unless you really need to manually adjust the flatness values, letting Corel take care of this will give you the best results.

Fountain Steps: Choose a low number of fountain steps for quicker printing; choose a higher number for better image quality (printing begins to slow with values over 40).

Number of Points in Curves: The default setting is 1,500, and you can specify a maximum of 20,000.

Download Type 1 Fonts: This option downloads fonts from your hard drive (or other source) to your printer.

Convert TrueType to Type 1: Converts TrueType fonts to Post-Script Type 1 fonts.

Color Manager

Choose File, Color Manager to open the System Color Profile dialog box.

The Color Manager lets you modify your monitor, printer and scanner settings so that what you see onscreen more closely approximates your printouts.

Current Profile: Corel uses a default color profile called _DEFAULT.CCS. You can create different profiles for different printers.

Notes: Lets you add notes to color profiles. This is an option you should definitely take advantage of—it's really easy to forget what you had in mind when you created the profile.

Monitor: Choose your monitor from the drop-down list and choose Edit to open the Monitor Calibration dialog box. Specify your monitor characteristics—adjust Gamma levels to control the brightness of midtone gray levels; adjust Chromaticity to control hue and saturation.

Printer: Choose the printer for which you want to make adjustments, then choose Edit to open the Printer Calibration dialog box. Following are some of the options you can set:

▶ Printer Type: Choose CMYK to print using four colors; RGB to print using three colors.

▶ UCR (Undercolor Removal): First choose Film or Printer, depending on your output device. Then adjust the TAC setting to control the amount of cyan, magenta and yellow ink in very dark areas of a printed piece. If you have saturated areas of dark color, use UCR to prevent problems such as slow ink drying.

▶ Black Point: This controls the blackness of black. Choose a higher value for darker CMYK shadows, or a lower value for lighter shadows.

▶ Color Match: Lets you match your printer and monitor colors for more accurate results.

Scanner: Select your scanner from the drop-down list and choose Edit to open the Scanner Calibration dialog box. This dialog box allows you to adjust the color accuracy of the systems scanner. Following are some of the options you can set.

▶ File: Choose a pretested scanner setting.

▶ Image: Build a custom scanner profile tuned to your printer's characteristics.

▶ Scanned Target: Adjust for skews or misalignment.

Using CorelDRAW's Densitometer

DRAW's printed densitometer lets you assess your four-color separations. When you print a CMYK separation, the densitometer, or density scale, prints on each page. For example, on the magenta page, a scale indicating the densities of magenta will print along the border of the page. If you're already experienced with color separations, or with a little practice, you can tell immediately if the magenta is too dense, affecting, for example, flesh tones. You can also have the densitometer print progressively, combining two, three or all four colors on a grid.

To get a printed densitometer, click on the Densitometer icon in the Print Options dialog box.

4.0 Choose Densitometer Scale from the Print Options dialog box.

Printing Fills

When you assign a fill to an object that sits on top of another filled object, CorelDRAW automatically "knocks out" (removes) the color on the lower object where the two objects overlap. However, if you want two spot colors to overprint:

1. Click the top object with your secondary mouse button.

2. At the Object menu, choose Overprint Fill.

Overprinting can be used to create special effects, but it is most often used to trap. Trapping occurs when two side-by-side colors slightly overprint at the edges. This avoids any show-through of the underlying page (usually white) that can occur due to poor color registration in the plate-making and printing processes.

To create a trap:

When you create a trap, remember that the darker color will always dominate the lighter color.

- If you want CorelDRAW to apply an automatic trap, at the Print dialog box, choose Options, Print as Separations, then Separations. Select Auto Spreading (for filled objects with no outline) or Always Overprint Black (when you want type or objects to overprint).
- Add a fine (0.30 points) outline to your interior object and color it the same as the object. Set to Overprint the outline.
- Create your objects with a slight overlap. Set the top object to Overprint.
- If the object doesn't have a fill, duplicate the object, increase its size slightly, then designate the duplicate to overprint. If the top object is darker than the background, give the duplicate a fill of none and an outline the same color as the background.
- To Overprint filled text, simply select the text, access the Object menu and choose Overprint Fill.

SERVICE BUREAU SMARTS

If you use CorelDRAW to create commercially printed design work, your artwork invariably ends up passing through a service bureau on its way to being published. The more you can predict about how your job will be processed, the more accurately you can budget time and costs and therefore avoid undue anxiety. Although all the elements of prepress can't be fully covered here, consider the following recommendations, precautions and preparations when ordering PostScript imaging.

Service bureaus can use any combination of a growing number of industry-competitive PostScript devices that incorporate a wide variety of processing speeds, image quality and page-size capability. These features and processes are calculated into the cost you must pay for the bureau's services. For example, there are five Linotronic models, ranging from the older model 200SQ and 230 to the newer, more enhanced 300, 330 and 530. Each imagesetter is controlled by one of several raster image processors, or RIP (a microprocessing unit that acts as a translator between the imagesetter and the PC or Macintosh computer that feeds it). As you can imagine, it takes a great deal of expense, dedication and expertise to keep everything up-to-date and working compatibly and reliably with a staggering array of graphics software.

Thoroughly investigate several service bureaus in your immediate area. Having several choices will provide you with a menu of services that can save you time and money, depending on whether you need more technical support or require less quality. Don't rule out bureaus located out-of-state, as long as they are reasonably priced and still affordable after adding on the costs of the shipping, modeming and faxing you will incur.

To ensure that you get the final image you require, make sure to clearly communicate to your service bureau what you want.

▶ Be sure your service bureau accepts CorelDRAW applications files and has a current version of the software.

▶ Find out as much as possible about a service bureau's hardware and software capabilities. Can they support your re-

Some service bureaus offer a 24-hour bulletin board service (BBS) for transferring files by modem during non-peak hours. (Make sure your communications software is compatible.)

When you're having an image professionally output, use areas bordering an image for a grayscale or color reference, or a job number and contact information.

movable storage device? What is the extent of their font library? Ask these questions at the outset to prevent incompatibility problems later on. Better still, when possible, send along your CorelDRAW application file (.CDR) to assure font compatibility.

▶ Whether using a modem or supplying disks, it may be necessary to compress files using third-party software. Many programs are available as inexpensive shareware and will compress or archive your CorelDRAW or PostScript file into a copy totaling one-half or less of the original size. If you can supply compressed files, make sure that the service bureau knows the type and version of the software you used. PKZIP is a standard compression program.

▶ Service bureau technical support should be well-versed in all aspects of the PC platform—hardware, DOS, Windows and PostScript—in addition to CorelDRAW.

▶ Ask questions about how they do business. Can you establish a credit account, or is payment due at the time of service? Know their responsibilities and yours. How are conflicts resolved? Can portions of a job be rerun, or must you output the entire job? Do they offer pick-up and delivery?

▶ What kind of quality control policies do they practice in case a conflict must be resolved? Mistakes often occur somewhere, especially if you are inexperienced. You should know up-front if a technician is constantly on the lookout for errors and can alert you to them before the job is delivered, or if you must simply pay for whatever comes out of the processor. Keep in mind that the latter, while admittedly a bit riskier, might be significantly cheaper in cost if you are absolutely confident about what you supply for output.

When working with fine halftone screens, check with your service bureau technician for advice on the best screen-lines-per-inch setting to use when creating the piece and on the dots-per-inch output resolution you should specify.

▶ Make sure you know their business hours—is this a 24-hour service or an 8-to-5 business?

▶ Always send files on clearly labeled, freshly formatted disks.

▶ Send a hard copy of your artwork (fax it if you've modemed the files) as a reference for their production staff.

▶ Keep detailed and accurate records of every job you send to the service bureau. Not only will this protect you in case of conflicts, but you'll be documenting specific outcomes that you may want to recreate later on.

▶ If you have peak periods, choose a service bureau that can help you with design and production support.

Getting the Most for Your Money

▶ Be aware that a service bureau offering a cheaper price per page doesn't mean much if the service bureau has a slower or outdated imagesetter or RIP and still charges for extra time beyond a set minimum. (You'll really pay for guesswork here.) On the other hand, expect to pay more for more expertise—but you may be spending less in the long run.

▶ If you are planning to transmit a large file to a BBS via modem, plan the operation at off-peak hours if possible. You'll save on tolls the same way you would with a phone call. Keep your system free for other, more productive work during the busiest times of day. (This procedure can also reduce error-causing line noise that may occur during the business day.)

▶ Plan to gang jobs whenever possible. You can usually image two-letter pages in a tabloid page without paying twice the cost. Of course, you can split output expenses with an associate and save even more money, especially if there's a minimum charge that must be met for the service. Include your own custom register/crop marks around your design and make sure they are set up to print on multiple pages if separation work is involved.

▶ Remember that you don't need to print separation negative films for every multiple (spot) color job. If the colored objects or text elements don't touch each other, you can place all the art on a single film and instruct the offset printer to block out the appropriate parts when making the plate.

▶ Some projects can be produced more economically and with similar quality using a 300 dpi laser printer and a graphics camera. A simple graphic or logo printed at large scale at 300 dpi yields high quality when reduced 20 percent to 50 percent and mechanically imaged as a negative film stat.

Complex & Oversized Illustrations

Preplanning can save time, money and frustration when building large or complex files.

▶ Before starting a large project, consider how your files will be output, delivered to the service bureau and archived for future use. For files too large to fit on a 1.44mb disk, you might want to transmit them via modem during off-peak hours. You could also explore file compression software and mass storage units.

▶ Another preliminary to starting a sizable project: clean up your system to be sure it's running at maximum efficiency. Compress your hard disk files for optimum running speed (see "System Setup & Maintenance" earlier in this chapter). Check to be sure you have enough disk storage space to hold files and their backups. If you're getting low on disk space, disable the "make backups" and "auto backups" features. Consider copying unused directories off to floppies for the duration of the project.

▶ Use letter-size pages as the basis for your design, no matter what its final size will be. You'll be able to proof using your laser printer, then combine the parts of your final piece before sending them to the service bureau. Use the Print Options tiling feature to print letter-size sections that can be assembled for proofing.

▶ Research the output device you'll be using. Each imagesetter has advantages and limitations—for example, Linotronic's 500 series machine will output using paper or film up to 18 inches wide, while other imagesetter brands are limited to 11.7 inches. Check with your service bureau for specifications on their imagesetter; if it doesn't meet your needs, shop around.

▶ Use paper and pencil to preplan your oversized projects. Lay out your design to final proportions. Take into consideration bleeds, folds and special printing processes such as die cuts. And look for complex elements that will affect your computer file sizes. If desired, you can transfer your sketch to your computer by scanning; or visually scale your design by overlaying the drawing with a grid that matches your computer grid.

▶ Make maximum use of your grid and guideline layers. For complex drawings, create lines and shapes for use as guides, but keep them on a separate layer that can quickly be made invisible for viewing.

▶ Create complex artwork in sections in a master file. Export each section and complete it in a separate file. When all sections are finished, import them back into the master file where they will be automatically positioned correctly.

▶ CorelDRAW limits objects to 3,000 nodes. As you approach the node limit, you may experience problems in printing. If you run into this situation, try decreasing the PSComplexity Threshold in your CORELDRW.INI.

▶ If your service bureau uses both Mac and PC platforms, find out which offers faster processing and/or costs less. If your service bureau suggests using the Mac, be sure to check the For Mac option when printing to file.

TECHNICAL SUPPORT

In addition to telephone support, Corel provides free bulletin board service (BBS): registered users can download free upgrades to portions of CorelDRAW as they become available. Also, users can access a variety of reference documents that cover topics ranging from fonts to supported peripheral device drivers.

Corel also runs very active support forums on CompuServe and America Online. When you post a question on these forums, chances are you'll get answers not only from Corel's technical support staff but from several Corel users as well, some of whom have probably run into and solved exactly the same problem you're experiencing. If you have a CompuServe account, just log on and type **GO COREL** at any system prompt. To obtain a CompuServe account, call 800-948-8199. If you're an America Online user, use the keyword: Corel. To obtain an America Online account, call 800-827-6364.

MOVING ON

All the power of CorelDRAW lies in your finely tuned system, your knowledge of the program's features and your own vision. We've designed *Looking Good With CorelDRAW!* to further your progress in all three areas.

We hope you refer to the how-to sections of this book whenever you encounter a question regarding the best way to translate vision into reality. We have no doubt you'll return often to view the inspiring works by the artists in the black-and-white and color galleries.

Your fellow artists around the world look forward to seeing what magic you can render with CorelDRAW.

SECTION IV: APPENDICES

Corel's Creative Collection

In this appendix, we offer a brief overview of Corel's exciting auxiliary programs: CorelPHOTO-PAINT, CorelCHART, CorelSHOW, CorelMOVE, CorelMOSAIC, CorelTRACE and CorelQUERY (new in Version 5.0). And we'll tell you a little about Corel Ventura, Corel's full-featured page layout program that is now bundled with your CorelDRAW 5.0 package. Finally, you'll get a quick look at ARES Font Minder, which is a terrific font management utility that's now included with CorelDRAW (starting with Version 5.0).

Those familiar with DRAW or other draw-type programs may puzzle over the inclusion of this diverse collection in the Corel-DRAW package. But Corel's logic is solid: while each of these programs is distinct, together they provide a comprehensive graphics "toolbox." In today's competitive visual environment, where artists benefit from skills in a variety of media, the Corel collection gives you a power-packed graphics studio right at your keyboard.

To make assimilation of these programs as easy as possible, Corel built the best features of DRAW into each program. You'll find familiar visual cues and the same intuitive interface. There are pull-down menus and toolboxes similar to the ones in DRAW. Most features are accessible via easy-to-recognize icons.

PHOTO CD:
High-Res Photos on the Desktop

Before we get into Corel's package, let's review the PHOTO CD technology available from the Eastman Kodak Company. It's important to look at this technology because it is an important part of this collection's value to the desktop communicator.

Eastman Kodak spearheaded the convergence of several late twentieth century technologies when it introduced its PHOTO CD system in 1990. This system digitizes regular 35mm photographs and stores up to 100 images on a compact disk. With a PHOTO CD player, you can view photos on your television set. As PHOTO CD imaging becomes available wherever photographic film is processed—including your corner drug store—and as high-density television becomes the standard, the vibrancy of digitized images and the efficiency of CD storage will open up a new era in photography and computer imaging.

For desktop publishers, the news is even better. Until now, color photos on the desktop were less than satisfactory. But with digitized photos and image manipulation programs such as PHOTO-PAINT (discussed below) you get tremendous control—control well beyond what was previously available in the darkroom. The digital format allows manipulation at the smallest level, opening up exciting possibilities for masking, merging, retouching, filtering and other special effects.

PHOTO CD's benefits to desktop designers are tremendous. Whole libraries of photographs are available on compact disk, and each image will be editable. Communications, from comp layouts to boardroom presentations, will improve in quality. The cost of color photography in publishing, especially for high-density layouts such as catalogs, will be reduced.

Kodak has established the Kodak Color Management System to control photographic color on the desktop. A universal color standard for computers, PHOTO YCC, ensures color consistency across platforms and devices. High-resolution color photo images can now be delivered quickly, efficiently and consistently—on your computer screen, from your printer or from a service bureau. Major hardware and software manufacturers are incorporating this new standard into their products.

Digitized photography stored on CDs sounds great, but what does it have to do with CorelDRAW? Corel's digital image processing program, PHOTO-PAINT, takes advantage of this technology, putting the power and possibilities of digitized high-resolution photographs at your fingertips.

PHOTO-PAINT: Creating Bit by Bit

Whether you're an artist, designer, photographer or desktop publisher, CorelPHOTO-PAINT is a powerful and exciting creative tool. PHOTO-PAINT gives you bit-by-bit control of color, grayscale and black-and-white images. This makes PHOTO-PAINT a versatile tool for creating artwork from scratch or for manipulating digitized photographs. PHOTO-PAINT is compatible with the most popular graphics file formats (see Figure A-5) and supports a variety of scanners and printers. You can also export images for desktop publishing, presentations and multimedia applications.

The detailed control offered by digitization and PHOTO-PAINT's variety of tools promises some exciting experimental artwork over the next few years. PHOTO-PAINT lets you access the digital images on a PHOTO CD, such as the Corel PHOTO CD Gallery, while the program's tools give free rein to your imagination: spray-paint an image's background, color a black-and-white photograph, clone and reverse an image, or merge several photos into an illustrative collage. We suspect that these two technologies—digital manipulation and PHOTO CD imaging—will keep computer artists busy experimenting for quite a long while.

With PHOTO-PAINT, you create and manipulate images using a toolbox plus a variety of roll-up windows similar to those you use in CorelDRAW.

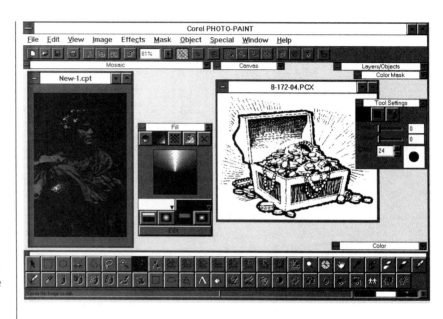

Figure A-1: CorelPHOTO-PAINT screen display showing workboxes and multiple window picture windows.

PHOTO-PAINT's toolbox contains your working tools for controlling display, selection, drawing, painting and retouching. Simply double-click on an icon to access each tool's individual adjustments.

You can customize the display of PHOTO-PAINT's toolbox. When you open the program, the toolbox displays as a single column with tools grouped by function on fly-out menus. To display the entire tool set, select Floating from the View menu's cascading Toolbox menu. Then click on the toolbox's Control-menu icon and deselect Grouped (if you leave Grouped selected, only the initial icon of a group will show, while the others are accessible from fly-out menus. When the toolbox is floating, you can resize it or drag it anywhere on the screen.

4.0 In Version 4.0, the Control-menu icon appears on the default toolbox. Make any changes you want by selecting items from the menu.

In PHOTO-PAINT, several special effects are accessible via the roll-ups. The Canvas roll-up lets you apply a textured surface to your artwork. With the Color roll-up, you can choose the colors displayed onscreen from the full available palette. You can use the Fill roll-up to load an image to the Tile tool. With the Tool

Settings roll-up you can adjust the size and shape of most tools, including width and shape of the Paintbrush tool and shape of the spray on the Airbrush tool. In addition, filter and transform commands—now accessed via the Effects and Image menus— let you apply darkroom-style graphic effects.

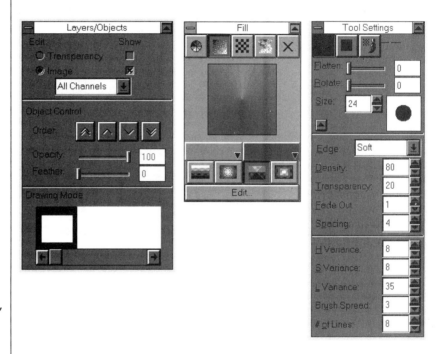

Figure A-2: Layers/Objects, Fill and Tool Settings roll-ups.

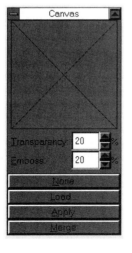

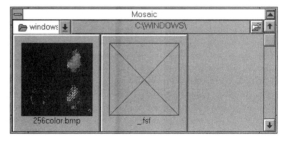

Figure A-3: Canvas and Mosaic roll-ups.

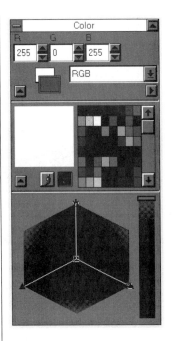
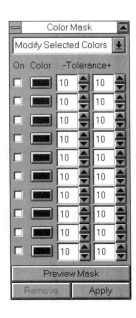

Figure A-4: Color and Color Mask roll-ups.

Three new roll-ups have been added in Version 5.0: Layers/ Objects, which lets you adjust the order of objects and apply effects to selected objects; Color Mask, which you can use to edit or protect colors in masked areas; and Mosaic, which allows you to access CorelMOSAIC from within PHOTO-PAINT.

PHOTO-PAINT File Formats

You can open a variety of image types into PHOTO-PAINT. The program supports 24-Bit Color, 256 Color, Grayscale, and Black & White pictures. In PHOTO-PAINT, artwork with fewer than 256 colors is automatically converted to 24-bit color. Black-and-white artwork can be converted to line art or halftone screens.

Figure A-5: Graphic file formats.

Below is a table of graphics files you can use in PHOTO-PAINT.

Extension	Name	Import	Save—256 Color	Save—24-Bit Color	Save—Gray Scale	Save—Black & White	Description
BMP	Bitmaps	yes	yes	yes	yes	yes	Windows's internal graphics file format—supported by OS/2.
EPS	Encapsulated PostScript	no	yes	yes	yes	yes	Creates bitmap image in PostScript (vector) code—save as .PCX to view.
GIF^{SM}	Graphics Interchange Format	yes	yes	no	yes	yes	CompuServe graphics format
PCD	Photo-CD	yes	yes	no	yes	yes	Kodak Photo CD-ROM Image format (Compact Disk-Read Only Memory
PCX	PC Paintbrush	yes	yes	yes	yes	yes	Universal PC industry format and PHOTO-PAINT's default save extension. Use with Ventura Publisher, PageMaker, MS Word 5.0.
TGA	Targa	yes	yes	yes	yes	yes	Truevision graphics format. Extensions also available include .VDA, .ICB, .VST
TIF	Tagged Image File	yes	yes	yes	yes	yes	Suggest for halftones. Some versions incompatible. Use compression to save disk space.

With PHOTO-PAINT you can do all this:

- Open up to 8 image windows.
- Make up to 20 duplicates for working in multiple views.
- View changes simultaneously in different magnifications.
- Adjust a single color or your entire palette.

- Color grayscale pictures.
- Access more than 16 million colors (in 24-bit Color mode).
- Customize picture windows and toolbox arrangements for optimum control.
- See which tool is selected with a cursor icon.
- Zoom to 1600% for pixel-by-pixel editing.
- Choose from the complete Windows font library.
- Adjust the intensity of special effects and colors.

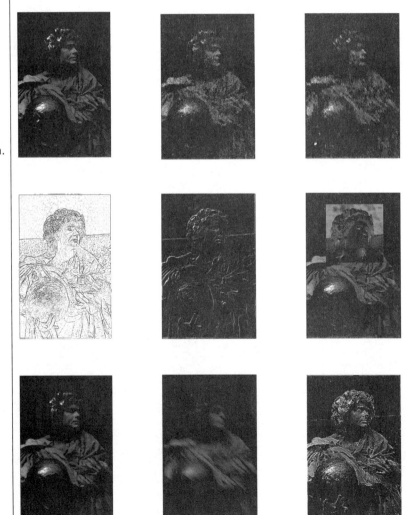

Figure A-6: Halftone, Pointillism, Impressionism.

Figure A-7: Edge Detect, Emboss, Invert.

Figure A-8: Jaggie Despeckle, Motion Blur, Outline.

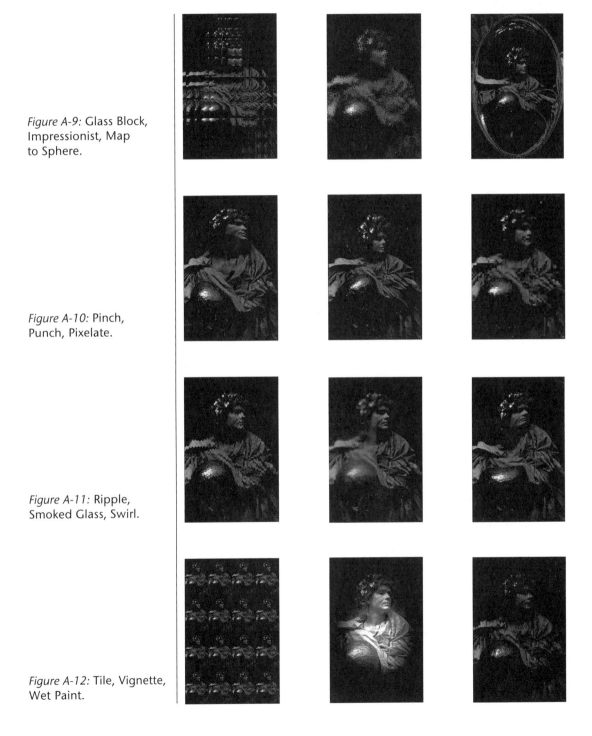

Figure A-9: Glass Block, Impressionist, Map to Sphere.

Figure A-10: Pinch, Punch, Pixelate.

Figure A-11: Ripple, Smoked Glass, Swirl.

Figure A-12: Tile, Vignette, Wet Paint.

Figure A-13: Wind, Sharpen, Convert to B&W.

Figure A-14: Posterize, Psychedelic, Solarize.

Figure A-15: Mesh Warp, Perspective, 3D Rotate.

PHOTO-PAINT's Tools & Special Effects

Here is a brief description of some of the program's most interesting features.

Selection Tools

Use to define and cut-and-paste areas of your artwork.

- Rectangle selection: selects area with rectangular bounding box.

- Magic wand: selects areas with similar colors.
- Lasso: selects areas with irregular bounding box.
- Scissors: selects polygonal areas.

Display Tools

Use to change your image's view, display size and position.

- Zoom: reduces or enlarges image view.
- Locator: when you have an image in several differently sized views, displays the same part of the image in each view.
- Hand: moves your image horizontally, vertically or diagonally on the screen.

Painting Tools

Use to paint with brush-type strokes, to clone and to add color and special effects.

- Paintbrush: creates brushlike strokes.
- Impressionism paintbrush: creates stylized brush strokes.
- Pointillism paintbrush: creates Seurat-style "dots."
- Airbrush: adds color in a soft "spray."
- Spraycan: adds color in wide, coarse spray.
- Flood fill tool: fills closed object with color.
- Tile fill tool: fills closed object with tile pattern.
- Gradient fill tool: fills closed object with gradient fill.
- Clone: copies a color to a new area.
- Pointillism clone: clones Seurat-style brush strokes from one area to another.
- Impressionism clone: clones stylized brush strokes from one area to another.

Drawing Tools

Use to draw lines, curves, and hollow and filled shapes and to add text to your artwork.

- Line: draws lines.

- Curve: draws curves.
- Pen: draws shapes.
- Text: adds text.
- Rectangle: draws hollow, filled or rounded rectangles.
- Circle: draws circles or ellipses (hollow or filled).
- Polygon: draws hollow or filled polygons.

Retouch Tools

Use to adjust colors and shades and apply special effects.

- Contrast paintbrush: adjusts contrast.
- Brightness paintbrush: adjusts intensity of color.
- Tint paintbrush: changes a color's shade.
- Blend paintbrush: smooths areas of color.
- Smear paintbrush: smears colors.
- Smudge paintbrush: smudges colors.
- Sharpen paintbrush: sharpens colors.
- Eyedropper: selects a color.
- Local undo: reverts to previous image style.
- Eraser: erases areas of an image.
- Color replacer: replaces outline color with fill color.

Filters

Use a variety of filters (from the Effects menu) to achieve special effects, including

- Artistic filters such as pointillism and impressionism filter.
- Emboss, invert, pixilate, posterize, psychedelic and solarize filters.
- Edge filters, such as edge emphasis, contour and outline.
- Noise filters, such as add noise and remove noise.

Transformations

Use this selection on the Effects menu to automatically apply effects such as 3D Rotate, Perspective and Mesh Warp.

PHOTO-PAINT & OLE

You can import artwork created in PHOTO-PAINT into other Corel programs, such as SHOW and MOVE, or into your publishing program. When your image and application are linked via OLE, any changes to your image made in PHOTO-PAINT will also be made in the other program.

Corel users will enjoy using PHOTO-PAINT to create art and illustrations; but when it's facts and figures that need visual interpretation, Corel provides another powerful program.

CORELCHART: Create High-Impact Infographics

If knowledge is power, the way you present information determines just how powerful its impact will be. CorelCHART makes it easy for you to transform basic data—statistics, sales figures, comparisons—into provocative visuals.

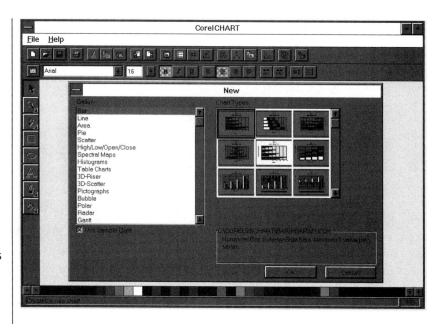

Figure A-16: CorelCHART's extensive menu of chart styles, plus thumbnail visual preview.

With CorelCHART you can do the following:

• Enter information into CHART's full-featured Data Manager.
• Edit in side-by-side views, one with Data Manager and one with Chart View.
• Clone and revise existing templates.
• Build custom templates.
• Layer information—use one for data, one for highlighting.

Using the Data Manager

CHART's Data Manager is a sophisticated way to organize information, whether it's sales figures or demographic comparisons. Access the Data Manager icon: the screen displays a spreadsheet-style data field. You can customize spreadsheet cells for both the x and y axes, enter field titles and control text style and placement. Use the Text Ribbon to style type. Print the spreadsheet or access Chart View to see the information presented graphically. A screen icon toggles between the Data Manager and Chart View, or you can display both on a split screen.

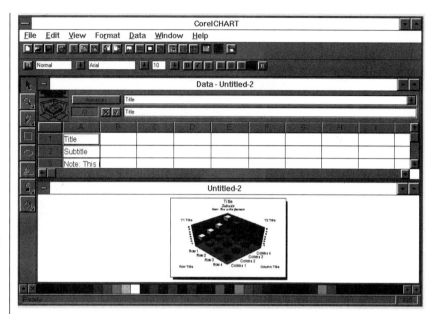

Figure A-17: Enter your CHART information into a Data Manager spreadsheet. Then select a chart style. CHART converts your data instantly.

Corel has added over 300 new spreadsheet functions to Version 5.0.

Data access: use information stored in popular spreadsheet software, or key in data in CHART's own Data Manager.

Math functions: set up cell-by-cell relationships to automatically perform mathematical calculations, from simple addition and subtraction to complex statistical and financial calculations; numerous math and financial formulae are available.

Spreadsheets: create spreadsheets as well as charts.

Cell control: format and edit your spreadsheet cell by cell.

Interprogram toggle: switch back and forth between Data Manager and Chart View instantly.

OLE client: In Version 5.0, CorelCHART is an OLE client, which means that you can place charts in DRAW (or any other Windows program that can act as an OLE server) and edit them in their original CHART format just by double-clicking on the chart from within DRAW.

4.0 Version 4.0 uses DDE (Dynamic Data Exchange) linking to achieve similar results.

Figures A-18 through A-23 show some of the many chart styles that CorelCHART offers.

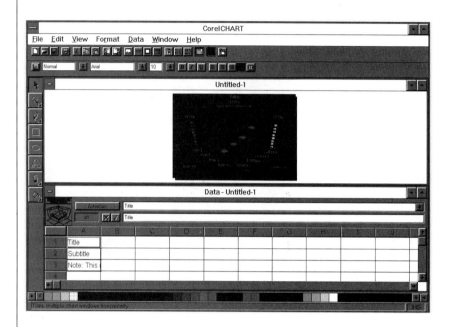

Figure A-18: Vertical bar chart.

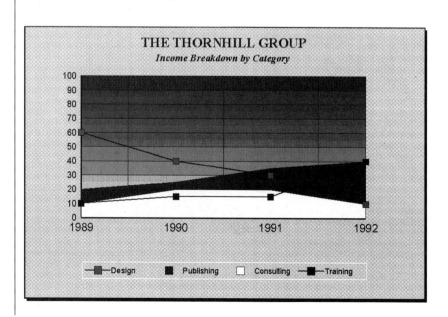

Figure A-19: Vertical area chart.

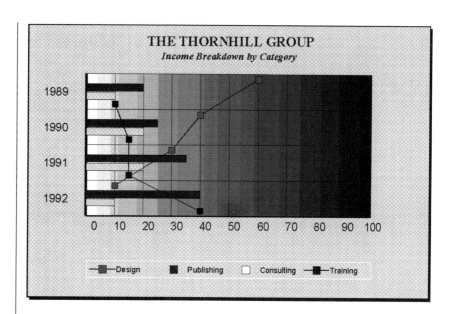

Figure A-20: Horizontal bar chart.

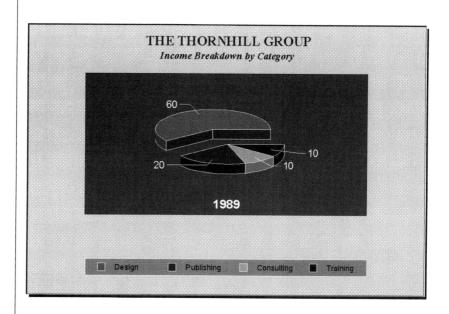

Figure A-21: Pie chart.

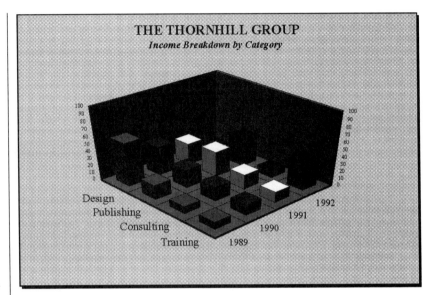

Figure A-22: 3D riser chart.

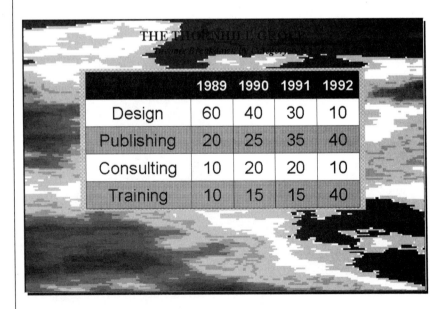

Figure A-23: Table chart.

Using Chart View

Once you've entered data into CorelCHART's Data Manager or another data program, you're ready to convert that information into a graphic. CHART offers more than a dozen basic chart styles, with several variations within each style. When you select New, a menu of chart styles, including a thumbnail gallery, previews your options. Once you've given CHART some simple instructions about converting your spreadsheet data into chart form, just click on the Chart View icon and your information appears in the form you've selected. When you have the chart style you want, you can modify the chart's colors and title styles; add grid lines, scale range or 3D perspective; and add pictographs. Use the Text Ribbon to style type. The toolbox lets you add type, draw lines, curves and shapes, add backgrounds and pictographs, and change the size of your view. Once a chart has been created, you can use it as a template for future charts.

CorelCHART files can be printed or processed as slides, transparencies or posters for presentations (see the Autographix Slide Service information in Appendix B, "Resources").

Chart Options: Choose from dozens of chart styles, including 2D and 3D.

Onscreen Color Palette: Click to choose the color you want from the palette at the bottom of your screen.

Chart Preview: Includes a thumbnail gallery of chart styles.

Roll-up Menus: Use for quick and easy editing.

Graphics: Add pictographs, color, patterns and textures and borders.

Font Library: All Windows and ATM fonts are available.

Chart Editing: Edit heads, subheads, footnotes and data in Chart View.

3D Editing: Roll-up makes it easy to adjust light source, perspective, axis, etc., on 3D charts.

Using OLE

CHART lets you use OLE technology in several ways.

- Spreadsheet data is linked to charts, so when you update data (in Data Manager or an outside program), your chart is updated automatically.

- Charts can be linked to other programs, such as DRAW and SHOW, so that when you update a chart, all linked versions are also updated. Or, charts can be embedded in other programs and edited without your original chart being affected.

What if you could put your DRAW, PHOTO-PAINT and CHART images together, combining them into a sophisticated sales presentation, onscreen portfolio, educational tool—or a family album George Jetson would envy? As usual, Corel is one step ahead.

CORELSHOW: Direct Your Own Production

Multimedia presentations have become a standard business tool. CorelSHOW makes creating dynamic presentations on the PC a snap. You can pull together elements from several Corel applications into a single presentation that may be a document, a slide show or even an automated onscreen display. You can select your elements from DRAW, PHOTO-PAINT, CHART or any OLE Server program, including animation software such as CorelMOVE, Quicktime for Windows or .FLI/.FLC programs.

If you want to share your onscreen presentation with a business associate, client or friend, CorelSHOW includes a runtime player (Version 3.0 or later). You are allowed to include this shareware program whenever you distribute a CorelSHOW presentation. The user will be able to view your presentation, make some modifications (such as changing onscreen times and transitional effects), but not change the body of the presentation.

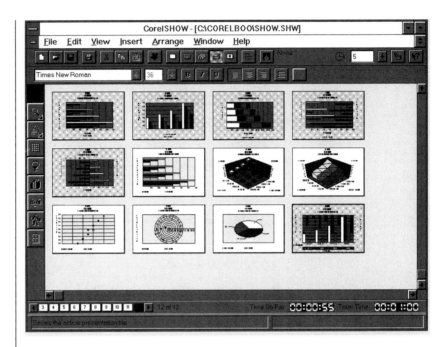

Figure A-24: Thumbnail preview gallery in CorelSHOW.

Use CorelSHOW's thumbnail preview gallery to select and order the slides in your presentation. Onscreen counters show Time So Far (to currently selected slide) and Total Time (of all slides).

Here's what you can do with CorelSHOW:

- Create elements and customize their assembly.
- Create support documents to accompany your visual presentations.
- Open multiple documents and display them side-by-side.
- Access DRAW, CHART, MOVE and other OLE applications instantly.
- Incorporate transitions and time-onscreen options to create dynamic presentations.
- Use onscreen counters to keep track of time elapsed to current slide, total time of presentation.
- Synchronize images and sounds.

- Use branching-style options to achieve interaction with the viewer.
- Loop the presentation for continuous play.
- Display an onscreen pointer to assist in presenting your information.
- Preview before you print or process film.
- Control the presentation from your keyboard, using keystrokes that let you pause, scroll backward and forward, go to the beginning and ending slide, etc.

SHOW Features

Page setup: choose from several standard page orientations and sizes, or customize.

Background: choose one or multiple predesigned backgrounds from a selection menu, or import a background created in DRAW or PHOTO-PAINT.

Assemble slides: pull finished images from a variety of sources.

Edit slides: customize individual slides with onscreen editing.

Reorder slides: add, delete and reorder slides in an instant; the thumbnail gallery gives you click-and-drag reordering; or use cut, copy and paste.

Transitions: choose from a variety of previewable animated and graphic transitions, including wipes, dissolves and curtains.

Save and Show: select automatic presentation or manual control.

Speaker Notes: attach notes to slides; the notes can be used as handouts or for reference during presentations.

4.0 Speaker notes aren't available in Version 4.0.

Using OLE

SHOW works by linking documents created in other programs, such as DRAW and CHART, through OLE. Any time you update one of these source documents (in the program where it was originally created), your SHOW files are also updated.

CORELMOVE:
Animate Your Corel Creations

An animation is a series of pictures, called frames. When shown in quick succession, these frames create the illusion of motion or action. Animators use actors (which move), props (which remain stationary) and sounds to create their animation movies.

Like all Corel applications, CorelMOVE is an intuitive, prompt-driven program. No matter what your level of animation experience, you'll find the CorelMOVE animation-building process both easy and fun.

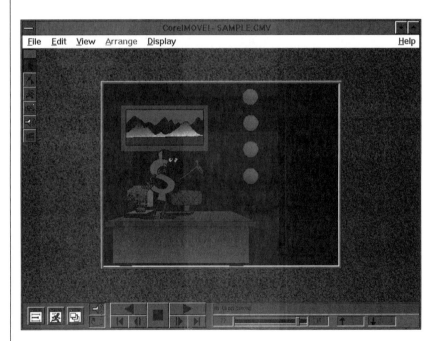

Figure A-25: CorelMOVE's animation screen display.

Creating Actors & Props

You can create animation actors and props directly in MOVE, or you can import from MOVE Libraries or other programs, such as DRAW.

When you begin CorelMOVE, you are given a toolbox with options to create a new actor or prop, set actors on a path, add

The Control Panel at the bottom of your screen gives you access to all roll-up menus, lets you play your animation as you're working on it, and lets you move through the animation frame by frame. Note that information on the currently selected object appears on the Status Line, and that the Frame Counter keeps a count of current and total frames.

sound or add cue. To develop movement, you must first create multiple cels for the same actor—each change in an actor's position requires a different cel. Use clone, delete and duplicate commands to create cels, then give your actors motion by adding a path.

New to Version 5.0 is *morphing*, which takes animation to a new level. If you watch "Star Trek: Deep Space Nine," you know what morphing is even if you don't know you know. Whenever Odo (the shape shifter) changes into another form, his original shape seems to dissolve bit by bit until the new shape is complete. With MOVE, you too can create effects like this by adjusting a series of control points between beginning and ending cels in a multiple-cel actor.

Paint Palette: Similar to DRAW and PHOTO-PAINT tools, the Paint Palette lets you "draw" and color your actors and props; choose drawing tools such as the pencil tool or box tools (for rectangles/squares, ellipses/circles and polygons), and painting tools such as brushes, spray can and paint bucket.

Layering: Each actor and prop are given their own layer; layers can be moved To Front and To Back.

Text Tool: This tool lets you add text to your animation. Text can be used for titles, balloons and labels, or as actors or props. Choose from over 750 type styles as well as myriad colors.

Pattern Fill: This roll-up window lets you choose predesigned pattern fills.

Library roll-up lets you create catalogs of actors and props in different libraries for future use. Each library gives you a Visual Mode that lets you see the library members as you scroll through its contents.

Foreground & Background: This roll-up window lets you choose from a full palette for foreground and background colors.

Special Effects: You can designate fills, tints, blends, rotate, flip, opaque/transparent, etc.; found under Options in the Paint Document Window.

Onion Skin: This cel appears beneath the working cel and shows either the previous or the next cel of the actor currently being worked on, providing a context for gauging your animation.

Cel Counter: This counter tells you the number of cels an actor has; number of cels creates the illusion of speed.

Zoom in to adjust your animation artwork at the pixel level. The Zoom button is on the Options menu.

The Animation Information dialog box (access through Edit menu in 5.0 and Display menu in 4.0) provides current information about your animation, such as number of actors, props, sounds and cues. It also lets you designate size of the animation window, grid, number of frames, frames per second, etc.

Zap! Boof! Blamo!

CorelMOVE lets you record sounds, link them to your animation and manipulate them. You can choose start and end frames; edit, cut-and-paste and repeat sounds; and apply effects such as fades and echoes.

Putting Your Animation Together

Once you've created your actors and props and recorded your sounds, you can merge these into a complex animated "movie." Use the Pick tool, Layering, the Edit menu and Library roll-up to place and manage actors and props. Designate when and how props appear and disappear from the screen; choose dissolve, wipe, scroll, iris, fade and other transition devices.

- Cel Sequencer: This roll-up window assigns frames to the actor's movements. Control cel order, size of objects within frame, etc.
- TimeLines: This roll-up window gives you an overview of the animation to allow fine-tuning of timing, sequence, etc.
- Cues: Use the Cue Information dialog box to set conditions that, when met, cue certain animation sequences. This allows you to create interactive animation.

Viewing Your Animation

When you've finished building your animation, you can play the finished product on CorelMOVE's player by accessing the MCPlayer icon.

MORE GOODIES

If Corel's package didn't go any further than what we've covered so far, that would be more than enough for most purposes. But there's much more. Following are brief highlights of the other additions to Corel's creative collection.

Corel Ventura

For years, Ventura Publisher has been one of the leading page layout programs. Now it's part of the Corel family and is included at no extra cost in your CorelDRAW 5.0 package. Its interface has been completely overhauled to make it more compatible with DRAW. If your page layout needs go beyond the plentiful desktop publishing features in CorelDRAW, take a look at Corel Ventura. Ventura includes some features you won't find in DRAW, such as cross-referencing and indexing. Creating your drawings in DRAW and laying them out in Ventura gives you the best of both worlds.

CorelMOSAIC

Use CorelMOSAIC to organize and manage all of your graphics files. MOSAIC has been part of Corel's arsenal for a while, but Version 5.0 has added a MOSAIC roll-up to DRAW and most of the other Corel programs, making it much easier to access.

CorelTRACE

Use TRACE to convert bitmap graphics to vector images. And you're not limited to straight conversions—for example, you can do woodcut and silhouette traces, which add effects during the tracing process. Version 5.0 also includes an OCR (optical character recognition) feature that lets you take bitmapped text files and convert them to characters that can be worked with as text in CorelDRAW.

CorelQUERY

New to Version 5.0, QUERY allows you to access database information in other programs and extract any portion of that information into Ventura or CHART.

ARES Font Minder

This is a totally cool font management program that's been garnering high praise for some time. With Version 5.0, Corel has graciously included this terrific tool to help you handle the myriad fonts on your system (the fonts included with Corel as well as any other fonts you have). Font Minder takes the headaches out of installing and organizing fonts—it handles True-Type and PostScript fonts at the same time, and you can even create and install different font groups without exiting Windows. With Font Minder, improving Windows's performance by loading only the fonts you actually use is a snap!

THE VALUE OF THE CORELDRAW COLLECTION

Without a doubt, CorelDRAW is an excellent tool for computer artists. But we're still deep in the Information Age, so Corel has given us many more ways to present information visually—right at the keyboard. The 5.0 package expands every Corel user's creative reach—into the range of digital image and color control, dynamic screen presentations, powerful infographics and animation.

B

Resources

Slide Service

Autographix Slide Service: Included in the CorelDRAW package is software that allows you to have your Corel artwork processed as high-resolution 35mm slides, continuous-tone prints, transparencies and posters (up to 42 inches wide). You can send your PostScript color file, plus a work order you create with the software, for processing via disk or modem.

The Autographix Slide Service has bureaus throughout the United States and in several foreign countries, with new bureaus being added each week. Phone 1-800-548-8558 (U.S. only) to locate a service bureau near you.

Organizations

ACAD - Association of Corel Artists & Designers
1309 Riverside Dr.
Burbank, CA 91506
818/563-2223

This international association for CorelDRAW users at all levels of ability sponsors monthly meetings, *Corelation* magazine and local job banks. Annual fee (U.S.) is $48.00 ($60 Canada or other international), which includes a subscription to *Corelation*. ACAD currently has over 75 chapters worldwide ($24 additional local chapter fee). For information on an ACAD group near you, write to the address listed above.

Applications & Utilities

Many other applications, from page layout to spreadsheet programs, work effectively with CorelDRAW. Here are the programs we used to create *Looking Good With CorelDRAW:*

Graphics:

CorelDRAW!
Corel Systems Corporation
Corel Building
1600 Carling Ave.
Ottawa, Ontario
CANADA K1Z 8R7
613/ 728-8200
Cust. Svc.: 800/772-6735
BBS: 613/ 761-7798

Page Layout Program:

PageMaker
Aldus Corporation
411 First Ave. South
Seattle, WA 98104-2871
206/622-5500

Word Processors:

DOS—XyWrite III Plus and XyWrite 4.0
The Technology Group
36 S. Charles St., Ste. 2200
Baltimore, MD 21201

Windows—Windows Write
Microsoft Corporation
One Microsoft Way
Redmond, WA 98052-6399
206/882-8080

Windows—Microsoft Works for Windows
Microsoft Corporation
One Microsoft Way
Redmond, WA 98052-6399
206/882-8080

File Management:

XTree Pro
XTree Company
15220 NW Greenbriar Pkwy., Ste. 200
Beaverton, OR 97006
503/690-8088

Publications

Artists' and illustrators' magazines have been somewhat slow
to herald the importance of computers in the overall scheme of
creation, but *How* and *Step-by-Step*, mentioned below, are devot-
ing more and more space to portfolio and how-to articles on
electronic artwork.

The rapid birth and death rates among desktop publishing
magazines over the last few years have been phenomenal.
Several are outstanding resources and we are pleased to recom-
mend them here. One caveat: some magazines listed here may
no longer be available, while other good ones may have appeared on the scene since our book went to press.

There are several publications devoted specifically to Corel:

Corel Magazine
980 Anderson Mill Rd.
Austin, TX 78750

Corelation
1309 Riverside Dr.
Burbank, CA 91506
Publication of the Association of CorelDRAW Artists

Chris Dickman's Mastering CorelDRAW Newsletter
PO Box 123, Station Q
Toronto, ON
CANADA M4T 2L7

Other useful publications:

How
1507 Bena Ave.
Cincinnati, OH 45212-0575

Step-by-Step
6000 N. Forest Park Dr.
Peoria, IL 61614-3592

These how-to magazines for traditional graphic artists have been including more and more computer articles.

Step-by-Step Electronic Design
6000 N. Forest Park Dr.
Peoria, IL 61614-3592
Publisher of a how-to newsletter for all flavors of computer artists and very rich in useful information. Highly recommended.

Publish!
501 Second St.
PO Box 55400
Boulder, CO 80322
Tracks developments in the desktop publishing industry.

Pre-
470 Park Ave. South, 7th floor
New York, NY 10016
Covers prepress issues and technologies.

Computer Graphics World
PO Box 122
Tulsa, OK 74101
Especially informative for high-end users.

NewMedia
901 Mariner's Island Blvd., Ste. 365
San Mateo, CA 94404
Tracks trends in desktop multimedia technologies.

Computer Artist
PO Box 3118
Tulsa, OK 74101

Color Publishing
PO Box 3118
Tulsa, OK 74101

Additional publications are listed in the "Further Reading" section of this book.

Clip Art

High-resolution electronic clip art is available from the following sources:

3G Graphics, Inc.
114 2nd Ave. South, Ste. 104
Edmonds, WA 98020-3595
206/774-3518
800/456-0234

Image Club Graphics, Inc.
727 24th Ave. SE
Calgary, Alberta
CANADA T2G 1P5
403/262-8008
Cust. Svc. 800/661-9410

Cartesia Software
5 South Main St.
Lambertville, NJ 08530
609/397-1611
800/334-4291 (sales only)

One Mile Up, Inc.
7011 Evergreen Ct.
Annandale, VA 22003
703/642-1177
800/258-5280

Totem Graphics, Inc.
6200-F Capitol Blvd.
Tumwater, WA 98501
206/352-1851

Innovation
41 Mansfield Ave.
Essex Junction, VT 05452
800/255-0562

Artbeats
PO Box 1287
Myrtle Creek, OR 97457
800/444-9392

Linotype-Hell Company
425 Oser Ave.
Hauppauge, NY 11788
516/434-2000
800/223-1564

Shareware

More graphics professionals are discovering the wealth of inexpensive, quality shareware programs. CorelDRAW artists will be interested in file compression and graphics viewing utilities, TrueType and Type 1 typefaces, and art files ranging from designs, patterns, backgrounds and clip art images. These products are available through downloading with your modem from either locally based bulletin board systems (BBS) or national online services. They also may be purchased for a nominal fee from various shareware distributors. After the initial expense incurred in obtaining the programs, users are asked to send a fee (usually in the range of $5 to $50) to the authors if they find the product useful.

Local BBS phone numbers usually can be obtained from a local computer retailer or user group.

The leading national online services provide toll-free numbers for local access numbers, rates, etc.:

America Online   800-827-6364
CompuServe   800-848-8990
GEnie   800-638-9636

Catalogs from shareware distributors are available from:

Reasonable Solutions   800-876-3475
The Software Labs   800-569-7900

Companion Disks
Sneak Preview

To help you get the fullest use from *Looking Good With Corel-DRAW!*, we've created a special set of companion disks. These information-packed disks—available in both 3½- and 5¼- inch sizes—feature an onscreen gallery of selected artwork from the book, a special collection of clip art and fonts from top-name manufacturers, and a start-up template collection. We've included a comprehensive README.TXT file detailing the disk's contents, sources and instructions for using our Installer. You can transfer the information to your hard disk in a single quick-and-easy session. **You'll find ordering information for the *Looking Good With CorelDRAW* companion disk set in the back of this book.**

ONSCREEN GALLERY

We made a careful selection of artwork from the *Looking Good With CorelDRAW* galleries. We wanted to include artwork on the companion disks for two reasons. First, we wanted you to see these special creations in full size and in electronic color. More importantly, we wanted you to be able to watch as these works build up on your monitor. As you see the layers compose on your screen, you'll learn a lot about how the artist constructed the elements and how the final piece came together.

CLIP ART

We've collected an eclectic gallery of useful clip art from some of the industry's top sources. Each image is ready for immediate use in CorelDRAW, and you can keep them handy to use for all your art and publishing projects. The *Looking Good With CorelDRAW* disk set includes

Backgrounds – Croppable, scalable, stretchable full-page images from *ArtBeat*'s superior library of background designs and patterns.

International Symbols & Icons – A collection of useful standardized symbols from *Innovative Advertising & Design*.

Graphics – A sampler from *Image Club Graphics*'s library of design and illustration clip art.

Illustrations – A variety of detailed line drawings from *Totem Graphics*'s extensive image collections.

FONTS

Your disks include a special collection of TrueType fonts supplied by Linotype-Hell.

TEMPLATES

To get you started designing with CorelDRAW, we've included a gallery of basic customized templates, including

- 3$\frac{1}{2}$-inch disk labels
- Corporate stationery & forms formats
  Letterhead
  Business card
  Memo
  Envelope
- Report covers

Further Reading

Books

Some older titles in this listing may be out of print but can probably be found in public or specialty libraries.

Beaumont, Michael. *Type: Design, Color, Character & Use.* Cincinnati: North Light Books, 1991.

A fine text complements excellent illustrations on how to use type effectively.

Cavuoto, James, and Stephen Beale. *Linotronic Imaging Handbook.* Torrance, CA: Micro Publishing Press, 1991.

The desktop publisher's guide to using service bureaus for high-quality output.

Cole, Bruce, and Adelheid Gealt. *Art of the Western World.* New York: Summit Books, 1991.

Collier, David, and Bob Cotton. *Basic Desktop Design & Layout.* Cincinnati: North Light Books, 1989.

A brief but thorough treatment of design principles and techniques for all types of document design in the context of desktop publishing. Well illustrated.

Cook, Alton, ed. *Type and Color: A Handbook of Creative Combinations*. Rockport, MA: Rockport Publications, 1989.

Acetate overlays allow you to preview more than 800,000 combinations of type, background color and grayscale. If you plan to work in color, you need this one.

Escher, M.C. *29 Master Prints*. New York: Harry N. Abrams, 1983.

Gosney, Michael, John Odam and Jim Schmal. *The Gray Book: Designing in Black & White on Your Computer,* 2d ed. Chapel Hill, NC: Ventana Press, 1993.

Labuz, Ronald. *Contemporary Graphic Design*. New York: Van Nostrand Reinhold, 1990.

A comprehensive survey of the design innovations of the 1980s. An excellent introduction to current typographic trends.

LeBlond, Geoffrey. *Windows 3.1 Power Tools*. 2d ed. New York: Bantam Books, 1992.

An excellent source of information on getting the most from Windows 3.0. Includes a disk of Windows utility programs.

Mansfield, Richard. *Desktop Publishing With WordPerfect 6.* Chapel Hill, NC: Ventana Press, 1993.

This is a book of suggestions, guidelines, examples and make-overs, not a book a rules. The focus is on creative desktop publishing design, but the author provides step-by-step Word-Perfect 6 keyboard and mouse sequences as well.

Parker, Roger. *Looking Good in Print: A Guide to Basic Design for Desktop Publishing*. 3d ed. Chapel Hill, NC: Ventana Press, 1993.

A treasure trove of design information and illustrations for a variety of publication formats.

———. *The Makeover Book: 101 Design Solutions for Desktop Publishing*. Chapel Hill, NC: Ventana Press, 1989.

Features more than one hundred makeovers from desktop publications.

Pedersen, B. Martin, ed. *Graphis Letterhead*. New York: Watson-Guptill, 1990.

A sumptuously produced full-color collection of more than 250 stunning letterhead suites (letterheads, business cards, envelopes, etc.). *Graphis* is a world-renowned magazine dedicated to graphic design.

Prueitt, Melvin L. *Art & the Computer*. New York: McGraw-Hill, 1985.

Rand, Paul. *A Designer's Art*. New Haven, CT: Yale University Press, 1985.

A collection of writings, copiously illustrated, by one of America's best-known graphic designers. This book offers visual inspiration and a look into the great designer's mind and heart.

Sosinsky, Barrie. *Beyond the Desktop: Tools & Technology for Computer Publishing*. New York: Bantam Books, 1991.

Explains in everyday language how to properly use available technology to enhance your desktop publishing projects. Also an excellent reference resource.

Swann, Alan. *How to Understand & Use Design & Layout*. Cincinnati: North Light Books, 1991.

Profusely illustrated, this volume briskly reviews the theory and practice of page layout.

Tufte, Edward R. *Envisioning Information*. Cheshire, CT: Graphics Press, 1990.

(See comments in the following book listing.)

———. *The Visual Display of Quantitative Information*. Cheshire, CT: Graphics Press, 1983.

Envisioning Information covers the visual issues involved in the presentation of complex, dense data such as timetables, scientific diagrams and maps, while *The Visual Display of Quantitative Information* focuses on creating visually successful statistical graphics, maps, charts and tables. Tufte's standards of book production are so exacting that he published these titles himself.

With meticulous typography, color printing and exquisite paper, they are examples of book production at its best.

Periodicals

Before & After: How to Design Cool Stuff on Your Computer, Page-Lab, P.O. Box 418252, Sacramento, CA 95841-9855. Bimonthly.

This exciting, full-color publication is a timeless reference tool and daily workbook for desktop publishers of all levels. Concisely written and profusely illustrated—not an inch of wasted space.

Business Publishing, Hitchcock Publishing, Carol Stream, IL 60188. Monthly.

Balanced treatment of both Macintosh and PC desktop publishing issues, along with up-to-the-minute reviews of the latest desktop publishing products.

Communication Arts, Coyne & Blanchard, 410 Sherman Ave., Palo Alto, CA 94303. Eight issues/year.

This traditional "required reading" for art directors and graphic designers now devotes an increasing amount of space to desktop publishing. Special focus issues showcase samples of the year's best designs in advertising, illustration and photography.

Print: America's Graphic Design Magazine, RC Publications, 3200 Tower Oaks Blvd., Rockville, MD 20852. Bimonthly.

Focuses on techniques and economics of professional graphic design, including advances in desktop publishing. Its annual regional design and advertising design issues alone are worth the subscription price.

Publish, Integrated Media, Inc., 501 Second St., San Francisco, CA 94107. Monthly.

In-depth critiques of the latest publishing hardware and software, along with design- and technique-oriented articles.

Step-by-Step Graphics, Dynamic Graphics, 6000 North Forest Park Dr., P.O. Box 1901, Peoria, IL 61656. Bimonthly.

Advertising-free, technique-oriented advice for advanced desktop publishers and anyone who aspires to greater expertise in layout and design. The *Step-By-Step Graphics* staff has also produced a book, *Step-By-Step Graphics: Designers' Guide to Typography*, containing an excellent collection of articles published in the bimonthly issues.

Glossary

24-Bit Color — Computer display capable of generating more than 16 million colors; also called True Color.

256 Color — Limited color palette selected to represent the entire color range when displaying and printing.

Aa

Adobe Type 1 font — PostScript specification.

Application — Software that performs a specific function: Corel-DRAW is a draw application; Ventura Publisher is a page layout application; Excel is a spreadsheet application.

Artistic Text — Words, usually in a large point size, used as a graphic device as well as to convey information. (*See also* Paragraph Text.)

ASCII — (The American Standard Code for Information Interchange) The most commonly used computer character coding set. ASCII text is free of all word processing formatting codes.

Attribute — Appearance characteristic applied to an object: e.g., bold and italic are text attributes.

AutoJoin — DRAW feature that automatically joins two nodes in close proximity. (A setting in the Preferences dialog box that lets you specify that distance.)

Autotrace — Utility in DRAW that automatically traces bitmapped images as an editable outline.

Bb

Bar — Selection on a dialog box or roll-up window represented by a rectangular bar.

Bézier line — Line created by choosing two points with the mouse; DRAW then joins these points.

Bitmap — Method of storing, displaying and printing a graphic image that represents the image as a series of black or white dots ("bits").

BMP format — (Bitmap format) Windows's internal graphics file format.

Bounding box — Box created in DRAW by dragging with the mouse in Pick Tool mode; used to select an object.

Button — Selection in a dialog box or roll-up window activated by clicking a square box.

Cc

Cell — A unit of data or information on a spreadsheet.

Closed Path — In DRAW, a continuous line. (*Compare* Open Path.)

CMYK — (Cyan, Magenta, Yellow, blacK) A method of specifying color; a printing method that separates full-color artwork into these four colors, with each color printed from a separate plate.

Combine — A DRAW menu call that converts a group of objects into a single object without visually altering the image's appearance.

Constrain — A limitation on movement, usually accomplished by holding down the Control key. (A constrained angle can be specified in the Preferences dialog box.)

Control Point — Points on a node of a curved line where you can modify the curve. Double-click on a node to access its associated control points.

Corner Cap — Round, mitered or angled finish on a corner.

Corner Threshold — DRAW Preference setting that controls the accuracy of curved lines.

Curve Flatness — DRAW setting that lets you specify *accurately* or *roughly* drawn complex curves. (Specifying roughly drawn curves saves time in screen drawing and printing.)

Curve Object — Object made up of curved lines.

Dd

Data Manager — Program that organizes specific fields of information (for example, names and addresses, sales figures, demographics) for use and manipulation.

DDE — (Dynamic Data Exchange) Windows feature used to link data entered in one program and used in other applications; CHART supports DDE-linked data.

Default — A program's preset selections.

Densitometer — A printed scale that shows the density of ink printed for each separated color (cyan, magenta, yellow or black).

Dialog box — An onscreen menu that lets you make certain choices regarding how the program will function.

Dithered colors — Screen display that approximates intermediate shades or colors between actual shades or colors.

Ee

Embedding — Windows system of marrying information created in one application to another application; embedded material must be edited at the source application. (*Compare* Linking.)

EPS format — (Encapsulated PostScript format) A graphics format used to convert bitmapped images to vector images.

Ff

Fountain Fill — A fill that changes gradually from one color to another or from one shade to another. (Same as graduated or gradient fill.)

Freehand drawing — Using DRAW's Pencil tool to create lines by dragging your pointing device; similar to drawing with a pencil.

Gg

GIF^{SM} format — (Graphics Interface format) CompuServe's proprietary graphics format.

Grayscale image — A picture that incorporates a range of gray tones — the more levels of gray, the more detailed the image.

Grid — An underlying framework used to ensure consistent sizing and alignment; you can specify grid measurements and Snap-To-Grid.

Group — A DRAW command that lets you link several objects so that they can be manipulated as a unit.

Guide — A (usually) nonprinting line used to ensure correct placement of an object; you can specify the position of Guides and Snap-To-Guide.

Hh

Handles — Small boxes at the corners and midpoints of the box surrounding a selected object in Pick Tool mode; you move the handles to scale or stretch the selected object.

Hot Zone — A DRAW type specification that limits right-hand ragging by specifying the point where the end word of a line will be either hyphenated or dropped to the next line.

HSB — (Hue, Saturation, Brightness) A color model that lets you specify levels of a color's hue, saturation and brightness.

Ii

Icon — A symbol that represents a function or option.

Intersect — DRAW command (Arrange menu) that creates an object the shape of the area common to two or more overlapping objects.

Kk

Kerning — Refining spacing between letter (or character) pairs.

Keyboard shortcut — Key combinations that access a menu, tool, dialog box or roll-up window (in lieu of using the mouse for access).

Ll

Layer — A DRAW device that lets you assign an object or objects to groups on different imaginary levels; visually, layers overlap without being physically connected.

Lens — DRAW roll-up (new in Version 5.0) that provides quick access to effects such as transparency, magnification, color filtering, color adding, complementary colors, negatives, grayscale and infrared imaging.

Line cap — A round, pointed or mitered ending on a line.

Linear Fill — A fill that gradually changes shades or colors in stripes. (Same as a Linear Fountain.)

Linking — A Windows system of marrying information created in one application to another application; linked material can be edited at either the source application or the destination application, with edits occurring simultaneously in each. (*Compare* Embedding.)

Mm

Marquee — Dotted-outline box created when dragging in the Pick Tool mode ▲ or the Shape Tool mode ⋏ ; used to select an object or node.

Mask — An object created with a see-through area that allows an underlying object to be seen.

Menu — A pull-down box that lets you access a variety of functions; e.g., the Type menu gives you access to type-related functions.

MSP format — (Microsoft Paintbrush format) Microsoft graphics format used by pre-3.0 Windows applications.

Nn

Node — A point along a line or curve that controls the contour of that line or curve; nodes appear at the beginning and end of a line segment and at the corners and midpoints of a selected object.

Nudge — To move in small increments using the arrow keys ⬇ ⬆ ➡ ⬅. Increment of movement is set in the Preferences dialog box.

Oo

Object-oriented program — A program that describes objects using mathematical formulas; a vector program.

OLE — (Object Linking & Embedding) A file device that lets you share information, such as a graph, photograph or graphic, among different Windows applications. OLE allows you to edit information in a destination file without having to return to the source file in which the information was originally input or created. For example, you can embed or link a source file (such as a photograph) into a destination file (such as a page layout program). Embedded information can be selected and edited within the destination file, whereas editing linked information changes the source file. (*See also* Embedding and Linking.)

Open Path — A line or series of lines with a beginning and an end. (*Compare* Closed Path.)

Pp

Paragraph Text — A large block of text whose primary function is to convey information. (*See also* Artistic Text.)

Path — A line or series of line segments.

Pattern Tile — A portion of an image marquee selected to create a repeating series; each unit of the pattern is one tile.

PCX format — A graphics format that is the PC industry's standard bitmap file format and CorelDRAW's default format.

Pictograph — A chart illustrated with simple graphic images.

Pixel — The smallest unit of screen display.

Pointing device — Device such as a mouse, trackball or pen-and-tablet that lets you move around your computer screen.

Posterize — A PHOTO-PAINT special effects filter.

PowerClip — DRAW feature (new in Version 5.0) that places one object (the contents) inside another (the container). The container and its contents can be a closed path, a group of objects or artistic text. PowerClip can also be used to place bitmaps in irregularly shaped containers.

PowerLine — A line with varying widths and contours.

Preset — DRAW roll-up (new in Version 5.0). Use this macro-building facility to save series of actions (like adding effects or formatting) that you use frequently. The preset can then be called back and replayed as needed.

Process color — A printing method that uses four-color plates (cyan, magenta, yellow, black) to create the illusion of full color.

Rr

Radial Fill — A fill that changes concentrically from a center point outward. (Same as a Radial Fountain.)

Resident font — Font information that *exists* in the printer (rather than being downloaded from a computer file) for use when outputting a document.

RGB — (Red, Green, Blue) Color model that uses percentages of red, green and blue to create colors.

Ss

Scale With Image — A DRAW call that links an object and its outline, so that when the object is scaled, the outline is scaled proportionally.

Segment — (line segment) Line section between two nodes.

Snap — Computer graphics device that forces objects to align with specified points (usually a grid or another object).

Spot color — Solid color applied during the printing process; printing press color created by mixing ink as specified using the Pantone or other color-matching system.

Spreadsheet — Visual representation of statistical data in a simple columnar format.

Status Line — Screen area that displays vital information concerning the selected object and functions being performed.

Submenu — A menu accessed via a main menu found on the Status Line.

Tt

Thumbnail — Small, sketchy, undetailed representation of a drawing or photo.

TGA format — (TARGA format) The standard format for several paint programs for color images.

TIFF — (Tagged Image File Format; TIF) Graphics format used for bitmapped images.

Tint — Percentage of a color.

Toggle — A key or onscreen "button" that switches back and forth between two functions or applications.

Trim — DRAW command (Arrange menu) that removes the area common to overlapping objects. This feature can be used to generate a complex shape very quickly by using simple objects.

Uu

Unconstrained — Free to move in any direction and in unlimited increments.

Uniform Fill — Fill that is a solid color.

Vv

Vanishing point — In perspective, an imaginary point at which lines illustrating an object would meet.

Vector — Method of describing a line by specifying two points and joining those points mathematically.

Index